MENTAL TOUGHNESS COLLECTION

3-in-1 Book

How to Influence People + Daily Self-Discipline + Stoicism in Modern Life.

Gain Perseverance, Resilience, and Overcome Procrastination + 30 Day Plan

HOW TO INFLUENCE PEOPLE AND BECOME A MASTER OF MANIPULATION

Proven Methods to Analyze People, Control Your Emotions and Body Language, Leverage Persuasion in Business and Relationships

Table of Content

Introduction

Everyone has a little manipulator living inside of them. If you're feeling insecure about your life, it might be hard to recognize this quality and the power it can have over others. As humans, we have a wide variety of methods we instinctively fall back on when we want to exercise our influence over others. We might make people doubt their own judgment in lieu of our personal advice when we want something; we could make people feel guilty about something we don't like, or we might put on the charm to entice someone to do something they are reluctant to do. It's all part of daily communication and we start relying on it very early in life.

However, somewhere along the line, we become convinced that manipulation has somehow become immoral; that there is something inherently indecent about it and so they change their means of communication. Sadly, this leaves them vulnerable to the devices of those who recognize that the skill is merely a tool that can be used for both good and bad purposes. As a result, they find themselves being manipulated and pushed to do things they don't really want to do. They end up feeling powerless, frustrated, and out of control.

What they are failing to recognize is that manipulation, like any other craft, is a skill that can easily be developed and used in a positive way to help them achieve their goals. Just by making a few tweaks to their body language, speech, and behavior, all of us can position ourselves to become masters of our own lives. It doesn't matter if you're a parent trying to get your child to clean his room or the CEO of a major corporation trying to motivate a massive workforce, getting past your own insecurities and learning how to use this skill can change the whole dynamic of your life.

It has sometimes been referred to as a form of "dark persuasion" as if to imply that there is something mysteriously evil about manipulation. On the surface, it may seem like that is true. After all, when you hear the word 'manipulation' the mind automatically conjures up intriguing ideas. Visions of science fiction movies on mind control play out in your head, hypnotists attempting to get you to do strange or embarrassing things you wouldn't normally do, and unethical people who want to persuade you into some form of questionable acts. But these are all misconceptions of what manipulation is all about.

The most common belief about manipulation is that it involves one person taking control over another as if they were a puppet with them controlling the strings. But what most people are missing is that the true art of manipulation has nothing to do with getting people to do things against their will but is instead a gentle form of persuasion that will convince them to want the same thing that you want. In other words, manipulation is simply deep form of persuasion, something that all of us do in our everyday lives.

Your goal is to get others to believe that whatever action they are taking was actually their idea all along. While there are always going to be people who will use this skill for questionable purposes but doesn't mean that the art of persuasion itself is wrong.

A person can use a knife to prepare a meal for their family or they can use it to cause harm to someone else. The knife itself is not the problem, it is how someone chooses to use it. If you follow the media then you know that historically there have been an endless stream of charismatic people that have put forth a lot of effort to influence and maneuver people to do their bidding. They look to control the behaviors of the masses in subtle ways that may be difficult to notice.

All of us have heard of the horrific stories of the Nazi oppression of the Jews during World War II. How many normally peace loving and kind Germans were duped into believing that the Jews were really a threat to their way of life? Or you may have heard about the record number of suicidal deaths committed at the persuasion of charismatic people like Jim Jones or those that participated in the pact formed in the wake of the Hale-Bopp comet. Our history books are riddled with such horror stories that show just how evil and dangerous psychological manipulation can be. However, those cases are not the norm and do not reflect the reality of what the art of manipulation truly is.

All of us practice manipulation in some form or another. We do it every day and never give it a second thought. In fact, the main definition of the word 'to manipulate' is "to manage or influence with skill," in some process of treatment or performance."

Manipulation is not the evil itself; it is how it is used that can become questionable. Do you have a religion? Do you have a clique that you belong to? Were you ever a part of a fraternity? Or a member of an exclusive club? Did you follow the rules at school? Is there office politics where you work?

All of these things groups were formed and grown by using some level of manipulation. The members were giving you gentle pressure to follow a certain norm, to fit into certain expectations, and to please a certain group of people. You just didn't realize that you were being manipulated because you wanted to be a part of the picture.

But after reading this book, you can be on the other side of that equation. Gently pushing people in one direction or another. The tricks are all there in your mind and how you think. All of that may need to change and our goal is to help you to do that. In this book you will learn:

9

- What manipulation really is and how to recognize when you're being manipulated
- Non-verbal language you're always sending out to the rest of the world
- How you EQ (Emotional Quotient) plays a part
- How to find out if you're lacking in EQ and how to get it back
- What attracts most people
- How to identify a person vulnerable to manipulation
- How to read body language and micro-expressions
- How the way you walk tells people a lot
- How to stock up your manipulation toolbox
- And how to manipulate others like a real pro
- And so much more

The question you have to ask yourself is why are you here reading this book? What is your goal in learning how to manipulate people. Keep in mind that to effectively manipulate people it will take a serious commitment in time. You will have to be patient and cultivate your art. It may seem easy, but in order for the strategies used here, you must practice them until they feel natural and effortless. This kind of skill takes time to cultivate and involves overcoming your own mental barriers and creating a very specific mindset.

That involves a lot of work and commitment. However, once you have mastered this skill, you will be able to accomplish amazing things. It will be easier for your new business to gain traction and pull ahead of the competition. You will be able to get the kind of support you need to overcome any obstacle. You'll have access to a wide source of resources, and you'll be able to communicate and connect to the rest of the world on your terms.

If you've ever wondered how someone with just the clothes on his back can seem to take on the rest of the world and win, then you've witnessed first-hand the power of manipulation. You don't need a basket full of tools or a lot of tricks up your sleeve. Whether you're looking to convince your kids to make certain life choices or you're a CEO trying to motivate a team of employees to follow your ideals, the strategies are the same.

What does that mean for you? It means a lot. With the art of manipulation, you'll find it easier to get the job you want, get the types of loans you need, and even negotiate the kind of deals you're seeking. Your goal is not to get people to go against their will and help you, but to convince them that what you have to offer to the world is worth them taking a risk on. That's a powerful tool that anyone can use to get what they need. And it's all about learning how to use your own personal strengths to your advantage. So, if you're ready to take on the world and finally get the things you need and should have, then it's time to turn the page and learn to be a master manipulator in your own right. So, let's get you started so you can take the rest of the world by storm.

Chapter 1: A Beginner's Guide to Persuasion

Most people think of manipulation very negatively. They feel that anyone that is manipulative has a malevolent purpose and can't be trusted. Unfortunately, this is at least partially true. There are definitely those out there who wish to do you harm or take advantage of anyone who gets in their path.

One of the reasons we often associate manipulation with negative intent is because we don't have the ability to look into someone's heart and determine what their true motive is. So, rather than thinking someone is genuinely complimenting you, the mind often becomes suspicious and will adopt the worst case scenario.

Everyday Ways You're Being Manipulated

It would be nice to feel that when we make our own decisions that we are doing it of our own accord, but that is rarely the case. We live very busy lives and as a result, we often defer to the influences of others and use them as a sort of a shortcut or as a guide to drawing our own conclusions about a given situation faster. For the most part, this can work well, but it is rarely the wisest course of action.

For example, you come home and turn on the TV news to hear the latest events going on in the world. You see a media photo of Prince Charles holding up his middle finger to someone in the crowd. People are outraged that someone in the royal family would adopt such an action in public and you agree. Are you being manipulated or is it a real news report. The image in the picture is clear so you join in the crowd and are incensed by the photograph and launch your own protest against an insensitive member of the royal family.

However, while this incident did actually happen, the media did not show the whole story. The same image taken from a different angle, shows that Prince Charles was actually holding up three fingers as if he was counting something while talking calmly with someone in the crowd. It was not the single middle finger and his gesture was completely innocent.

That major example of manipulation had millions of people weighing in on the state of the royal family before the truth was really revealed. However, all manipulation does not come out in such a public way. It can come on a smaller scale as well. Consider those people who act as if they are better than you. Perhaps they have a higher education, or they make more money than you. Some even act that way because of their family line. When they talk to you, they take on a condescending voice as if speaking with a child. Their facial expressions make it clear that they see you as inferior.

Does this strategy work? Only if you accept this behavior and go along with it. If you become nervous and jittery in their presence you are giving them signals that you agree and you do see them as superior to you. How you respond to that type of behavior will let you know if they are manipulating you or not.

Other manipulating strategies may be seen in a person's body language, tone of voice, or even in what they don't say (silent treatment for example). There is a myriad of ways that one can try to manipulate you. If you take the time, I'm sure you'll find countless forms of manipulation being played out with you every day. It's a perfectly normal strategy that we all us throughout our lives.

Manipulation: A Tool for Both Good and Evil

It is cases like these that make people question whether manipulation is ethically sound or not. The media is notorious for these kinds of tactics. They use photography, carefully worded phrases, and other clever tactics to persuade people to feel a certain way.

However, while the message they deliver has some degree of truth it is not always the whole truth. Because someone uses manipulation for bad doesn't mean it is all bad. A closer look at our communication styles helps us to understand how manipulation has been used far more for good purposes. Once you recognize this, you'll not only be able to recognize it when you see it playing out around you, but you'll want to apply it in your own life as well.

Because our subconscious mind is usually the force that is driving our behavior, we don't often recognize what is really happening during our mental processes. The subconscious mind is always at work, every second of every day, it is collecting information from our senses and putting it through filters, deciding what is important and what is not.

So, as you are scrolling through your computer, checking your social media pages, things are happening in the back of your mind that you're not even aware of. This is a strategy that marketers use to draw you in. A business' marketing team understands that if they put the brand name in front of you often enough, you'll eventually make a connection to it. Have you ever wondered why Coca-Cola has become the number one brand in the world of carbonated beverages? Little things like a catchy phrase, little blurbs in between scenes of your favorite TV show, and their logo plastered at every sports event and entertainment venue.

This crafty art of manipulation isn't something new. It has been around for decades. It is used by businesses, political parties, religions, and even social interest groups. Your employer uses it to get more work out of you, your parents use it to get you to come home by curfew, your teachers use it to get you to want to study, and your spouse may use it to get you to agree with him on any number of things. Simply put, manipulation is the skillful use of persuasion to achieve a desired result. It is the oil on the squeaky wheel that moves our society.

Bottom line, if you're a part of this world, you are in one of only two classes; the manipulator or the one being manipulated. There is no middle ground here. So, in essence, it is one of the most useful skills a survivalist can use to get what he needs.

If you're thinking that you need to have a special amount of charisma or certain talents to employ the strategies we will use in this book, then you'd be wrong. The fact is that everyone has an inborn talent to be a master manipulator. You already have the qualities to get the job done. So, let's start with the basics.

6 Golden Rules of Manipulation

So, how can you tell when you're being manipulated? There are a lot of ways this can happen. Chances are, by now you're starting to get the idea, but let's get a little more specific here. After years of study, researchers have narrowed down exactly how manipulation works.

In the beginning, you probably felt that people made decisions based on the information they have gathered, but that is not always the case. Evidence shows that manipulations has very specific characteristics and the decision-maker uses those characteristics as a kind of ruler to measure the information they collect. This allows them to come to a conclusion by bypassing all the analytical steps involved. There are at least six different rules of manipulation that are commonly used on you every day.

- Reciprocity
- Scarcity
- Authority
- Consistency
- Liking
- Consensus

Once you understand how each of these works and how they can be used you will not only be able to spot when someone is trying to manipulate you but will be able to harness this strategy and use it on others.

Reciprocity: The art of reciprocity allows the manipulator to tap into an inborn characteristic of all of us. If someone does something for you, you automatically feel compelled to do something in return. Even if their gift does not come with an expectation in return, you will still feel as if you have to do something for that person before your mind will rest.

Still, don't expect it to be an equal exchange of gifts or favors. The manipulator may not even ask or expect something from you, but instead will create a situation that will make you feel connected to them in some way. Later, when the circumstances are favorable and they need the service or product you provide, your mind will automatically bring up their name and put it at the top of the list and the odds are good that you're going to throw your business their way.

A perfect example of reciprocity is a practice found in most restaurants today. After you've had your meal, the waiter will usually bring you the check along with a mint for each person in your party – a gift. In most cases, the gift is something small and seemingly insignificant. How do you feel when you receive this gift? What do you do? While the mint costs the restaurant a tiny fraction of the meal you just had, you begin to feel a sense of indebtedness. Your subconscious mind tells you that you have to return the gesture in some one. Evidence of this has been revealed in a number of studies that have shown that diners who receive a mint after their meal often increased the amount of their tip by at least 3%. If they received two mints, they size of the tip actually quadrupled to around 14%.

Another surprising result of reciprocity is if the waiter gives you a mint with the bill and then starts to walk away, pauses and then returns to compliment your party by saying something nice, the tips increase even more up as much as 23%.

This reveals something interesting. That it's not just the gift that makes a difference. Yes, giving a gift will increase your chances of getting what you want, but attention should also be paid to the manner in which the gift is given. This will give you the maximum possible results you receive.

Scarcity: It is a well-known fact that when there is only a limited supply of anything, people will want it more. This natural reaction is built into all of us. We may not even be aware of this inclination, but psychologically when something we desire becomes scarce, we feel compelled to try and get it as soon as possible.

We see how marketers use the art of scarcity in campaigns that have deadlines. You'll receive emails or text messages with phrases like "only 12 hours to go" or "just five seats left." To put it simply, once you realize that you no longer have infinite access to something you want you will be driven to take action and secure it for yourself before supplies are exhausted.

The important thing to remember here is that nothing has changed about the product. It isn't improved nor is it offered at a lower cost. The only difference is that there is a good chance that the resource would no longer be available. That fact alone made people want it all the more.

So, when you really want to motivate people to action, the Principle of Scarcity is very effective. When people learn about the benefits they would be missing out on, they will be clamoring to get it while supplies last.

Authority: We have been programmed from a very young age to respect and accept the words and advice of people in authority. This is the reason we take the advice of medical professionals without question, we listen to the voice of a teacher, and we comply with the badge of authority whenever it gives us direction.

We do this on a conscious level. It is a decision that we all make at some point in our lives. However, few of us realize that we also do this on a subconscious level. Even a professional who we know nothing about, we give more weight to their opinion and place it higher than any others. It is because it is our way of acknowledging their experience, position, and knowledge.

It is interesting to note that this automatic acceptance can be seen not just in numbers but also in social settings all around the world. Doctors are able to get their patients to follow certain regimens of treatment if their diplomas are openly displayed in their offices when they make recommendations. People are more likely to obey traffic laws if there is a uniformed officer present, and most are inclined to listen to an expert on any subject if there is some indication that he is indeed an expert.

Of course, this strategy can also backfire on you. If you were to go around boasting about your accomplishments or you were to tell everyone that they have to listen to you because you're the expert, it can be off-putting to many people and shut them down. However, if someone else was to point to your level of experience in a particular area and recommend you, people are more inclined to respond favorably.

This is why you see countless testimonials on webpages that want to sell you something. Interestingly enough, you don't need to know the trustworthiness of the person who is making the recommendations. In most cases, just the suggestion from an outside person is enough to convince people of the weight of the authority is all that is needed. Studies that have shown that this type of referral strategy can yield an increase of as much as 20% results in many cases.

Consistency: People generally will always follow the same path they have traveled in the past. They defer to something familiar and comfortable. Therefore, if someone naturally has done something for you in the past, it is quite likely that they will do it again; in most cases, their next action will even be bigger than before.

If you can get someone to make a small and insignificant commitment the first time, then it is likely that they will make an even larger gesture later on. Businesses tap into this natural desire by asking first for small but voluntary commitments like filling out an online form or answering a simple survey question. In one such health center, patients were asked to fill out their own appointment card rather than the staff. As a result, they had an 18% drop in missed appointments. But the act was so miniscule and minor the patient never even realized they were actually making a commitment.

Liking: We all naturally gravitate to the people and things we like. This is because of three essential elements. First, we want to be with those who are similar to us and we can relate to. Second, we are attracted to those who compliment us, and third those people who are willing to work with us and help us to achieve our goals.

Many have become successful by finding ways to point out similarities between their goals and their potential customers. By taking the time to engage in some form of small talk, sharing personal information with each other, you create a bond that will bind the two of you together on some level. The stronger you can make that bond before you begin to make a request, the better chance that the person will be willing to grant your request. Businesses that have used this strategy have seen as much as a 90% positive response as opposed to those who had a 55% response when they just got right down to business.

To use this skill to your advantage, look for common ground that you might share with others and give them genuine compliments rather than canned platitudes, and you should see better results.

Consensus: Consensus is the gentle use of peer pressure. People tend to follow the crowd in their actions and beliefs, especially if they are not sure of themselves. All of us take notice of what other people are doing. We often choose a restaurant because of how busy it is. We assume that if it is always busy it must be good. McDonald's displays the number of customers they've served over the many years they have been in business and you've probably already noticed how Amazon has a list of other products customers are buying when they choose anything you've searched for.

It's all part of our culture of socialization. Applying this to our art of persuasion gives people a sense of camaraderie with us and helps people to connect to not just what we have to offer but also to others who have already become a part of who we are. Whether you're selling a product or you're just trying to get someone to agree with you, one of the simplest ways to get people on board is to let them know that if they join you, they will not be alone. It feels less risky when they know they have someone to join forces with.

Any one of these strategies can help you to achieve better results when you're looking to get certain things. You've probably already begun to realize how many times you've been manipulated in your everyday life. No doubt, you believed you were making your own decision, which is probably true to a certain extent, but there's no question that the idea that germinated in your mind was planted there by someone else.

How to Use Persuasive Body Language

One thing that few people realize is that when you communicate with others, it is not the words that most people connect with. The foundation of your communication style lies not on what comes off your lips but on what your body is doing. Careful attention must be given to how you present your message. A poorly delivered speech can do so much more damage than a poorly developed presentation. To get the most of your message, your aim should be to tap into their subconscious mind on a more physical level. Here are just a few of the most commonly used body language signals. As you read through them visualize them in your head, practice them in a small scale when with others and watch how easily you can bring people into your fold.

Be Superman

The Superman pose works because it makes you stand out from the rest. Practice this in the privacy of your home before going out. Slip into the bathroom and try standing erect, puff out your chest (not too much), and place your hands on your hips with your elbows pointing out to the sides. Your goal is to make yourself look as big as possible. Do this pose before you begin your presentation and notice how your confidence and poise begins to grow.

Stand Up Tall

It can be pretty easy to slip into a slouch but fight the urge. It's important for you to stand tall so you project the best possible image you can. When you speak publicly with your body erect, your shoulders pulled back, and your body straight you'll not only look more confident but you'll feel it too. However, there is another benefit to standing tall that is not so readily seen. When you stand up tall, you align your airway so that your breath flows in and out freely. With all the potential blockages open, you'll naturally speak louder, your voice will be cleaner, and you'll sound as well as appear more professional.

Keep Your Body Open

You do need to be careful with the standing tall pose. You can overdo it and instead of displaying poise and confidence you could come off as being cocky and arrogant. To avoid this, resist any temptation to cross your arms as that will make you appear closed off. Try not to stuff your hands in your pocket, and if you are sitting don't cross your legs. You want to appear confident but also trustworthy so the more open you can keep your limbs the more people will want to respond to your message.

Make Eye Contact

If you want to give your presentation a more personal touch, work hard at making true eye contact. When you look directly into someone's eyes, you are basically inviting them into your inner fold. Direct eye contact creates an unspoken bond that feels more receptive than just talking at a person.

Of course, you don't want to stare into their eyes because that might make them feel a little uncomfortable. So, make eye contact with them, but only hold it for a few seconds. If you're speaking to a group of people, pick out several people in the crowd and make eye contact with each of them. After a few seconds move to the next person and continue this with as many people as is reasonably possible. It makes listeners feel that you're giving them a personal touch and that you are genuinely interested in them.

Move Around

If you're giving a presentation, resist the temptation to stand there like a statue. Whenever possible walkaround and use as much space as you can. It will reflect a more natural movement and give you more confidence. If you are nervous, movement will help you to relax in the environment and get your message across more easily. Movement also makes it possible for you to project your voice into different areas of the room so more people can connect with your message.

Use Your Hands

Remember, let your whole body talk. Communication involves more than words. Keep your hands free so that you can gesture freely. This will draw more people from your audience to you. Let your hands move freely to emphasize the points you want to make. Common gestures you can include could be pointing to your palm to stress a specific point, palms open wide and spread out to the sides to indicate openness or to create a question in the audience's mind and pointing outwards to stress other matters.

It would help a great deal if you were to take some time and observe how you communicate naturally with people you know. Very few people speak comfortably without gestures, you just don't realize you're doing it. However, if you start to take note of how your hands and body move when you speak with friends, you'll know which gestures you can incorporate into any presentation you make to give it the extra push to take your message over the top.

Use Facial Expressions

We say a lot with our face and when people speak to you, they will subconsciously look for those cues to fill in the blanks of what you didn't or can't say verbally. When they ask you a very basic question like, "how are you?" they immediately watch your face when you give the answer. Our faces are like blank canvases and when we speak our message is reflected on it projecting our inner feelings. Without saying a word, a person can tell how we are feeling, what we are thinking, and whether or not they want to trust you.

When you make facial gestures, keep your face relaxed. A calm and relaxed face can give you the appearance of authenticity and make you feel more human.

Keep these facial gestures to a minimum. Too many and people will feel uncomfortable – too little and people will think you are uninterested.

Becoming a master manipulator is just a matter of perfecting an art that we have been learning since childhood. It is not something new, unique, or questionable. It is just refining our way of communicating with the outside world. What we've just discussed in this first chapter are the basics of this skill. Now, let's roll up our sleeves and look a little deeper under the surface to see what really drives people to follow a true master in the art of persuasion.

Chapter 2: Emotional Intelligence 101

For years, the common belief was that the key to success lies in your Intelligence quotient or your IQ. Whether you are book smart or street smart, there is no question that having some level of mental acuity will help you navigate the obstacles that you must overcome to achieve your goals.

But that leads us into a long-standing debate, which one is more important? Those who advocate for IQ as the most important argue that your mental intelligence is what will help you to navigate the system will definitely pave the way for you but evidence is now emerging that shows that emotional intelligence is equally as important in preparing you to deal with people. To clarify this though, we need to fully understand the difference between the two.

Well known psychologist, Howard Gardner points out that one's intelligence is not limited to mastering one single ability. His years of study in how the brain works has identified several different ways one can show intelligence. Read any of his writings and you'll come across his well-known expression:

It's not how smart you are but how you are smart

Where IQ focuses on one or a few abilities, commonly referred to as the "G Factor," he points out that the ability to recognize emotions, understand, and express them clearly is key to how well one may be able to navigate the challenges in life.

If you've ever taken an IQ test then you know that it only focuses on certain skills. Your IQ score was based only on visual, spatial, working memory, short and long-term memory, quantitative and fluid reasoning. In essence, you were tested on the general topics commonly taught in school.

Your EQ, however, is measured on your ability to perceive an emotion, evaluate, manage, and express it. When you have emotional intelligence, you are able to see and identify the emotions in others, reason on your observations to determine how others are feeling and use those emotions as a means of facilitating communication all while keeping your own emotions in check.

For years, we've always placed great store in our IQ and it is still viewed as important even today. However, as our knowledge of how the brain works continues to grow, there is increasing evidence that the IQ alone is not a guarantee of success. It's true, people with a high IQ will usually do better in school, they get the better jobs, and even seem to be more physically healthy. But throughout history, we have repeatedly seen many with high IQs that seem to fail at everything they attempt. It is clear that IQ alone will not get you to where you want to be. Rather it is an entire battery of factors that include your EQ that will give you better assurance at success.

What Is Emotional Intelligence?

We've already determined that at the heart of it, emotional intelligence is the ability to identify and recognize emotions in others and manage your own, but there is more to it than that. In order to have good emotional intelligence, you need to master three skills.

- **Emotional Awareness:** The ability to recognize emotions in others and label them. It's not enough to say that person is upset, you need to know whether they are angry, sad, frightened, grieving, or embarrassed.

- **Redirect:** Once you've identified those emotions, you need to skillfully redirect those emotions by thinking things through, use them to solve problems, and apply them to the tasks or skills you need to meet.

- **Manage:** The skill in managing your own emotions goes beyond just not throwing a fit when you don't like something. As long as you can manage those feelings and use them to your advantage, you will become a master of emotional intelligence.

When you have a high EQ, you are able to identify a wide range of both negative and positive emotions, even when they are not obviously displayed. You will be in-tune with how other people are feeling, which can give you insight into what they are thinking, and you'll be able to pick up on even the subtlest of cues when you are interacting within a particular social environment. All of these skills can be used to help you become a better spouse, friend, parent, teacher, lover, leader, boss, or anything else you might wish to do.

It would be difficult to get someone to respond to you if you don't know what moves them to take action. There is a delicate art to managing emotions, but it is necessary for anyone who is looking to expand their horizons.

Emotions are extremely powerful and are the force behind all of our behavior and by extension the behavior of all people, triggering both positive and negative reactions. Your EQ will help you to focus on not just your own personal feelings and thoughts, but also on those of others.

If you take the time, you could probably look back and find plenty of examples of how others have used their EQ to manipulate you in the past. The tactic was subtle, you likely had no idea it was happening. For example, how many times have you been watching TV and saw a commercial showing young children from a third world country with distended bellies and flies and mosquitos buzzing around them. It pulls on your heart strings, doesn't it? Or perhaps you met up with a friend who was visibly distressed and after some prodding, told you how he was in a bad financial state and needed some help to pay off some financial obligations.

In each of those cases, the manipulator pulled on your emotional heartstrings because they knew how it would affect you emotionally. They were able to get you in a position to want to help them. In fact, you probably thought that it was your idea all along. Every day, we see these kinds of emotional manipulators all around us, most of them are used in a positive and beneficial way, but there are plenty examples of negatives ones as well.

Consider one example of one manipulation master that caused extreme harm to others. Before Adolf Hitler began his reign of terror as the head of the Nazi regime, he spent years observing human behavior and how his own body language was affecting those around him. He observed the emotional impact of every gesture and position and honed those skills until he turned himself into a mesmerizing speaker.

A leader who wants to take unfair advantage over others will use many things to get them to buy into a specific idea.

They may try to control you by using your own fears against you, even going to the point of exaggerating the truth or telling you outright lies to back you into a corner where you feel they are the only ones you can trust.

They could also resort to outright deception to put you at a disadvantage. They may tell you the truth but only part of the story; the part that shows them in a more positive light. They will say all the things you want to hear. So, they may be the yes person in the office, always agreeing with you on every point, regardless of the logic. They will do you small favors in an attempt to get you to be indebted to them. They will try everything they can to maneuver things to their advantage. This strategy puts you in a setting where they have the power and you are not as at ease as you would be otherwise. Meetings will be at their home, office, club, or any other location of their choosing.

They are not afraid to ask the hard questions. This is an attempt to uncover your weaknesses or to gather information they could one day use to manipulate you further. Often the questions are about personal matters or things you are less likely to discuss openly.

They talk fast to try to throw you off track and may even use uncommon vocabulary in order to undermine your confidence. Think of those fast talking infomercials you see on late-night TV. They usually throw extensive vocabulary at you in the hopes that you won't be able to follow their storyline fully. And the rapid-paced speech doesn't give you enough time to process all the information they are giving you, leaving you unsure of yourself.

They are not afraid of showing their emotions or causing a scene when it will work to their advantage. Negative situations often make people uncomfortable which can give them a huge advantage that they can exploit.

They will pressure you to respond to situations quickly so you don't have time to think about it. They want you to react on impulse even to what may seem like unreasonable demands.

They may even cut off communication altogether in order to unnerve you and give them the upper hand. This gives them a sense of power and forces you to wait until they are ready to continue the relationship.

All of these are tactics that negative manipulators use at will. As you read through them, there is a good chance that you have seen these used on you from time to time. In fact, you may have even used them yourself on other people.

As a master manipulator, it is important that you recognize these tactics. None of these would work if you recognized them firsthand, and if you had a high enough EQ, you would know how to respond in order to avoid being manipulated in ways that you're not comfortable with.

If they try to use fear – take the time to examine the bigger picture, gather more information so you would have all the facts to make a decision.

If they are being deceptive – ask questions to uncover the truth or speak to someone trustworthy to verify the facts of the situation.

If they are being too agreeable – focus on having a more balanced thinking process.

If they are always doing you small favors – don't hesitate to say no and refuse them.

If they always want to control location – insist on a neutral meeting place.

If they ask too many personal questions – avoid saying too much.

If they speak too fast – stop them to ask questions for verification.

If they are prone to emotional outbursts – avoid impulse reactions. Wait for them to calm down and speak to them in a slow and purposeful manner to balance the situation.

If they are pressuring you to make a decision quickly – request more time or refuse.

If they are giving you the silent treatment – be willing to walk away or at least wait until they come to you, giving you the advantage.

Another masterful manipulator of the 20th century was Martin Luther King, Jr. Take some time and read over his *I Have A Dream* speech and ask yourself why it was so powerful. Why decades later, the words continue to resonate with everyone who reads or hears them. It was his choice of words, meant to stir up and touch on the emotions of his listeners. At the same time, as he delivered his message, he was able to keep complete control of his own emotions, letting out only what was needed to stir the audience to align with him.

So, while your IQ may be instrumental in positioning you in the right place to achieve some level of success, it is your EQ that will be most effective in getting others to go along with your grand plan so you can get the results you seek. No doubt, you'll need both, but your EQ will be the bigger indication of success.

Why Master Manipulators Need Emotional Intelligence

Lisa Nowak was a highly intelligent person. By the time she had applied for her job at NASA, she had met all the qualifications. She had completed a Master's program in aeronautical engineering and a postgraduate study in astrophysics at the US Naval Academy. She had spent more than five years accumulating five years of piloting experience. She was physically fit and had all the book knowledge she could have possibly need. She was selected to be in the astronaut program with no problems.

Unfortunately, things didn't work out well for Lisa. In 2007, her inability to control her emotions caused her to make a rash decision that destroyed her chances completely. When she discovered that her then romantic partner was involved with someone else, she took matters into her own hands. She took the 15 hour drive from Houston to Orlando to confront and kidnap the other woman, which lead to her having an emotional breakdown, going to jail ending her career completely.

The evidence is clear, one's EQ dictates how we behave. Our behavior is the end result of a linear process that is played out in our brains.

1. A triggering event occurs
2. Our senses pick up the event and transmits it to our brain
3. We mentally process the event and produce thoughts and opinions about it
4. The thoughts trigger an emotional response
5. The emotion we feel triggers a specific behavior
6. The behavior then triggers another inciting event
7. The cycle starts all over again

The key to becoming a master manipulator is to control behavior and since all behavior is triggered by our emotional state, it is important to manage emotions well. No matter what we do with others, communication, relationships, business, or anything else, the emotions are behind the entire process. If you have a high EQ it will be easier for you to read other people and manipulate situations in order to get them to do what you expect.

Most of us can identify and recognize our own emotions and how they cause us to react to triggering events in our lives. However, where we often find ourselves lacking is in the ability to see those same reactions in others. One of the most important factors in mastering a high EQ is to identify emotional reactions in others.

According to one study conducted by Johnson & Johnson, higher performers in the workplace were those who showed a higher emotional intelligence. The numbers were quite impressive showing 90% of the best workers were those with a high EQ and 80% of the lowest showed a low EQ.

No matter what your goals are or how you plan to use your manipulation skills, a high EQ can be one of the most significant factors in getting you to where you want to be.

9 Ways to Develop Powerful Emotional Intelligence

Because emotions are so powerful, they have a direct effect on how well you interact in social situations. They can also dictate your coping strategies, the amount of money you spend, and what you do with your time. As you can see controlling your emotions could be one of the most important factors in determining your success no matter what you do.

Keep in mind that there is a big difference between developing emotional intelligence and suppressing your emotions. If you feel sad or you try to hide your feelings, it could cause you more harm than good. Suppressing emotions are generally what leads to damaging coping skills like over-eating, gambling, and drinking.

Managing your emotions and developing a high EQ is not hiding or suppressing your feelings but is recognizing those feelings and not allowing them to have the power to control you. In other words, you control your emotions not the other way around. So, if you find yourself in a bad mood, you need to take the helm and change it by choosing to display another emotion. But learning how to manage them will take an investment in time and practice. Here are a few skills that will help you get started on the right path.

1. Identify Negative Emotions First

Generally, the emotions that are most likely to get us into trouble are the negative ones. When our negative emotions take control, we often make impulse reactions. We need to take the time to analyze what is going on inside our heads. By taking the time to stop and think about what's happening internally before you become overly emotional, you are less likely to have a knee-jerk reaction to a triggering event. Learn to breathe a little and try to look at things more objectively. Practicing the art of mindfulness can help you to slow down and analyze a situation objectively from different perspectives. Once you have identified your emotion and labeled it, you cross a mental threshold that makes it easier to move forward.

2. Change Your Vocabulary

Your choice of words you use to communicate says a lot about who you are inside. Analyze your language to see which words you're using to relay what you want. Those with a higher level of emotional intelligence are very specific when they speak while those with a low EQ tend to be very vague, sounding like they are skirting issues rather than addressing them. The next time you're in a conversation with someone else that didn't go well, take the time to analyze the words you used. How could you have been clearer in your communication. Chances are you will start to see your own communication deficiencies, but also recognize emotional triggers in others. This will give you a better chance of addressing the problem rather than allowing your emotions to catapult you into a cycle of negative behavior.

3. Learn to be More Empathetic

Start watching other people more closely. People subconsciously give you both verbal and non-verbal cues letting you know what emotions they are feeling. This can give you invaluable insight into what actions you need to take or words you need to say to change the dynamic. Before you react though, take the time to put yourself in their place and ask yourself how you would want someone to react. This can be a key communication tool that can lead to better connections with others and remind yourself that every situation is not always about you.

4. Learn Your Stressors

All of us have our own triggers, events that cause us stress and anxiety. These stressors are what can take you out of the game so, if you know what they are, you can develop strategies that can address them before you react negatively. So, if you know that looking at the bills gets your blood boiling, put it off to a time when you are less likely to have to interact with other people. If you know that the phone ringing during dinner time causes you to get angry, unplug the phone until dinner is over. By being proactive in these situations, you can avoid negative altercations with others.

5. Don't Allow Challenges to Bring You Down

No matter who you are, we all are faced with challenges. That in itself is not an indicator of the kind of person you are. It's the behavior that those challenges trigger that can tell the world who you are. How you address uncomfortable issues can either put you on the path to success or bring you down. So, when faced with unpleasant situations, learn how to take a more optimistic view rather than a critical one. For example, if you find you are having difficulties with your employer, you can either leave the office constantly complaining about what he or she said, or you can ask yourself constructive questions and try to come up with proactive strategies to diffuse the situation. Learn how to address the conflict before it arises and take on a more optimistic approach. This will gradually start to change your personal behavior and will start to draw more people to you.

6. Strive to Understand the Reason Behind Your Emotions

Once you have been able to identify which emotions you are experiencing, you need to try to understand why. Your goal is to discover the triggering event that caused these emotions to form. It may take a little time, but rarely is the triggering event the true cause of the feelings. You may find that you have to look further back in your life to find out why certain events cause you to react the way you do. Quite often it is not the event that causes your distress but the fact that the situation does not honor your personal values in some way. This will require you to develop some cold hard honesty to help you uncover your own hidden truths.

7. Resolve the Issue

Sometimes all that is needed to diffuse a difficult situation is to learn how to look at it from a different perspective. Remember the cycle – thoughts lead to emotions which lead to behavior. If you are feeling bad about something, go back to your thoughts to change the dialogue. After you've identified the triggering thought, try to think of different possible thoughts that can change the outcome. Focus on the positive and the negative feelings usually will go away. Other times, you might find that much of the negativity you've built up can be alleviated simply by understanding what's happening. This redirect process is key to gaining command over your emotions and usually leads to a much calmer personality.

8. Make a Different Choice

After you've resolved the issue in your mind, you need to make the decision to react a different way in the future. This can be quite difficult, because we know that in the heat of the moment, rational thinking is never truly the case. But a lot of our behavior is actually the result of habits; we have automatically behaviors with certain situations and we have done so for so long that we don't even stop to consider if our response is working or not. No one wants to be the guy that flies off the handle at the slightest provocation; it's stressful on everyone including him. Make a choice today, to not allow your emotions to hijack you and lead you down the path towards destruction. Learning to master this skill is not something you can just read about and the next day you know exactly what to do. You will fail many times, you will struggle with restraining yourself, but you will gradually make a change.

9. Minimize Negative Moods

When you do find yourself in a bad mood, readjust as soon as possible, otherwise you could find yourself engaging in behavior that will isolate you. Avoid being evasive, this can actually work against your attempts to become a master manipulator. You might find yourself complaining about the people around you or slip into a scenario of not talking or lashing out at others.

So, it is smart to plan ahead. Think of the things that generally put you in a better mood so you can start doing those things when negative feelings start to rise up. For example, you might want to talk about pleasant things with a friend, listen to your favorite music, take a walk, or meditate. It will keep your mind focused on what's important so that you can get away from the negative feelings before they become a problem.

It is one thing to identify emotions and understand them but managing them can be very difficult. Our emotions are not constant and can rise and fall like the waves of the sea so it can be hard to keep them under control. No one is pleasant all the time and no one is always a hot head. We all have certain triggers that bring out the ugly in us, but if you practice these steps often enough, eventually you will begin to see the tide changing and you'll get the mastery over them. As you do, your EQ will become stronger and you'll be more in-tuned with your own inner demons. This will give you the needed confidence to handle uncomfortable situations by shifting your mood and give you more control over any situation you find yourself in.

How to Control Your Emotions Like a Boss

When you feel like the world is closing in on you, there is a powerful but overwhelming sense that you are losing control, which can be a very frightening thing. It doesn't matter if it deals with something at home or in the boardroom with a team of professionals. The pressure from a constant stream of things piling up can make you feel claustrophobic causing you to do something quickly to change it. It can be these times that cause us to make our biggest impulse reactions, which are usually the ones to get us into trouble.

At times, taking a few deep breaths or a walk around the block just doesn't cut it. As the cortisone in your body starts to increase, you feel your chest tighten or the knot in your stomach starts to grow. You start to yell and scream at anyone within your vicinity, whether they are responsible or not. You may threaten, or you could storm out of the room, slamming the door behind you in a child-like tantrum. That is the moment when you are on the verge of exploding. How can you reclaim your life and make sure that your emotions stay in check even when everything seems out of your hands.

We've all had that scenario or something similar happen to us. Later we are riddled with guilt and shame for our behavior. But what we may not realize is that your emotions have triggered a chemical reaction in your body, which started a snowball effect that once started was almost impossible to control.

On the other hand, we have all seen that one boss, parent, teacher, or other authority figure that seems to maintain their composure no matter how desperate the situation may seem. What's the difference? It comes down to one simple factor. They were able to control their emotions so that the negative behavior never starts in the first place. The truth is that managing your emotions can literally transform your life and personality, enabling you to bring out the best qualities within you rather than the worst.

If you can relate to either of these situations, it should become clear to you that emotions are not inherently bad. We all have them for a reason; they are there to warn us of situations that are uncomfortable, dangerous, or unpleasant. But, since schools are primarily focused on teaching us book knowledge, most of us have to learn to manage our emotions on our own and we never outgrow those temper tantrum habits we displayed as a child.

It doesn't have to be this way though. By making a concerted effort to take charge of your emotions, you can literally begin to take charge of the situation. Rather than allowing your own emotions to direct your behavior, you direct your emotions. How can you do this?

By developing something called emotion regulation skills. In essence, these are unique skills designed to manage those impulse urges and emotions that rise up in all of us. The more you master these skills the more confidence you'll have in managing your emotions and controlling them. This will be a major step in your training to become a master manipulator. It's a X step process:

1.   Identify your feelings and accept them for what they are

You can't manage what you can't understand. But it is not enough to say, "I'm angry" or "I'm frustrated." This is a starting point but aim to be more specific in your identifying process. Are you angry because you're afraid? Are you frustrated because of the workload or because you feel unqualified to manage it? By identifying the root cause of the negative emotion, you begin to understand what your true emotions are. Rarely, are the ones we reveal to the public a true image of who we are.

It is important that you get rid of the need to judge yourself. Your goal here is to merely identify the situation, not justify, explain, or judge. Acknowledge it for what it is, don't resist them, just accept them for what they are and move on. You'll address the correction of these habits later on.

It is important to do this as soon as you notice an emotional surge begin to rise. Work at expanding your vocabulary and go beyond just stating the obvious. As you work on developing these skills, you will soon be able to discern even the slightest changes in your mood swings.

a. Identify that you are having an emotion
b. Pause and analyze
c. What thoughts are running through your mind
d. What sensations are you feeling in your body
e. Identify the emotion
f. Try to discern the nuances and what changed
g. What is the reaction you are trying to suppress
h. Observe

Here, you are working as an outside observer. Rather than allowing the emotion to unfold within you, use your imagination and allow it to play out in front of you as if it was an actor on a stage. Let happen, watch it intensify and then dissipate without making yourself a part of it.

2.   Take Positive Action

Once you are familiar with the emotion, you will find it much easier to manage it. As you observe the emotion playing out in front of you, pull back the curtain to see the bigger picture. In most cases, you will be able to bring your mind to a calmer state. Often just taking the time to identify and look at the bigger scope is enough to bring you into a more stable frame of mind.

If that doesn't work, you can take the next step and find something that can distract you from your negative feelings at the time. Try to have a calming task you can do on hand to bring your mind back into balance. Many people turn to something they instinctively enjoy like walking, journaling, deep breathing, crafting, or coloring. The key here is to have something that will naturally relax you. All of us are different so your calming activity may be something unique to everyone around you.

By mastering your emotion regulation, you will naturally become more confident and empowered. Once your emotions are no longer controlling you, it will be easier for you to see how you can master manipulation. The bottom line is that you can never hope to manipulate others until you are able to manipulate yourself. Once you have developed your EQ well, you will not only see how it changes you internally, but by extension have a positive effect on everyone around you. It will take dedication and hard work. You won't be able to accomplish it right away and it will take a lot of practice, but the results will pay off for you many times over and you will be able to see the advantages in the changes as you progress.

Chapter Three: Choosing Your Target

After going through the process outlined in the last chapter, chances are you've come to learn something new about yourself. Most people are surprised to learn what really makes them tick, and it's even more surprising to discover what their triggers actually are. Now that you understand yourself better, it is easier to determine exactly what you need to change your circumstances and move towards your goal. You can't manipulate or influence other people, if you can't manipulate yourself.

Another advantage of mastering the skills in the last chapter is that you become more aware of others around you. By paying more attention to both verbal and non-verbal cues they give, you will almost feel like you're a mind reader. You will be able to discern their moods, wants, fears, desires, etc. This knowledge can be used to find your first target for manipulation.

When choosing a target, look for certain traits that the individual demonstrates to show they are open to receiving and responding to your powers of influence. So, as you scope out potential prospects, look for these characteristics. Don't assume that if someone is displaying these qualities that they are in some way inferior to you or others. To the contrary, many of the following qualities are quite admirable. As we've already stated, any facet of a person's character can be used in both a positive and a negative way. We are only looking for a doorway to enter and implement a possible means of exercising your powers of persuasion.

They are Conscientious

People who are conscientious are not likely to be focusing entirely on themselves. Conscientious people are concerned about the quality of their work, the welfare of others, and their commitment to any task that has been assigned to them. While they may be concerned about how events will affect them, their primary concern will be determined by their moral compass. In order to exercise some level of influence over them, you need to tap into their powerful sense of morality. Once you can show them how they can achieve their goals in relation to that, you will have a powerful means in which to persuade them to do what you want them to do.

They Have Empathy

A good target will have strong empathetic tendencies. Empathy can be viewed as the emotional fuel that you can use to propel you towards your goals. People with empathy often are given praise, attention and valuable resources freely, putting you in a state of comfort as you make your requests or needs know.

Empathetic people are excellent at putting themselves in your shoes. They can feel your pain in their heart and because of this, they will do everything within their power to relieve you of it. You can use that empathy to your advantage by telling a store, apologizing, or carefully framing a scenario to gain their sympathy.

They Have Integrity

A person with integrity is true to their word and can be of immense value to you. They are not inclined to cheat or steal, nor are they likely to break off a relationship until it is absolutely necessary. Even if they realize later that you have taken unfair advantage of them, their sense of integrity is usually what keeps them from retaliation. The relationship you build with them will be strong and their entire sense of being will keep them from betraying it no matter what.

They are Resilient

A good target will be resilient enough to bounce back from any incidents that may cause them harm. This resiliency makes them strong enough to stand up against of the pressures you can put on them. Even if they are faced with difficult challenges these are the people who are less likely to give up. While all their instincts may be telling them to run the other way, they are more likely to stay the course in spite of it all.

Establishing a relationship with them is the same as obligating them to you. They are unlikely to turn on you even if they discover that they are being manipulated.

They are Sentimental

A person who is very sentimental leads with his heart in everything he does. A manipulator can use flattery and praise to position the target and set them up for persuasion. The words used need to address their unique needs and desires. By idolizing them from the very start of the relationship, you can garner their trust and appeal to their most basic need for love. Creating pleasant memories together pulls at their heartstrings and bonds them into a relationship you can use later to get what you want.

They best way to influence a sentimentalist is to carefully study them, determine their individual qualities and the things that they value the most. By establishing a relationship with them and picking up on their verbal-and non-verbal cues, you can uncover their insecurities and weaknesses.

These are the basic characteristics you will find in those who are easy targets for manipulation. It doesn't mean that they are the only one you will be able to work your magic with, but these are the ones you will most likely find success with as you start to apply the manipulation strategies will we be discussing throughout this book.

What Hooks People In?

Anything that draws our attention can be used as a key tool of manipulation. So, when choosing a target to persuade in one way or another, it is important that you use those things that will naturally hook people and draw them into you. Your hook, however, needs to be something that your target won't have to think too much about. In fact, you don't even want them to get even the slightest inkling that you're pulling them in. With the right skill, you will be able to subtly draw them into your circle without ever making them consciously aware that they are caught in your web.

Whether you're trying to entice a love interest or you're trying to get your foot in the door of your next job, your first task is to draw the person in. This can be tricky and the answers can vary depending on your target. However, there are common threads you can find in all sorts of people. Since most people are more inclined to listen to you when they feel respected it's a given that if you can tap into their personal sense of self, you'll be halfway there. Consider these very basic qualities and test them out to see if they will work with your intended target.

Become a Good Listener: People will naturally be drawn to you if they feel that you are listening to what they have to say. But this involves more than just giving the appearance that you are interested in what they have to say. When you are a dedicated listener, you are fully engaged in their message.

This does several things that can work in your favor. First, you'll become a better communicator but you will also be building up a level of trust between you and the other person. That rapport will work on a subconscious level slowly building up a deeper and more meaningful connection between the two of you.

An active listener requires commitment and focus. It may not be easy at first, but to show keen interest in what the other person is saying. That means not responding to distractions or interruptions but being completely present in the moment. You may have to ask questions for clarification, regularly insert words in the conversation so they know you're still with them, turning off or not answering your phone when calls come in, and giving your whole attention to them.

Being Observant

Active listening also means watching the other person's non-verbal cues as well. You will be paying close attention to their body language and verbal intonation. In other words, you want to not only hear what they are saying to you but how they are saying it. This will give you valuable information about their emotional state of mind.

For example, if they are whimpering or speaking in a low tone of voice it may be a sign that they are worried or fearful. However, if they are shouting it could be an indication that they are angry or frustrated.

But in order for these observations to draw them in, you need to find ways to show them that you are committed to them. By mirroring back some of their expressions, and clarifying your understanding of those points, you are demonstrating to them that you are kindling a new relationship with them. It will endear them to you on a subconscious level. The more they are able to believe that you value their input and their message, the more attractive you will be to them and they will respond to you accordingly.

Kindness

We live in a world where true and genuine kindness is hard to find. If you want to really hook people in, just a simple act of kindness may be all that is needed. Kindness does not necessarily mean the giving of gifts. While that may be a part of it, sometimes just the habit of saying kind words, smiling, or showing a genuine active of consideration may be all that is needed to show people that you care.

This should not come as a surprise to you. You've probably already experienced how you respond to people who are kind to you. You should think no less of those who you are trying to lure into your circle. In fact, it has been scientifically proven that both men and women are more drawn to people who are compassionate and selfless. It is actually quite a powerful means of attracting others and can literally influence a person even if the kindness is not shown to them. In other words, it can also work if they are just mere observers of your acts of kindness even if they are not the recipient.

The concept of kindness can be extended beyond the obvious. A 2013 study showed that both men and women were drawn to people who had a more helping spirit, actually finding them to be more attractive on all levels. Demonstrating a preference for others in a helpful manner can appeal to people on the most basic of levels as this is an indication that a helpful person will fill need for protection in a dangerous world.

Smiling

Hooking people can be as easy as smiling. It is the one act that will cost you nothing but can yield you lots of results. Smiling not only makes you stand out as kind and helpful, but it also releases your own endorphins and serotonin in your body. Both of these naturally produced chemicals will not only improve your own mood but is infectious enough to improve the mood of those around you, including your target.

Studies have shown that just seeing a smiling face can activate the pleasure center of the brain giving your target a sense of satisfaction and reward. According to the School of Psychology conducted at the University of Aberdeen in Scotland, those who received smiles from others (even if indirectly) were naturally drawn to the smiler.

Consistency

People crave stability in their lives. If you're serious about drawing other people to you then consistency is the key. Instability in jobs, home life, even our diets cause people distress. Life becomes unpredictable and confusing. A person who has an inconsistent person in their lives never gain the ability to feel secure.

Your target will naturally be drawn to you on a subconscious level if your behavior is consistent and reliable. To reinforce this gravitational pull, if your consistency is in line with their personal attitudes, beliefs, and core values it will be that much easier to draw them in.

Obligation

People can also be hooked and drawn over to you by obligating them to you. This is interesting in that quite often the obligation starts even before you do anything directly. Think of the company that offers a free gift of very little value. Sometimes referred to as the theory of reciprocity, it is a concept that is deeply ingrained in us from a very early age. When someone does something for us, we feel indebted to reciprocate in some way. They may not expect anything in return, but the power is so strong that it compels us anyway.

This power is so strong that there is only one way to rid ourselves of this need to return like for like is to do something for the other person. Even if you don't want or even like the gift or favor, you feel compelled to follow through quite often with a sense of urgency. It is a kind of psychological debt that can sometimes be so strong that it drives a person to sometimes exceed the original gift many times over.

Connection

It's a natural inclination in all of us. The more connected we are to others the more influence they have over our decisions. By creating a bond, you create comfort in others. Even if you've known them only a short time that bond can make it seem like a lifelong relationship.

There are four main elements to a strong connection:

- Attraction: By choosing a single positive quality and using it to influence the general perception, people will naturally feel connected to you. By displaying qualities like kindness, intelligence, and loyalty, people will find you more attractive.

- Rapport: Rapport is a little bit more difficult to define. It is a hidden quality that puts you on the same mental wavelength as the other person. It's that feeling you get when you meet someone and instantly hit it off. That secret something that automatically bonds you to another person. Sometimes rapport is readily recognizable as in a physical attraction or a common understanding. Other times it is a little harder to identify. You've probably seen cases where two people have no obvious common ground but they develop a rapport just the same.

- People skills (EQ): Your ability to work well with people can forge a strong bond with them. According to some research, at least 85% of your success will depend on how you interact with others; the other 15% can be related to your intelligence and specific training. As we discussed in the last chapter, your EQ is crucial to your ability to take that knowledge and skill base and connect it to other people.

- Similarity: People are naturally drawn to things they are familiar with. So, by utilizing those characteristics that people feel comfortable with, you can connect to more people. Studies have revealed that people are naturally attracted to things they can relate to and understand. By matching your personality traits with their lifestyles, they will be impelled to connect to you.

When all four of these elements are in play you can build a strong bond that long-standing relationships can be founded upon.

Social Pressure

Because we are social creatures by nature, all of us, no matter how shy, have an inborn desire to belong to something. A good manipulator will definitely look for someone who is searching for some form of inclusion to his advantage. For all of us, if the desire to become a group is strong enough, it can easily cause us to change our viewpoint and perceptions just so we can fit in.

We all care to some extent, about what others think of us and we all seek validation, even if we don't want to admit it. It is this inborn desire to fit in with the main crowd that determines our view of what is considered "correct" behavior. If our actions go against the mainstream of the masses, our behavior is frowned upon, but the more we fit in, the "correct" others will perceive us and the more likely they will be willing to conform to what you want. It is a natural part of human nature, and the more you can create an approved form of social pressure, the more your targets will feel validated and bond with you.

Scarcity

People have an inner drive to not miss out on things. This is why limited time offers usually work very well when it comes to sales. The natural tendency is to put things off until a later time when there is no real immediate need, but by creating sense of urgency, you can trigger an impulse reaction that will compel people to move even if their own minds tell them it's not necessary.

Scarcity triggers that inborn fear of missing out or FOMO. Think of how things work in an auction. Usually at an auction, there is a limited supply of a specific item (often only one). When another person outbids you, a sort of panic starts to set in. What if you can't find this item again, what if someone considers the item more valuable than you? Perhaps you missed something? All sorts of thoughts start to running through your head and suddenly, the drive to obtain that item becomes more powerful than your own common sense. No matter what you planned before the event, it can quickly go right out the window when this factor starts to put pressure on you.

This factor can be extremely powerful when played the right way. The more scarcity you can create, the more valuable it will be in the eyes of others.

Language

Your choice of words also has a great deal of influence on other people. Because we are social creatures, at least 60% of our daily lives is spent on oral communication. By choosing words that appeal to the ears of your target, you can capture their attention and bring your story to life. Words can generate a powerful source of energy and convince people to respond to your message. By the same token, the wrong words can crush all of your hard work in mere seconds.

The more adept you are at using the spoken word, the more persuasive you will be. While body language makes up the lion's share of our communication skills, do not underestimate the power of your words. They have a direct impact on the beliefs, attitudes, and perceptions of those around us. Used in the wrong way, you could lose a lot more than you bargained for. Even newscasters are specifically trained to use certain inflections in their voices to project a sense of authority and knowledge.

Elements of voice control also influence people. Consider how you emphasize words, your pitch, pace, fillers, volume, articulation and even where you pause when you speak. Even your lack of words has power. Knowing when to speak and when to let the silence have power says a lot about your own level of confidence.

Creating Contrast

Contrast is usually something that is better understood in art, but when applied in persuasion can literally bond someone to you with little effort. When you present someone with two scenarios that seem like they are worlds apart you are creating a contrast. Imagine realizing that you need thousands of dollars to redecorate your home, and then later learning that most of the cost can be eliminated by using a different designer. This is creating contrast. Chances are you will feel indebted to the new designer or contractor that saved you all the money, even if you later learn that none of the other expenses you thought you needed were even necessary.

They key to the success of using contrast is to use the two scenarios close together. If too much time is allowed to pass before the favorable option is presented, contrast loses much of its power. Because people will naturally be drawn to positive news, when they hear negative reports they are usually emotionally thrown. Here, timing is key. If you submit your concept in quick succession with another great idea, your message will have little impact. There is not enough contrast between the two ideas. However, if you submit your idea immediately after someone else presents a bad idea, the power of your message will cut right to the heart of the listeners and you will see an immediate reaction.

Creating Expectations

Many people make decisions based on what they know others will expect them to do. We see this often in children. If the parents expect them to behave poorly in a given situation, they will usually oblige them. The same is true of all of us. If your target is aware of your expectations, they will usually act accordingly.

People have all sorts of ways to show what they expect of you. Some will tell you directly what they want and others will use more subtle means. For example, if you are meeting someone for the first time, how you introduce yourself lets them know exactly how you want to be addressed. If you use your title and surname, then they know you want to be addressed that way. However, if you tell them a nickname or just a first name, they are more likely to feel more at ease and comfortable around you. The casualness of your words can put them at ease.

Whenever you communicate with others, you're letting them know what your expectations are.

Involvement

You have much more influence over another person when they are involved in what you are doing or saying. Efforts to engage the other person requires you to tap into their sensory perceptions. We all have five senses that is continually feeding the brain. The more of these senses we are able to engage in, the more involved and committed to you the other person will be. By creating a very specific atmosphere you can yield a powerful influence over them.

Just talking to the other person is not sufficient enough to influence people because listening is merely a passive exercise. It doesn't evoke any emotions or connection. However, if the other person is listening, smelling, tasting, and feeling all at the same time, it would be nearly impossible for their mind to drift off and focus on something else.

There are several ways you can create a sense of involvement in the other person. If you're in a discussion with them, make sure the conversation is not one-sided. Ask information questions that will naturally compel them to contribute to the discussion. You can engage their creative mind by telling stories designed to touch them emotionally. By creating an atmosphere of suspense, you can keep them hanging on to your every word until you achieve your set goal. The more involved a person is in your goal the more likely they will do whatever is necessary to give you what you want.

Build Self-Esteem

One might think that a person with a weak self-esteem is easy to manipulate but that would not be entirely correct. The general belief is that anyone that is lacking in self-esteem craves acceptance. The reality though is that acceptance, praise, and recognition is a common need shared by all of us. It speaks to the core of what it means to be human.

Watch what happens when you praise anyone, even with the smallest and most insignificant expressions. You can literally see their spirits lift and their mood change. All humans need praise and recognition. In fact, it is the only way a person gets built up psychologically over time. Praise from others satisfies our need to be a part of something bigger than ourselves.

When persuading others, presenting your message in a way that edifies your listeners will take you much farther than you might imagine. The more you build them up, the more they will be inclined to follow you through to your goal. This rule is true for everyone regardless of their level of self-esteem. But the mere fact that self-esteem is key to their connection with you, your goal should be making your listener feel needed and respected.

You will have to walk a fine line here though. There is a big difference in helping to build someone's self-esteem and boosting someone's ego. So, don't go overboard when it comes to this practice. Make sure you understand the difference because this quality could easily backfire on you.

Association

As social beings, our brains subconsciously look for connections in everything we do. We do this so quickly we rarely recognize that we have automatically categorized people as soon as we make a connection. These categories instantly put some people closer to us and others far away. We categorize based on a myriad of options. We might decide where they fit in our lives based on the colors they wear, the people they are with, the jobs they have, the music they listen to, or even emotions they express. We use these associations to make judgments about them and how deep our relationship with them will be.

When you are trying to apply your powers of persuasion you utilize this internal and instinctive need to create the type of relationship you need. You can tap into it to bring out certain emotions you need them to employ to bond them to you. Obviously, everyone's idea of association will be different so before you can use the art of association, you need to learn enough about that person to figure out what kind of associations you need.

Balance

When you are manipulating your target, your focus needs to be on their emotions but that does not mean that you can neglect their ability to reason on things. There has to be some level of balance in order to get your desired results. You may be able to evoke a powerful emotional response that may last for a while but no one can maintain intense emotions all the time. By the same token, you may be able to use careful reasoning and logic analyzing a certain situation but that will eventually become boring and they may lose interest.

Emotions can stimulate a person to action, generating the necessary energy to move them in the direction you want them to go. Logic works by laying a foundation they can rely on to make their decisions. By creating a careful balance between the two, you can create the perfect environment for evoking the right response.

To become a master manipulator, you will need all of these qualities, but you will use them each to different degrees depending on your target. Everyone needs them in order to tailor their message for the best results.

7 Qualities That Signify the Perfect Target

With the above qualities, just about anyone can be manipulated. However, there are some people that will stand out as the perfect target for persuasion. These people will show some express vulnerabilities that will be easy to identify.

The need to please: Some people crave attention so much that they will be more than eager to please others. This may stem from a need to be accepted or a low self-esteem, but these people are pretty easy to pick out from a crowd. Push just a few of their buttons and they will usually fall in line pretty quickly.

Fishers of compliments: Along with that need to please, many will also be constantly fishing for compliments. In other words, they will constantly be creating scenarios where they will earn praise and approval from those around them.

Fear of their own negative emotions: They will fight very hard not to display any sign of negativity in their lives. They may resist the tendency to express disapproval of something they seek, their disappointment, frustration or anger. They will apply avoidance techniques in order to not show that they feel uncomfortable about a given situation. They may work hard to find the right words to say what you want to hear in order to not lose their connection with you.

Lack of assertiveness: Assertiveness is one's ability to feel self-assured and confident about themselves and to have the kind of control that keeps them from being aggressive and overpowering others. People who are assertive do not need to demand or force others to do things. They have a quiet and controlled demeanor that naturally draws people on. However, those who lack assertiveness are very unsure of themselves, struggle with saying no to anyone even when they are uncomfortable about the situation making them the ideal target for manipulation.

No clear personal boundaries: Those who are willing to compromise on their personal boundaries can make easy targets for manipulation. They lack an established sense of identity and therefore are inclined to bend to the whims of others. When anyone is not clear on who they are or what they should stand for, they tend to stand for everything. They have no firm grounding to base their decisions on and therefore are easily swayed.

Low self-reliance: They lack independence and therefore are always in need of help from others. In essence, they are always in need of other people to help them get through even the most basic things in life. They struggle to survive if someone is not there to provide the basic necessities for them.

Belief in their own self-control: Sometimes referred to as locus of control, it does not reference one's level of control over certain events but rather to one's belief that they have control. This is a very big difference. When one believes that outside factors have more control over a situation than they do it leaves them open to all sorts of persuasions.

A person that believes he has control will more likely believe that anything he does has in some way been caused by him. When something goes wrong, he'll accept the blame rather than shifting it to someone else. However, if he believes that the fault lies in external factors, he will likely not want to take responsibility even if it is pointed out that he is responsible.

Any one of these qualities will make a person a pretty easy target for manipulation. In most cases, they won't be hard to find, they may even have a form of nervous behavior that will put their low self-esteem on display. An effective manipulator should first take the time to observe potential targets and look for these specific characteristics to identify them.

The Targets That are Harder to Win Over

No matter how careful you are in choosing your targets, there will inevitably come a time when you're going to find someone who resists your attempts to manipulate them. It's true, everyone will fall for the strategies of manipulation at one time or another, even those who you might feel are relatively wise. However, there are those few that will not succumb to your attempts no matter what you do. Trying to influence these targets can literally leave you with a headache as you struggle to overcome their resistance.

However, there are those who have been "burned" before by past manipulators. So, while you may be able to overcome their objections, their defenses will be up and they will be on guard for any other possible forms of influence.

Think about it. A common manipulation strategy is to promise them relief from whatever stresses or worries they are trying to overcome. However, those who have been burned have a highly suspicious nature and will question everything, even seeing ulterior motives in your efforts. You will have to work pretty hard to overcome those objections.

Their past baggage will cause them to approach every new relationship with an anticipation that something is wrong. It will take a lot of work to get them to believe in any promises you make, no matter how reasonable you sound. They may even insist on solid evidence, physical proof, or even more time for you to show that you are worth the trust you are asking for.

Another person you may have trouble reaching are those who are "loners." It is human nature to find a place within a social network. The common and often unspoken belief that there is safety in numbers is what makes a person an easy target. People who are loners, content with their own company have somehow overcome that need and are less likely to succumb to the same tactics that others may follow.

A person who is not part of a family, team, religion, or tied to any other group does not feel the need or is resistant to inclusion. While this is a natural inclination that we are all born with, they have learned to survive without it. In order to reach those people, you will have to rekindle that need in them in order to get them on your side.

A good manipulator seeks out weaknesses and works at them until they can trigger an emotional reaction. Your main goal is to get them so emotionally involved that they develop a sort of tunnel vision that gets them to push their own logical reasoning ability aside and respond emotionally to your needs. In essence, you are creating a narrow-minded focus in them, so they only see what you want them to see.

Those people who are resistant are strong willed enough to carefully think through every scenario will be your most difficult targets. They may actually be manipulators themselves and will therefore recognize your tactics as soon as you apply them. It doesn't mean that they can't be overcome with these strategies, but you will likely have to work longer and harder to get them to where you want them to be.

It's true, there are some targets that will seem impervious to your efforts, but don't let that discourage you. Where you can't find success with one person there are plenty others that you will be able to influence.

Chapter Four: Decoding Body Language

Communication is much more than just words. Inside of all of us there is a hidden code that we inherited at birth that allows us to communicate even when words are not available. In fact, this hidden form of language is far more reliable than the words we choose to speak. Through it, we let others know how we are feeling, what we are thinking, and our innermost desires.

Body language is more than just gesturing because its roots are embedded deep in our subconscious. One movement can relay more meaning than a thousand words strung together, no matter how poignant. Still, few of us have learned how to read this language and use it to our advantage. We are often so focused on the verbal message people are delivering that we fail to notice what is right in front of our eyes.

This form of non-verbal communication is done on a subconscious level and the messages others are sending to you can be very valuable to a manipulator. Not only can you read and interpret what others are saying, you can learn from your own actions what kind of messages you are sending out. Either way, understanding the underlying mean of these body signals can give you a wealth of information that will make it easier to create a persuasive strategy you can rely on.

Reading the Body's Subtle Signals

There are two kinds of body language cues you can look for: positive and negative. Positive body cues tell you if the person is feeling confident about what he is saying or comfortable in his surroundings.

You will see them in all sorts of settings so whether you're talking one to one or you're in a group, these will easily be observed.

- Standing erect with head high and shoulders back
- Making good eye contact and smiling eyes
- Comfortably gesturing with hands and arms while engaged in conversation
- Speaks clearly with a moderate tone of voice
- Nodding his head to indicate is listening and interested in the conversation

Negative body cues are an indication that there is some level of discomfort either with you or with the setting. Look out for these signs:

- Avoiding eye contact
- Minimal hand or arm gestures. They keep their arms close to the body as if in a defensive mode.
- No nodding or smiling while listening or when speaking
- Arms folded across the body – this tells you they are closed off or are unwilling to accept what is happening.
- Nervous tapping of hands or feet
- Clenched fists
- Speaks quickly or at a high pitch

There are signs that may not relay comfort or confidence, but rather how interested a person may be in your message. Recognizing these can help to determine if you are really reaching a person or if your words are falling on deaf ears.

- If they're head is down and there is no eye contact it usually indicates a lack of interest

- Signs of active listening or concentrating on what is being said involves getting the whole body involved in the conversation. Signs of active listening:
    o Repeating or paraphrasing your words
    o Leaning forward or to the side while listening
    o Slight tilt of the head or if sitting, resting the head on one hand
    o Mirroring your facial expressions
    o Steepling the fingers – sign of authority and control

When there is a lack of interest, you will see other signs.

- They may be easily distracted
- Constantly checking the time
- Doodling
- Playing with their hair
- Picking at their fingernails
- Not asking questions
- Staring at something else
- Fiddling with small objects

Before you can become a master manipulator you have to become a master at body language. Skillful use of it can help you to decide on the spot whether you need to change tactics or not. It doesn't matter what your goal may be, knowing the message can tell help you to land that perfect job, negotiate the best price, win an argument, or whether you should proceed with a relationship.

It is important to note here that these are the subtle cues founded in modern western culture. Body language signs are not universal and therefore can vary from one culture to the next. If you are not living in the modern western culture like in America, the UK, or Canada, it would be smart to take the time to learn these cues before you attempt regular communication. One gesture in one area could mean something entirely different where you are.

The Secret Messages of the Face

Our faces are also very expressive sending out messages that words can never convey clearly. We all know about smiles and their meanings, but did you know that there were different types of smiles, each one with its own unique message? A smile can show you're happy, shy, warm, or fake. There is one smile called the "Duchenne" smile that is considered the most genuine of all. It is the one that the corners of your mouth pull upward while you squeeze your eye muscles making crow's feet in the corners. Fake smiles do not have the crow's feet in the corner of the eyes – when you see that, you know that the person is not sincere in his expressions. Fake smiles tend to show more teeth than genuine smiles.

Frowns on the other hand, show disapproval, unhappiness, or doubt. A person may tell you he's feeling good about something but the look on his face could be sending you an entirely different message. Body language can tell you a lot about what someone is feeling but facial expressions tell you clearly how a person is feeling.

Unlike gestures and movements in body language that do not cross cultural boundaries, facial expressions are universal. No matter what background or history a person has these expressions can clearly be seen in every part of the world. Research has even indicated that most of us, without realizing it, make judgments based almost entirely on a person's facial expressions. We conclude that if someone's face reflects joy and happiness, they are more intelligent than someone who is constantly showing anger. This helps us to understand how valuable it can be to learn and understand true facial expressions. It speaks to the core feelings of your target so that know exactly what you are dealing with.

Eyes: There is a reason why people have described the eyes as the window to the soul. There is so much expression in them that sometimes people do not have to say a word but their thoughts and feelings come across very clearly. When you are involved in a conversation take the time to observe their eyes. The way they move will give you a glimpse into what's going on in their brain.

- Gazing: When they are making direct eye contact with you, they are showing interest to what you are saying. However, the length of time they gaze can also reflect meaning. Have you noticed how uncomfortable you become if someone gives you prolonged eye contact? That's because we naturally perceive this type of gazing as a threat, much like a predator would feel uncomfortable if a dog was watching you intently.

  Breaking eye contact also shows you that your listener is bored, distracted, or is trying to hide his true feelings about the discussion.

- Blinking: We all blink frequently throughout our waking hours, but when you notice someone blinking too much or not enough, they are sending you an unconscious message. Too few blinks means that they are deliberately controlling their eye movements. Gamblers often do this to resist the temptation to appear too excited about a potential outcome. If you notice rapid blinking it is usually an indication that they are feeling nervous or uncomfortable.

- Pupil size is an amazing sign that most people have no idea they are using. Pupils react to environmental lighting but beyond that, they also reflect emotions in their small changes in size. If they are highly dilated, it could be a sign that they are keenly interested or aroused.

- If they are moving up and to the right when answering a question, it could mean they are lying. Up and to the left usually means they are being honest with you.

- Disgust can be seen when the eyes narrow. It is a negative response and when it is accompanied by tight lips it can mean anger or hostility. Usually the narrower the eyes become the more intense the negative emotion.

- Eye blocking or the covering his eyes after you've made a request usually indicates that they are uncomfortable with something you've just said or that they disagree with your viewpoint.

- Arched eyebrows often show happiness, especially if it is accompanied by a smile or by the pupils getting larger. You will notice mothers do this often when they see their children.

- Fear is also showed with arched eyebrows but is accompanied with wide open eyes and the absence of a smile. There is also a quick and fleeting look and the pupils will dilate as a result of a quick burst of adrenaline flooding the system.

- Probably the most important thing you want to see in the eyes is their focus. When they are keenly interested in your message, their pupils will start to constrict. The opposite is also true, if they are not interested you can expect to see the pupils dilate.

These non-verbal cues can be awesome tools when it comes to reading people's emotions. The next time you are engaged in conversation, start to take notice of these subtle little glimpses into their soul. You will begin to see a whole new world unfold right before you and what you learn can help you to understand exactly what you need to do in order to achieve your goals.

The Mouth: The mouth also says a lot even when the person is not speaking. Every expression has a meaning and learning how to read them is essential for anyone who is looking to persuade someone.

- Covering the mouth: This is usually an attempt to be polite. People do this when they are coughing or sneezing, but they also do it when they are bored or yawning, which could be a warning sign that you need to change tactics. One thing you want to watch out for is covering the mouth as a sign of disapproval.

- Pursed lips: When they tighten the lips, it is a sign of distrust or disapproval of some kind.

- Biting lips: This is a cue that they are worried or stressed about something.

- Turned up at the corners: Indicates that they are happy or optimistic.

- Turned down at the corners means sadness or disapproval. If the gesture is prominent it could mean extreme distaste.

Gestures: Gestures, like the eyes, are usually some of the most obvious signs that reflect a person's inner feelings. We automatically read gestures without giving them a second thought. No one would question the meaning of a wave or pointing or even counting on the figures. Those are quite easy to understand, but there are also cultural gestures that you might encounter. If you've traveled a lot, you'll notice that a gesture in one country does not always translate to gestures in another country. These are common gestures found in the United States.

- *Clenched fists:* in some instances, it could be a reflection of anger. However, if it is made with the arm upraised it usually means solidarity or unity.
- *Thumbs up:* approval
- *Thumbs down:* disapproval
- *Pinching thumb and forefinger together:* This is a sign of approval or saying everything is okay.
- *The V sign:* This sign, made by holding up the index and middle finger in the shape of a V means victory. It some areas it can also mean peace.

The Extremities: Arms and legs are excellent communicators. For example, Crossing your legs and turning them away from the other person lets you know that the other person is taking a defensive position and is wary of you. By paying attention to what the extremities are telling you it will be easy to determine if what they are saying is matching their feelings.

- *Crossing the arms:* the person is feeling defensive or is closed off, not willing to open up to you.
- *Hands on hips:* a sign that they are in control. If the posture looks more defiant it could also be a sign of aggression.
- *Hands clasped behind the back:* this gesture could be a sign that they are bored or anxious. Sometimes could be a sign of anger and frustration.
- *Fidgeting or tapping fingers:* When done rapidly, it is a clear sign that they are impatient or frustrated.
- *Crossing legs:* indication that they are closed off or that they need some separateness or privacy.

Posture: Our posture is another way we unconsciously communicate to others, How we hold our bodies can reflect many things from the state of our health to our sense of confidence. There are two types of posture to watch for.

- *Open:* when the trunk of the body is exposed it tells others that they are open and friendly. An open posture usually means that they are willing and ready to comply.

73

- *Closed:* When the trunk of the body is closed off by stances like hunching forward or crossing the arms the legs, it can be a show of hostility or anxiety. Usually not a friendly gesture.

Personal Space: In America, people take their personal space very seriously. If you stand too close, they are likely to feel very uncomfortable. It is best to maintain a respectable distance between you and the person you're interacting with. A little too close and they will become defensive and wary, a little too far and they are likely to get the sense that you are being closed off and uninterested.

- *Intimate conversations usually require a distance between 6 to 18 inches.* This distance is acceptable for those in a close relationship and allows for more intimacy and private discussion. The close proximity allows for intimate touching, hugging, and whispering.
- *When it is not an intimate discussion but can still be considered a personal relationship such as with family and friends a distance of 1.5 to 4 feet is considered acceptable.* The amount of distance you maintain between the other person reflects on how close the relationship is. The closer you are the more intimate the bond.
- *In social or group settings, maintaining a physical distance of 4 to 12 feet is acceptable.* This is the acceptable distance for personal acquaintances like co-workers and business associates. When dealing with people who you are unfamiliar with or those you interact with infrequently, it might be best to stay on the further end of the range.
- *Public distance of up to 15 feet is maintained when you don't need to have direct personal contact. For example, when you*

are giving a presentation or speaking to an audience you wouldn't want to be too close to your listeners. The distance allows you to make brief eye contact with different people in the audience without making them feel like they have been singled out.

While you won't need to go out with a measuring tape to determine the proper distance to allow for personal space, you can take your cues from those around you. This is especially important when you are dealing with cultures from other countries. For example, personal space in most Asian cultures is not as important as it is in North America. The same is true with those from Latin America. The more you observe this distance the more effective you will be at reaching your target audience.

Understanding body language will naturally make you a better communicator but it will also help you to understand the signals you're sending out into the universe. This is by no means a full selection of possible gestures so it would be a good idea to do additional research on the topic. That said, just by applying these listed here you will be well on your way to understanding what needs to be done to persuade others.

Understanding Microexpressions

Before, we discussed the importance of facial gestures in understanding communication. However, one area of facial expressions that we are now beginning to get a better grasp on is that of microexpressions. These are involuntary gestures that happen very quickly when a feeling or emotion is first felt. These generally are more reliable than any other facial gesture as they are impulse reactions that the person has no time to think about. They happen quickly and usually occur within the first fractions of a second after the emotion arises generally starting at ½ of a the first second and lasting 1/15th and 1/25th of a second before fading. Because they appear and disappear so quickly, they are good indicators of any emotion that a person is trying to hide or suppress.

Learning how to detect these microexpressions is key to becoming persuasive but before you can master this skill, you have to understand the dynamics of the human face and what you should be looking for. According to Dr. Paul Ekman, these expressions are pretty universal. Everyone, no matter where they are from, shares at least seven common expressions that have exactly the same meaning. While there are plenty more microexpressions to learn, knowing at least these seven will give you a pretty good picture of the person you are dealing with and what to expect.

Surprise: This common expression is seen by the raising of the upper eyelids, the eyebrows raised and curved. You should also see the mouth partially open when the jaw drops but the lips and mouth muscles will remain relaxed. The length of this expression tells you if the person is surprised or fearful. If it lasts longer than a second it is more likely a sign of fear.

Fear: Similar to surprise, fear can be seen when the upper eyelids are raised up. The eyebrows are lifted and pulled together making a flat line. The mouth opens slightly and the lip muscles are tensed and pulled back tightly.

Disgust: This classic look is easy to recognize by the wrinkles that form around the nose. The eyebrows are drawn down and the eyes narrow. The upper lid, cheek muscles, and the lower lip are tensed into a sneer making the teeth visible.

Anger: When a person is angry both the upper and lower eyelids are drawn tightly together. The eyebrows are pulled down in the center and drawn together tightly. You'll see vertical lines appear between the eyebrows and the eyes themselves take on a strong stare or start to bulge out. Some people have a habit of thrusting the jaw forward when they are extremely angry.

Happiness: This emotion is seen when both sides of the mouth pull up in the corners making a symmetrical smile. Many people try to pretend to be happy by forcing a smile but you should be able to tell the difference by looking at the corners of the eye. Genuine happiness also shows in the eyes as well as the mouth. Look for the corner eye muscles to engage showing the tell-tale signs of crow's feet. Expect to see more engagement of the face muscles when happiness is genuine than you will with a forced display of emotion.

Sadness: This feeling can be seen when the corner muscles of the lips pull down at the sides and the lower lip juts out in a pout. You may also see the inside corner of the eyebrows lift slightly.

Contempt: This emotion can be clearly identified by the classic raising of one side of the mouth making a sneer or a smirk.

Microexpressions are universal and common. They differ from regular expressions in that they are very difficult to intentionally create. People can readily hide their innermost feelings with regular facial gestures but microexpressions are formed in a different part of the brain and are impulse reactions. They are fleeting at best and disappear as quickly as they come so to notice them and identify them will require you to pay very close attention to your target so you can catch that one instant that will reveal everything you need to know.

What Walking Styles Say About Someone

Most of us do not spend a lot of time worrying about how a person walks but a recent study published in *Social Psychological and Personality Science,* gives us good reason to consider it. The study conducted in 2017 by a health and wellness expert at Maple Holistics reveal that one's walking speed could tell us at least five different personality traits. These traits: agreeableness, openness, extraversion, conscientiousness, and neuroticism can tell us a lot about the kind of people we are dealing with.

There is a great deal to be learned when you analyze their speed, stride, and how they hold their arms when they are walking. By analyzing these characteristics, you can reveal something about them that you may not otherwise be able to pick up.

Fast Walkers: People who walk fast tend to be more outgoing and maybe even more conscientious. In fact, the faster they walk the more outgoing they tend to be.

Slow Walkers: Those who move at a slower pace reflect a more cautious personality. When they take shorter strides at a more leisurely pace it could reflect a little bit of me-ism as they are classic signs of a self-centered personality. However, this does not necessarily mean that it is a bad thing. It simply reflects a person who is looking out for his own best interests. Those who are more introverted may also walk slow but their body language reveals a lack of confidence. They keep their head down and pull into themselves. A cautious person is not an introvert but rather more careful about his decisions. He walks with his head held high so he can see and analyze everything in his environment.

Veering to the Left: People who gradually veer to the left as they walk tend to be showing signs of anxiety and stress. The further they veer off the straight path the more anxiety they are feeling. No one fully understands this phenomenon but it is believed that the right side of the brain is more fully engaged in solving problems or dealing with their worries or fears than the left side.

The Saunter: When someone takes a more leisurely stroll, literally sauntering down their path with their head held high but no clear destination in sight it is a powerful sign of confidence. These people fall into a slow and easy stride reflecting the calm state of mind.

Energetic Walker: Those who move with a high energy in their step are super conscientious and are more detail oriented. They walk quickly even when covering short distances. For instance, they may move just a few steps to a chair or across the room. Their gait is quick but it is not smooth. Their movements will be jerking as they switch their attention from one thought to the next.

Graceful Walkers: Graceful walkers reflect a quiet and inner sense of confidence, but how you read them will depend on the direction their feet are pointed. When their feet are pointing outwards as they walk it is a sign of high self-esteem. This position is not a natural gait but is one that is taught. Toes pointing inward is a sign of insecurity.

Slumped Shoulders: If their posture has them in a slightly bent forward position with their shoulders hunched over it is a classic sign of discomfort. It is a position that is designed to protect the vital organs of the body. They may have suffered some sort of trauma in their past either physically or psychologically but have not yet recovered.

When it comes to body language, the more you learn the more you realize that every movement, every nuance, and every slight little twitch or gesture is working like a mirror to the reflecting what is going on in the mind and the hearts of the people you are interacting with. While learning these things won't make you a mind reader, you can get pretty close to it when you apply them to your art of persuasion.

Chapter Five: Essential Manipulation Tools

The art of manipulation has a very specific goal. You want to change the mind of your target so that you can affect the kind of behavior you want to see. Learning how to read other people and detect their emotional state of mind is only half the battle. Once you understand your target it's time to select the proper manipulation tools to use to your advantage.

There are several different approaches that are very effective in persuading people. The ones included in this chapter work subtly on the subconscious mind so the target never fully realizes what's happening, but they yield the best results.

Everyday Manipulation Tricks

Foot in the Door: The main principle behind this concept is to get someone to do what you want them to do. In essence you are laying the groundwork to ask for a favor. It starts small by asking for a smaller and less important favor first. By doing this, you're building a small but simple connection between the two of you based on an unwritten rule of commitment that you can fall back on later.

The Chinese have been practicing this strategy for centuries. It follows that by doing small but insignificant favors for someone over time causes them to be indebted to you. It's like putting money in the bank so you can make a bigger request later on. While in China, this tool runs much deeper than in western society, it is a powerful weapon in indebting someone to you.

A good example of how this can be used can be seen can be seen in all walks of life. For example, you might find yourself in unfamiliar territory and ask someone for directions. This simple request creates a connection with you. After a simple and brief conversation, you might make your second request by explaining that you're not very good with directions so would rather they showed you instead of telling you. The person may decide to draw you a map or even personally walk you to your destination. There is a good chance of this working if you asked for the smaller favor first. However, if you had just approached a stranger and asked them to walk you to your destination, you almost certainly would have been unsuccessful.

This theory was tested by researchers back in 1966. A group of 156 women were divided into four groups. They started by asking the first three groups to answer a few basic questions about the kitchen products they used. After several days, they asked permission to go through their kitchen so they could catalogue the products they used. The fourth group was only asked the second question. The results showed the effectiveness of this approach with a 52.8% success rate for the first three groups and only a 22.2% success rate for the fourth one.

You can see this applied everywhere you look in marketing. Most online websites start by asking something that doesn't seem to cost you anything. They may ask you for your email address and then later ask for something bigger. Someone may ask you to "like" a page and then later ask you for a comment, which could later lead to a sale.

Door in the Face: The main principle behind this technique is to ask for something extremely big and unreasonable and then when declined, ask for something smaller. It works on the opposite scale of the Foot in the Door technique. In this case, you are requesting something so large that you know you're going to be refused and then you make a request for something that is much easier for them to comply with.

A case in point would be if you asked a friend for a large loan and then when refused, ask for a significantly smaller one. This works primarily because just by making the initial request, you have moved your relationship up to another level causing them to feel some sort of obligation to you. Then it becomes much easier for them to comply with your second request without hesitation.

This fact was verified in a case study performed in the retail market. Researchers used one saleswoman who was selling cheese to people in the Austrian Alps. She first offered hikers passing by two pounds of cheese for eight euros, and when they rejected the sale, she then downgraded her request by offering one pound for four euros. The results were impressive with only a 9% success rate with the first request and a 24% success rate after the second.

Anchoring: The main thought behind anchoring is to create a cognitive bias by creating familiarity with the same or a similar product so your target can make a decision based on this knowledge. There are several ways you can apply this technique from marketing to landing that dream job you want.

It works similar to the Foot in the Door technique. Stores often raise the price of certain products by 15% prior to a 10% sale. People see the price at a discount from the actual posted price not realizing that they are paying even more for the product than they would have before the sale.

Evidence that this works was seen in a study where 100 subjects were given three different options for subscriptions. The first option was an online cost of $59, the second option was for a printed subscription for $125, and a third option was for print and web combination for $125. The results showed that out of the 100 subjects only 16 chose the first option and 84 chose the third option. Then the second option was removed and the same exercise was given to another 100 subjects where only 32 chose the third option with the remaining 68 choosing the first.

The results showed that when option B was a factor it was merely used as an anchor. No one would seriously consider it, but it clearly showed the value of the other two options. This process is an effective means of transferring learning experiences. It its core, it gives people a stimulus or a personal experience from which to base their decisions on.

Commitment & Consistency: The basic principle here is to tap into your target's internal sense of consistency. As creatures of habit, if you are able to get them to commit to something small and insignificant, then you can use that to motivate them to do something more in the future.

All of us do this to some degree in real life. When we go shopping, we buy the same products we are familiar with, we take the same route to work every day, and we usually eat the same things with few variations in every meal. Because of this internal need for consistency, we rarely try things new. By getting someone to do something for you once you start a precedent that they will follow to maintain consistency.

Many online websites use this principle in their marketing efforts. They start by asking potential customers to sign up for regular emails from their company. You've seen them on the screen when you visit their sites with words like "Yes, I like free money," or "Yes, I want to know more." Sometimes they will even give you options that make you feel like you have to choose one over the other. For example, you may be given two options, "Yes, I want to know more about how to make option," and "No, I don't want to be successful." The second option is so far from the truth that you feel compelled to choose the first one. But once you've made the decision, no matter how insignificant, you will feel obligated to stick to it.

To get the best results, the first commitment should be easy to make. It won't cost them much or anything at all. A charity may send out a petition to get people to increase their commitment to their efforts. The initial cost is minimal at best. Later, they can ask for larger donations and most will comply just to keep their level of commitment involved.

Social Proof: We've all heard of peer pressure, right? Social proof is a perfect example of peer pressure at work. The prevailing principle here is that you don't want to be the odd man out. This concept is based on the thought that before anyone makes a decision, they will stop and think about what decision their peers will make and will usually act accordingly.

If you are working in a restaurant and there is an empty tip jar present, you could start the tips coming in by adding the first coins of your own. Customers are much more likely to add to a jar that already has money in it than to be the first to get the ball rolling. You are more likely to leave a comment on an article or video if you see others are doing it as well.

A 1935 case study bears this out. Researchers took several subjects and placed them in a dark room with the only source of light a pinpoint 15 feet away. They were asked to watch the light and give an estimate to how much that light moved. Each participant gave different answers about the movement.

The second day of the study, they were put into groups and asked the same question. This time they all came to a singular agreement that was far removed from the estimates they gave just the day before.

Authority: We learn from an early age to listen to those who have authority. Regardless of the area of expertise, establishing yourself as an authority on a subject will have a powerful influence on others.

Marketing experts use this very effectively with phrases like "9 out of 10" doctors approve this medication. Or they may say something like "our product won 8 out of 10 awards for being the best." Websites and blogs often enlist the endorsement of recognized authorities in their area of expertise, or they post testimonials from past customers to give evidence that they are the professionals they claim to be.

One Yale University psychologist proved this very effectively in a series of studies called the Milgram Experiment. The studies consisted of three different people, the experimenter, the teacher, and the learner.

The teacher's role was to ask the learner questions. If the learner gave a wrong answer, the teacher would give them an electric shock. The experimenter then would press the teacher to continue to use the electric shock even if there was evidence that the learner was in pain.

In the majority of the cases, the teacher would continue to administer pain even they it went against their conscience. In fact, 8 out of 10 teachers would continue to give the electric shocks regardless of the circumstances. This gives evidence that most people are willing to cross even a moral boundary if their instructions are given by someone in authority.

Scarcity: The fear of missing out is a powerful one and it is the principle that scarcity is built on. People use it to create a sense of urgency and compel their targets to make a decision sooner rather than later. In reality, the tendency to want something when it is in short supply is very strong so by convincing someone that soon something is going to run out within a certain amount of time is more likely to drive them to buy it.

Scarcity is probably one of the most often used persuasion techniques in the world today. We see it used in marketing, in relationships, and in the social world. If you've ever tried to book a vacation online, you'll probably be greeted with there are only a few seats left on this flight, or this offer expires at midnight, or you can only buy these at this time a year. The whole premise is what America's Black Friday is based on.

In one study, 180 student subjects were separated into two groups. The first group was given a product and told of its scarcity while the second group was told that there was an abundant supply. The result showed that most subjects were eager to buy simply because they were afraid that it would no longer be available.

A classic example of this is a case discussed by psychiatrist of a car salesman who made it a point to have several people show up for a car at the same time. This created an aire of competition and anxiety between them making the actual car seem more valuable than it really was.

When used successfully, there is unique sense of power for the victor. The theory is that this principle protects one sense of freedom to choose. Whenever freedom of choice is limited, we have an inborn desire to protect it. By increasing scarcity, we instinctively recognize that our access to that item is restricted unless we do something quickly.

Reciprocation: Reciprocation is the act of obligating one to you because of something you've done for them. Regardless of what the gift is, just the act of giving it generates a powerful need to return the favor. We automatically feel indebted to the giver and the manipulator can definitely use it to their advantage.

This can be used in a wide variety of ways. For example, you might offer a free gift for the first contributors to your cause or you could be given a free download of a book before being asked to make a larger purchase.

Evidence bears this out in a study conducted at a New York city restaurant where the waiter would give a small gift before providing the bill. In most cases, this saw an 18% increase in tips. In a similar setting, when the waiter would leave a mint and then walk away, turn around, and give them an additional piece the increase in tips went up to 21%.

These are not the only persuasion techniques there are but they are the most commonly used. Use these to lay the groundwork for your next persuasion strategy and see how much your power of influence will increase.

11 Persuasion Tricks to Start Getting What You Want in Everyday Life

We live in a dog eat dog world. It doesn't matter who or where you are, you will fall into one of two classes: the manipulator or the one being manipulated. We call them mind games and they are being played out all around us. You need to know them just to make sure that you're not caught in the latter group. Not that being manipulated is always a bad thing, but at least if you are being manipulated you know and recognize the signs and you can then use them to your advantage.

Once you learn these persuasion tricks, you'll be able to use them to get everything you want out of life.

1. **Hardly Evil:** By helping someone else to achieve their own goals you make them indebted to you. The general concept

that we all believe in is that you can get what you want from life as long as you help other to achieve their own goals.

2. **A Little Manipulative:** Asking for favors in a more public setting can make people feel more inclined to do things for you. Rather than asking in a more private setting, making a public request is less likely to be turned down.

3. **Bait and Switch:** Using a decoy offer to hook people then offering them something of higher value, and then making a final offer that seems to be of the same value but less effective in order to get them to purchase what you want.

4. **Focus on the Win:** Get your target to realize what he is gaining in the deal rather than what he is losing.

5. **Mirroring:** Mirror the other person's body language to get them to be comfortable with you. They are more likely to connect with you and do what you want.

6. **Watching:** Make them feel as if they are watched. This can be done by showing them an image of eyes. Subconsciously, when we see eyes as in an image or in a video, they will feel as if they are being judged, which will make them alter their behavior to something they feel will be more accepted.

7. **Tap Into Insecurities:** Your choice of words can tap into how they feel about themselves. People tend to think more of their personal identifies when they hear nouns but they think more of their behavior when they hear verbs. If you want to tap into their insecurities, choose more nouns in your conversations than verbs and you'll weaken their defenses.

8. **Deception:** Speak rapidly if you want them to agree with you. Use lots of words to overwhelm them so they will lower their guard. Many times, they will agree with you because they just can't keep up.

9. **Scheming:** Approach them at the end of the day when they are tired and ready to quit. When people are exhausted, they're more likely to comply with your request because their energy to resist is pretty much spent.

10. **Fear:** Tapping into their fears is an effective way to get people to comply with your request. Expose their fears and then immediately offer a solution.

11. **Confusion:** Deliberately confuse them. Most people's pride won't allow them to admit that they don't fully understand. The easiest response for them is to agree. Offering prices in unfamiliar terms will make them give up because they struggle to mentally process it.

How to Use the Six Laws of Persuasion

The laws of persuasion are constantly in use all around us. It is at the core of every business negotiation, every relationship discussion, every parent-teacher or parent-child debate, and the center of every social media interaction. It is a fact of life that is essential for every one of us whether we're in business or not. Every one of these aspects employs skill negotiations on some level.

To be successful at using these laws, you need to first understand yourself (your EQ) and the goals you want to achieve, but you also need to understand what's in the heart of your target. This will create a platform from which you can launch your influence over others and affect the kind of change you want to see in your world.

But successful manipulation should not be just about what you want. While you will be able to gain a modicum of success thinking only of yourself, your best results will come when you create a situation that will be mutually beneficial for both you and your target. How well you do this will determine the extent of your success and how efficiently you can ensure that all parties are winners in your negotiations. To do this, you need to develop your expertise in employing the six main laws of persuasion.

We don't realize it, but the average person makes around 35,000 decisions every day. Of course, the majority of these choices are made on the subconscious level and therefore do not require any conscious thought. They provide us with ways to simplify our lives, gives us shortcuts, and are designed to save us either time and/or money. However, it is those conscious decisions we all must make that will allow us to have influence over others and give us what we want. Here is where the six laws of persuasion can hold sway. We talked briefly about them in the last section, but we're going to examine them a little more closely here.

Law of Reciprocity: The law of reciprocity compels others to return favor for favor. By giving someone something they will feel obligated to repay you. To increase this sense of gratification, if you make sure you give them something, they want their connection to you will be even stronger.

Applying this in your life could be pretty simple. Keep in mind though that getting someone to agree to something without asking for something in return sets a pretty bad precedent that will cause the other person feel entitled and you feeling at a loss. By giving them something it gives them a sense of having some bargaining power. So, using a quid-pro-quo works best and can help to establish a longer standing relationship. The sooner you create this understanding, the easier it will be to persuade that person again and again. It is an extremely effective way of bringing your target into your fold and closing the deal whatever it is.

Law of Commitment and Consistency: Using consistency as a means of easing your targets discomfort is important. Once you've established a relationship with that person, it's important that you stick to it and not deviate. Showing the other person that you are committed to a decision (no matter how significant) gives them the assurance that you are not going to abandon them at the first sign of change. Salespeople are very good at this. By getting their customers to agree on several smaller things one right after another they set a precedent of commitment. So, when they do ask for the big sale, it is almost impossible for them to say no.

Law of Liking: Whether you want to attract another person and kindle a new relationship or you're looking to land that dream job of yours, you will probably use the Law of Liking. This basic law of human nature dictates that we are drawn to those people who are more like ourselves. The more similarities you find with someone else the deeper your desire to want to please them. When applying the Law of Liking work to establish a good rapport and make it clear that you are like two peas in a pod. The more similarities you can show them the deeper the bond will be. This works well with home-based sales parties, religious groups, and social groups. Remember the old saying, 'birds of a feather flock together.' Once you've made this type of connection with them, the less likely they will want to disappoint you by saying no.

Law of Scarcity: You don't necessarily have to have a limited supply of something to make the fundamental law of scarcity work for you. You can apply the same pressure without it. You could let the other party know that you will be available to answer questions for a limited time only. This works well for seasonal offerings or things only available during a certain time of the year. You just have to create the idea that something is scarce to get the result so they believe that if they hesitate, they may miss out on the privilege entirely.

Law of Authority: When applying this law, it is important that the other person knows that you are the "expert" in this field or you are acknowledged and recommended by recognized experts. This can be done in several different ways. Marketers often use the "testimonials" of past customers, bloggers use the credibility of other more well-known bloggers, and there is certainly nothing wrong with advertising or posting your own credential that establish you as a knowledgeable person in your area of interest.

Law of Social Proof: The dynamics is any social group is quite powerful. It can be quite unnerving to go against the crowd so people are more inclined to conform when necessary. Once people understand what is the accepted behavior in any social group, they are rarely inclined to go against it. Think about how you feel when you are in an unfamiliar social setting. Your first instinct is to look around you to see what other people are doing and then you copy them. Establishing a set of guidelines for your social group will almost always end in conformity that will be difficult for anyone to break.

All You Need to Know About Reverse Psychology

You've probably heard about using reverse psychology to get people to do things. The principle is very simple. You tell them something opposite of what you want and if they are resistant to your efforts, they will usually do what you desire. The tactic can be quite successful in many different forms of persuasion. However, while simple, it can backfire on you in a pretty big way.

Part of the reason for this is its simplicity. In fact, it is so simple that many will begin to rely on this strategy far too much. Once people begin to understand what you're doing, it can leave a pretty sad taste in their mouth. As a result, you may find that rather than connecting more people to you, it could end up pushing them away leaving a string of broken relationships in its wake. If you do decide to use reverse psychology, make sure that you use it only on rare occasions and not as a regular habit and even then, only in the most serious of situations.

That said, here are some simple ways to use this strategy to get what you want.

To Change Someone's Mind: To do this you have to think beyond the idea of changing the person's mind. Before you can begin, you have to implant your ideas into their head. Even if it is something you know they are resistant to they need to at least recognize the idea as an option.

- **The set-up:** start by presenting the two options they must choose from. For example, we have two options for dinner on Saturday night. If you know that your target has an affinity for Japanese food but you're more interested in Italian you already know what their preference will be.

  Casually present your idea in a matter-of-fact sort of way. You might say something like, "Did you know that there is a new Italian restaurant opening up on Fifth Street this week?"

  When you present your option downplay it to create a negative effect. "I've heard it's pretty good but it'll probably be packed by the time we get there. We might have to wait an hour or more to get a table."

- **Subtle Enticement:** Find subtle ways to build a desire in them. You could happen to have a menu from the new restaurant to look over. Point out some pictures and dishes that you would like to try. You could even start with an

Italian night to see if you can imitate true Italian food. This will help them to see just how flavorful Italian food could actually be.

You could also make everything else sound more appealing. Talk about past experiences in Italian restaurants, pleasant memories about the Italian culture, and how "real" Italian food should taste.

- **Add Non-Verbal Cues:** A few days before, start by adding in a few visual images about Italian culture. You could drive by the restaurant on the way home to plant the idea of going there. "It doesn't look as crowded as I thought it would be." Take them for a walk in the area where they can get a whiff of the aromas as they are wafting through the air.

- **Take the Opposing Viewpoint for the Choice You Want:** Once you realize that you have caught their interest, don't give up too quickly but be slightly argumentative. This will compel them to push harder for what they want. This works much better than immediate capitulation. When a person has the natural tendency to resist it gives them a sense of fighting for the choices, they make creating a win for them.

When the event arrives, chances are they will already have made their decision. Introduce the subject again by saying something like "What do you want to do? We can go to the Italian restaurant or we can go to the Japanese." If they are still resistant to Italian you can add something like, "We get to eat Japanese all the time so it won't be anything different, but how often do we really eat Italian?"

Finish with "what do you think?" "I can't decide so it's up to you."

- **Closing:** Finally, you want to resist long enough that the other person is forced to decide. While your goal is to get what you want, the other person must think that it's their decision. After you ask your last questions, wait for them to answer. It may create a bit of discomfort but resist the urge to fill in the silence. Your target is also feeling the pressure too so wait it out until they make the choice. If they are a naturally difficult person then in most cases, they will make the decision you want to do.

When to Use Reverse Psychology: Reverse psychology doesn't work on everyone. Some people are more likely to respond to a direct request while others will be more contrary. This is why it is so important that you understand the personality of the people you are targeting. They behavior will dictate which persuasive strategy you should use. This strategy works best with people who have a naturally obstinate and stubborn nature. Here are some questions you might want to ask before you decide.

- Do they usually go with the flow?
- Are they independent thinkers?

If they are naturally fluid and agreeable, using reverse psychology will likely backfire on you. But if they are more independent thinkers and are not usually comfortable with the status quo, they are more likely to be the best subjects for reverse psychology.

Make it Light: This works well when you're using reverse psychology on children. Keep the topic lighthearted and fun so that they will believe that they're actually smarter than you. Children love that.

For example, you're trying to get your child to clean his room without having to ask him to do it. Start by setting some rules.

"Don't start cleaning your room until I've finished cleaning mine." This sentence might start off sounding like that's all he needs for an excuse to "not" clean his room. He'll be happy. But then you will add something like, "I know you're too young to do it right so I'll come in and help you."

Then leave the room and go about your business. In about an hour, you can return to the room "to help" him and you'll most likely find that he has already finished or is well on his way to proving that he's not too young and he can do it on his own.

Using this same tactic with an adult can be similar. Your goal is to allow them to feel as though they are asserting their own independence in the situation. You might be trying to choose between two different TV shows; one may be serious dramatic film and the other could be a light comedy. Your preference is for the drama so you could say something like "I'm not sure I have the emotional stamina for a really serious drama tonight. If your partner is a naturally resistant person, he may want to convince you that you do have the emotional fortitude for it. He may even go as far as he could to prove it. By allowing him to apply a little resistance for a while then you'll most like end up getting exactly what you want.

Think About What the Other Person Needs: Whenever you choose to use reverse psychology, you need to consider what the other person needs or wants in the situation. In some cases, you may have to do a little bobbing and weaving before you get him to give up on his goals. Your strategy is not just to apply the opposing viewpoint but to assess of your desire for what you want is strong enough to overpower their need to resist. If you haven't thought this process through your efforts could easily backfire on you.

Your friend may be interested in visiting or driving through a rather seedy part of town that you know is dangerous. If his desire is extremely strong your efforts at reverse psychology may not work.

However, by analyzing the situation first, you could probably find other ways around the challenge.

As you consider the possibilities start by thinking about all the possible arguments you might come up against in the situation. Then think about the end result you want to achieve. Your goal is to help him to see the risks involved in his decision, not necessarily to prove that you are right or smarter. Sometimes reverse psychology will work and sometimes it won't. Possible things you could say.

"I can't tell you what to do and I can't make you do anything that you don't want to do. I pretty sure that the area is dangerous but only you can decide how much risk you're willing to take to get to where you want to go."

Your goal is achieved. Leave the decision in their hands. If you've applied the right amount of pressure, then there is a good chance that he will decide not to go.

Keep in mind that you won't win every argument this way. Reverse psychology works well only on those personalities that are naturally resistant to going with the flow. Strategies do not always turn out the way you expect them too. Occasionally the situation may escalate into an argument and in the heat of the moment you could lose sight of your goals. Try to avoid this and keep reminding yourself of what you're trying to accomplish and you'll find yourself having more successes in this strategy than not.

Remember, this strategy only works in certain situations and should be used subtly and rarely. It is easy, after achieving a few successes, to want to use it as a fall back but that could get you into trouble and could start to create negative inroads in your relationships. Once others realize this is your fallback position it could cause resentment. You have to learn to let the other person have their way sometimes or they may tire of you always having the power of them.

Try to use this type of tactic in situations where there is not much to lose. Don't use it on something that will dampen your relationship over time. For example, use it when deciding on what to eat or what to do for an afternoon at home. Don't use it when deciding on what car or house to buy.

Never Lose Your Temper: It is important to stay calm when using reverse psychology. It could easily escalate into arguments where you can become frustrated or feelings can get hurt. This is especially true when dealing with young people. Be patient, it may take a while before they come start to see things from your point of view.

Emotional outbursts are natural so make sure you can handle them yourself before you begin. If the other person loses it, you need to remain calm. All them to finish their outburst before you continue your discussion.

Most important of all, make sure this is not done in extremely serious situations. It could not only backfire but could cause irreparable damage as a result. A good example of this is someone with a serious medical condition who is resistant to going to the doctor. Your partner's resistance could be stronger than his desire to get help and you might find yourself supporting his fears rather than getting him to do what he seriously needs to do.

Chapter Six: A Master in Every Arena

Manipulation can be a pretty touchy subject these days. Never before in history have, we seen so many people trying to manipulate others to their advantage. People are constantly on guard against salespeople, bloggers, social media gurus, marketing experts and others. Everywhere you look there just seems to be someone who is trying to hold sway against others for their own advantage.

However, to become a master manipulator, you need to cut through all of that chaff and still find ways to get people on your side. It can be quite unsettling when you end up as a victim of some type of dirty negotiation tactics, especially when it's going to cause you to lose months or even years of your hard earned time and money.

Rest assured, if you're not manipulating there's a good chance that you are being manipulated. It's at the heart of every negotiation whether it is getting your two-year old to use the potty or getting your boss to give you a raise. In this chapter, we're going to teach you how to use manipulation strategies in any type of negotiation situation. That way, you can recognize manipulators when they're trying to sway you and you can hone your skills in a way that will turn the table to your advantage.

How to Secretly Manipulate Your Boss

If you're dealing with a rather difficult boss it can cause a great deal of stress. Difficult bosses are notorious for being die-hard narcissists, playing favorites, and at times even throwing a temper-tantrum or two. These kinds of people leave you feeling insecure and anxious and you end up spending much of your valuable time complaining rather than working towards achieving your own goals.

It's time to change all that. First, you must accept the obvious. Your boss is not going to change no matter how much you yell back or how hard you work to please him. It's because he doesn't want to change. His child-like antics have worked for him so far, so rather than wasting your energy working to get him into a new frame of mind, you need to change your own tactics.

No matter who you want to manipulate, it is important that you understand where they are coming from. You need to find out what is fueling his difficult and challenging behavior. What is he afraid of and what does he want? This goes back to building up your own EQ. You might have to spend some time observing him in his natural habitat in order to fully understand what he secretly wants.

What are his secret fears and/or desires: In nearly every case where a boss is a tyrant, those negative emotions spring from an underlying fear. In fact, desires and fears are the two strongest emotions to deal with. When you look very closely, everyone is either running or hiding from some secret fear that is buried deep in his psyche or they are running to something they secretly want. This is what drives our behavior. Once you understand what these two elements are in your bosses life you place yourself in a position of power. You need what he wants to avoid and you know what he wants to achieve. You can now predict his reaction to any number of situations so you can develop a strategy that will turn the tables in your favor.

Let's take a brief look at some different types of bosses to see how this works:

- The Finger-Pointer: This boss spends his time blaming those who work under him because he is afraid, he doesn't have enough of his own skills to be a success.
- The Egomaniac: usually believes he is perfect in every way. However, a closer look at his work will usually reveal someone who leaves behind a lot of projects that were started

but never finished. This person has a strong desire to be loved and admired but secretly feels he is not deserving of any of it. He feels if he loses his control everything will fall apart. He believes he is just merely an average person trying to pass himself off as being special.

Become his ally: Once you know your boss' fears and desires you need to use it to become his ally. You can do this by feeding his desire or shielding him from his fears. By becoming an ally, you are actually taking back the power he is trying to steal from you. It will give you leverage and put you in a position to demand more and likely get what you want and need.

For the boss that spends his time blaming his underlings, you need to learn to control your own emotions and not fight back when his ire is up. People who blame and shout are trying to instill fear in others, when you don't react in fear, he begins to realize that he cannot overpower you in that way. He will calm down.

Once he is calm you can present yourself as his personal problem-solver. Take the initiative and offer to "fix" the problem. When the problem is solved, he will feel like a success and you will gain his trust in the process. After several of these attempts, you will have become one of his most important assets and a tool he will need to achieve his own level of success.

For the egomaniac you will need a lot more strength and intestinal fortitude to withstand the pressure. Try going with the flow so you can fuel his need for employees that are loyal to him. This type of boss needs to feel like he is in control 100% of the time, by following his cues you can smoothly turn a world of chaos into peace and order. If you are good enough at it, you can position yourself as the trusted wingman that he won't want to do without. In time, when he moves up there's a good chance that you will move up at the same time.

Keep in mind that your goal is not to destroy your boss and let him know that he's not manipulating you. That would be counterproductive to your goals. You're trying to use his fears and desires in a way that will support your goals. As a result, you create a win-win situation that you both can gain from. It will relieve much of the stress from work and give you a higher level of job satisfaction.

The Meeting Hack: Sometimes your boss is intent on causing you embarrassment in a meeting or he is just set on refusing to hear your viewpoint. In that case, you'll have to prepare a strategy before the next meeting so you can get your point across.

Start by making sure that you have a consensus group before the meeting begins. In other words, find your friends and allies among those who will be attending. If you don't feel you have enough of those on your side, convince your boss to widen the scope and invite more people, make sure your supporters are on that list.

Prep your people and encourage them to support your ideas. When the meeting begins volunteer to be the one to take minutes. That way, you can frame the follow-up to support your ideas. After the meeting, send an email detailing the events of the meeting and make sure it is written to show that a consensus was reached in your favor.

It doesn't really matter what actually happened in the meeting. Based on the principle that most people will follow the flow; people will usually reframe their memory to match what is written in your minutes. However, it is important to make sure that when you submit your minutes, you have at least given some recognition to the points of view of the others in the meeting.

Be prepared if someone does accuse you of changing the flow of the meeting. In your minutes, cover you bases by using phrases like "the general sense of the meeting was...." Or "several alternative suggestions were put forth including...", "there was a difference of opinion on..." "However, there were no major objections to the concept that...." This will show that other ideas and suggestions were considered.

If you think this is an unscrupulous strategy then think again. Go back through your mind to consider how many meetings have already been planned to discuss one issue and in the end, the main topic of discussion was one thing but, in the end, the majority of people ended up discussing something entirely different. It is a common practice in business meetings and you probably thought it was just an accident that it happened. The only difference is now, you know that it was a planned strategy.

Bury Information: Another classic strategy for manipulation is to find ways to hide crucial information in order to create a basis for "plausible deniability." Information that may appear detrimental to you or to a case you're working on is, in most cases, essential that you inform your boss. However, there are ways you can do it without getting your or your boss into trouble.

If your boss is like most people, he is constantly on the run. If you give him a stack of papers, he will not likely have the time or the desire to read through them all before giving his signature. By adding the information you are required to report hidden a few pages before the end of the document you're pretty safe that he won't see it. In addition, if you add the document to another report as an attachment.

If your boss does take the time to read it, he's likely just going to give it a cursory glance and then move on to something else. Once he's made his decision, based on the information you made obvious for him to see or he learns of the negative information later, you can honestly inform him that you provided the data in said report and assumed that he had already read it and had no questions about it.

This form of manipulation may also seem a little dishonest but it is a common practice in corporate offices. How do you think that many of these corporations are getting away with millions if not billions of dollars from legal contracts that keep the average customer from figuring out. One telecommunications company has a contract they give to their customers for a simple monthly phone service that is sixty pages long. Don't think you're the first one to try this and don't expect that others are going to let opportunities slip through their fingers by not doing the same.

Create an Illusion of Choice: When you want to be sure that your boss will make a decision in your favor, you can create an illusion that makes him think he has a choice.

Start by preparing three possible methods for dealing with a specific situation. However, you want to be sure that at two of the options you give him only seem like possibilities but if actually put into force would prove to be non-starters. You might offer an option that puts his bonus in jeopardy, or you might present an option that everyone on the team would object to. The third option would be the one you actually want him to make. Your boss will usually consider all three options and then make his choice.

While this is a very effective approach, your boss will likely appreciate your hard work in doing such thorough research in helping him, you need to exercise this strategy with caution. You can't make what you're doing too obvious. If your two additional options are not believable or within the realm of possibilities, your boss will figure out what you're doing and it could end up causing you more harm than good.

Wording is key in this arena. By phrasing the two options that are not viable with words like "courageous" or "bold" it will give him the idea that you think he's strong enough to handle such a bold decision but will cause him to feel more cautious in his approach. The trick to success is in carefully creating seemingly viable bad choices that seem equal in nature to the one you want him to make.

Overworked: This one works well when you want to get out of doing assignments you don't really like. Start by adjusting your appearance. When you're in the office, make it a point to walk around with a large stack of papers in your arms. As a habit, walk fast and give the appearance that you're always on your way to do something, even if it's just a trip to the bathroom.

If he asks you how you're doing, answer with a roll of the eyes and a quick answer. "I'm frazzled," "I don't know how I manage to muster up enough energy to do this or that." "I'm muddling my way through it." If your office has additional meetings to sign up for, try to get in as many as you can so that you can honestly say you're too busy. Your goal is to give the appearance that you're just too busy to take on any additional work.

What usually happens is that you'll develop a reputation for always working hard and you'll gain the sympathy vote. Your boss will see this and as he hears comments from others about your diligence at your job, he'll be reluctant to add any more to your workload and give additional work to someone else in the office.

This is a very effective strategy but it will only work with the kind of boss who values hard work over measurable results. If you have the kind of boss that wants actual reports and solid proof of what you're doing, this is not going to be the best approach.

Wrong place at the wrong time: This is a deliberate strategy that puts you in the wrong place at the wrong time. Your goal is to make it inconvenient for your boss to respond as he usually would to your suggestions. You might pitch an idea at a time when he's in a meeting with a client or on the phone under the guise of being helpful.

Just before the meeting begins give him a large stack of information to throw him off balance. You could also make an expression just before he's ready to launch into his spiel. As you hand him the information add a phrase like, "I just heard that he didn't like the last presentation someone gave him, so it's up to you to kill it in there. Here, I thought this information would help."

The message will be so unnerving to him that he will lose his focus. He will go in the meeting but his inability to concentrate will cause him to fumble or make a major mistake as a result.

Here there are two things that are important to happen at the right time. First, your timing has to be exactly right. Too soon and you give him a chance to recover, too late and you miss your window. Second, your message has to be vague enough that he won't have any way to verify it.

Other than that, you need to make sure that he understands you're not trying to undermine his work, but that you only want to be helpful.

Killer Negotiation Strategies to Manipulate Your Way to Success

The art of negotiation is one area of business where manipulation can prove to be very powerful. If fact, it is the one place where manipulation is not only effective but also necessary. Whether you're buying a new car or you're closing a major multi-million dollar deal on a prime piece of real estate, learning the psychology behind manipulation and negotiation practices can save you a massive amount of money, time, and energy.

Disappointment: Letting the other person see disappointment in you can be very effective. Studies have shown that just the appearance of disappointment is all that is needed to boost the size of your concessions made in your favor. If you're considering a new car for example, you might notice the salesman appear like he isn't pleased with your offer. There is a method to his madness. He may be very happy with your offer but acting disappointed makes you feel guilty and compels you to offer more or opens the door for him to ask for more. It also lowers the chance of you changing your mind and having second thoughts about lowering your offer.

When this is done on the first offer, it puts you in the power position in the negotiation process. Since power people rarely accept the first offer given, the direction the offers move will be based on how you respond. Fake disappointment lets you decide which way the next offer will go.

The Anti-Negotiation Buster: When the other party plays the disappointment card on you, how you respond could put the ball back in your court. By responding with a statement like, "I'm sorry, I don't have the authority to respond to such a good offer, I'll have to defer to my superiors." They will usually respond with a number they want, and the ball is back in your court again.

"You can do better than that": Silence is a great tool for any negotiator. We are psychologically hard-wired to fill in the blanks when there is too much lag time between conversations. That's why when bill collectors call, they usually will say something like we haven't received your bill for this month," and then they will remain quiet.

The don't push or ask what happened, and almost always you will feel the pressure of the silence to say something. That's when you start to make excuses or explain why you haven't paid your bill.

This same tactic works well in negotiations. When you tell them that they have to do better and then wait, more often than not, they will make the concession. Silence makes you the master of the negotiation.

The Defensive Strategy: This strategy uses reverse psychology as its foundation. Manipulators use this when they are dealing with a person, they haven't been able to gain their trust or when other forms of manipulation haven't worked yet.

By telling them that they are "being defensive" and then follow it immediately with a joke at their expense, it takes much of the stress out of the situation. Think how you would react to a statement like this in the middle of a negotiation.

"My goodness don't be so defensive. Just relax a little, we're just discussing a great deal for you. If you accept it, you'll bankrupt us unless we can get you to put down your defensive walls se we can get something out of it too."

The statement is designed to get the other person to lower his guard and maybe even laugh a little. It also gets him to think that the negotiations are already going in his favor and he may lose the deal if he doesn't start making even more concessions.

If someone uses this tactic on you, how would you respond? In most cases, one might find himself compelled to let down his guard in an effort to prove him wrong. Don't fall for this trick. The best response would be to say something like, "The way you are pushing this deal is what is making me defensive. If you want me to take this a little further, this is why…."

This kind of defense puts you back in the driver's seat and you have control once again of the negotiations. You could also make a joke. "Don't take it so seriously. We're all friends here, if things don't go your way, you could always come over to my place. You do cook, don't you?"

Getting to the higher authority: In most cases, when a person says they have some freedom in deciding a price, you can pretty much bet that they won't have the final say on anything. In fact, it means that they don't have much power at all. You need to find the person who is really in charge of what happens in the negotiations. This is usually someone who is just pretending to be a small fry.

They may be the silent one at the table who is pretending like he has no control at all over the situation. They do this so they can use the "fly on the wall" strategy to find out information and play all sorts of games with you.

By presenting yourself as a fake higher authority, you can successfully:

- Delay the negotiations until a time when you're better prepared.
- Take a stronger stance without looking like the bad guy.
- Offer a last minute concession if necessary.

There are several ways to respond when someone uses this negotiation strategy on you:

- Go along with it but make a mental note of the game he's playing. You could respond by saying, "You're not going to play the good cop/bad cop game on me, are you?"
- You could agree and then tell them, "when you do meet with your boss let him know I'd like to meet him."
- Or you could call him on it and tell him you now he's the boss.

Last Minute Approval: On nearly every occasion if someone is pushing for a last-minute concession, you know you're dealing with a master manipulator. There are many ways, they can show their hand. They may agree to the transaction and then inform you that they need an additional approval from someone else. They will give the appearance that the agreement is done but then hold back on finalizing everything. Later, they will come back and tell you that their boss is being very difficult.

If this happens to you, when they return, tell them that you also have a higher authority and you need to defer to them for a final decision. When you return, ask for your own concession. If they need the deal more than you do, this could turn into a final showdown. You could put yourself into a position where you could easily blindside them with a little pressure.

For example, "Listen, I gave this some serious consideration and I really want to hold my position here. I don't like going against my word, but I think I need to ask for 10% more." Then later, you could feel guilty about it and then make a small concession. "Because I quoted you a different price before, I can give you a 5% break, but I need an answer soon. Can you get back to me by the end of the week?"

Good Cop/Bad Cop: This is an expression that all of us know and we usually associate it with legal authorities, but it works well if you have a partner at the negotiation table too. In each case, the bad cop is the one who is firm in his position and doesn't want to budge. When too much demand is on the table the bad cop feigns anger and storms out of the room leaving the good cop to play the nice guy. The good cop then plays the higher authority card and defers to the bad cop for the final decision.

If someone plays this game on you, don't be afraid to present your own bad cop. If that doesn't work, pretend like you're giving in and use what they do next to your advantage. For example, if the good cop presents an offer you then know what they consider a good deal and what they want, but you also know what you won't accept.

Fractionation: The Seduction Tool of Master Manipulators

Have you ever wondered why "that guy" was the one to always get the girl? Why he or she seemed to always have someone hanging off of their arm, but you never seemed to be able to get past first base with anyone? No matter who you are or where you're from, there always seems to be someone who is able to do what you felt was close to be the impossible when it comes to relationships.

In order to have a close relationship with anyone, you need to be able to draw people to you. The common belief was that attracting people was a matter of looks, mannerisms, and sex appeal. However, now according to studies in modern psychology, attraction appears to be well within the reach of anyone and everyone through developing the manipulative skill of fractionation.

The name is derived from its basic scientific definition: *a separation process in which one mixture is divided into a number of smaller parts.* This seems an unusual term to use when trying to attract the opposite sex, which most of us would agree needs some level of skill in the art of seduction, but if you stick with me here, you will see how it fits.

When it comes to relationships, fractionation combines several theories all into one. With the careful use of psychology, persuasion, and the mysterious art of hypnosis, you can attract almost anyone to you. Basically, when you boil it down to the basics, it is simply the manipulative side of seduction. Because of its power to attract, many will question whether it is right or wrong to use it. However, the decision of if or how you use it is entirely up to you. Many claim that you can attract another person in as little as 15 minutes.

With all the hype surrounding fractionation, it almost sounds scary and mystical as if it were a part of the dark arts. In reality though, it could just as easily be described as a conversation technique designed with the sole purpose of bringing out strong emotions in the other person. Emotions so strong that will automatically connect them to you.

The Preparation: If attracting someone of the opposite sex were as easy as just walking up and talking to them then everyone would have someone by their side. In order to effectively use this strategy, you need to dedicate some time to preparation. Before you begin, there are certain skills you should work on developing:

- Leadership skills: Especially if you are a man, most women are not interested in a follower. If you are a woman, most men are interested in an independent woman but not an overbearing one. Learn to be more balanced and flexible.

- Your uniqueness: You don't want to appear as someone that just fell out of a mold. You need an interest that will ensure that you stand out from the crowd.

- Social skills: Build up your confidence in speaking with the opposite sex while in a crowd. Practice talking to both men and women in different settings until you are able to comfortably develop a casual conversation no matter where you are.

- Know the playing field: Learn about all the hot spots where people you're interested in like to gather. Be familiar with various options so when these places come up in discussion, you can easily participate. It also gives you a few great places to recommend if you want to invite someone out.

All of these qualities can only be done if you approach every encounter with confidence. Note, the word used is confidence, not arrogance. Statistics show that confidence is the most attractive quality to people. If you seriously want to attract someone into your life, get rid of your awkward shyness and let to present yourself in a more positive light.

Your goal with this type of preparation is to position yourself so that you will look desirable in the other person's eyes. Note, all of these things should be done before you open your mouth and say your very first word.

Make it a habit to always look your best every time you walk out your door. Spruce up your wardrobe so you have something trendy and appealing. While looks don't account for everything when it comes to attracting the opposite sex, it does matter. No one wants someone unkempt and slovenly on their arm. This doesn't mean you have to wear the most expensive clothes or the latest styles, but at the very least, make sure the clothes you wear are or were stylish within the last decade and are net and clean.

Your Emotions: The art of fractionation is very similar to the style of writing used in those addictive soap operas watched every day. Ask yourself, why are people glued to the TV set to watch a fictitious story come to life. It's because it is easy, the characters are those they can relate to and the story line taps into their **emotions.** This works because at the core of seduction is always emotion. There can be no seduction if emotions are not involved. This means more than saying pretty words, you're evoking a form of mind control so you'll need to pull out all the weapons in your arsenal including using your body language, controlling your tone of voice, and even some subtle forms of hypnosis.

As you choose your target, don't let your own insecurities get in the way. Never downplay the value of what you have to offer to a relationship. That means, the general idea that "she's out of my league," should not be part of the thought process. Instead, you want them to think they are not in your field, but you want them to feel confident enough that they can reach for it. This creates an area of challenge that will have them believing that you are worthy of the chase.

When you have carefully chosen your target, you are ready to employ your skills in fractionation. Begin with your conversational style. This is where you will apply your excellent conversational skills. Remember, conversation is more than just spewing out the right words but you need to learn to speak with your body as well. Your aim is to not to create a physical attraction but to establish a relationship. Your new relationship should be built on trust, which will be vital if you ever hope the relationship to last more than just a few days. This will require having to ask a lot of questions in order to get her involved in the conversation but be careful. It is not a job interview, just enough questions to show that you are interested, but not enough to make them feel like you're prying, nosey, or a busybody.

Conversation should be compelling and emotionally diverse. What I mean by that is that it should never display one emotion, you want to stir up a range of feelings. Your goal is to build up the kind of conversation they would want to be a part of. Choose topics that will have the emotional ups and downs and use them as an anchor to hold them in. From there you can pivot in any direction you want and they will follow.

Getting started is the tricky part. Start by asking probing but non-invasive questions to get the conversation started. You could ask them to tell you about something that makes them happy. Or you could ask her about something relating to another powerful emotion. After skillfully doing that they will happily follow you through a whole barrage of conversational topics. By tapping into both positive and negative emotions one right after the other and employing your other conversational skills like voice inflections, tone, and body language, you've hooked them in.

So, how do you choose a topic that is going to be the initial draw and then keep it moving forward. Think polarity or focus on alternating with a sequence of opposite emotions. Pleasure/pain/pleasure/pain and so on. The longer you can keep this string going the stronger the bond you will build.

For example, "Have you ever been very close to someone. So close that you felt like you were two sides of the same person and then suddenly they were gone? They just died?" This sentence starts off with something full of joy and happiness and then ends with an emotional downturn of loss and sadness.

Another example: "Have you ever met someone and was sure that they were the one for you? That the two of you were destined to stay together? And then suddenly they left? Something happened to break you apart?"

As you can see from the above examples, your questions have to have some level of depth to them. Don't settle for the superficial expressions commonly heard. Look for ways to introduce topics that will be intriguing and get them to express their innermost feelings.

It's not always easy to find ways to weave these types of questions into a regular conversation and it will take practice. However, once you do, you have started a new relationship with someone that you can now start to build on over time. Fractionation can be a challenge but eventually you will be able to master it and as a result, make yourself more attractive and interesting to others.

The whole idea behind fractionation is to create an aura of suspense. Think soap operas. Don't charge in right away with statements like you're really into them. These rarely work because you can't be interested in someone you know nothing about. It only tells them that you want to get them into bed. People want a challenge they can work for so make don't make it too easy to gain your interest. If they feel too comfortable, they will quickly lose interest and move on to someone else.

Confusion can also be very effective in attracting others. If you're very interested one minute and nonchalant the next it creates a question in their mind. They'll want to get to know you better to find out what's really under the surface.

What to avoid: This is only the beginning of a relationship. As time passes, you will have to continue to find new ways to keep interest. As you build on the foundation you've laid, try to avoid the following:

- Using bad manners: we live in a world where manners have been thrown out the window but that should not be your excuse. Always fall back on courtesy and respect.
- Talking about your exes: no matter how much you've been hurt or disappointed in the past, it should never be part of a conversation with a new relationship.
- Downplaying their emotions: An angry person never likes being told to calm down. While you may not agree with how they feel, their emotions are real and valid to them.
- Posting pictures with other women or men

You get the picture. Remember, you are trying to draw them to you. Men complaining about women's monthly period or her mood swings is just going to put a damper on all your hard work. By the same token, women who challenge his masculinity will rarely be a basis for a long-standing relationship.

There is no question that starting a new relationship is difficult. The combination of nerves and emotions can be hard to cope with. However, if you feel you're ready to embark on this adventure, it is not impossible. Build up your confidence and give it your best shot. If once you've started, you don't feel comfortable in the new relationship, don't be afraid to walk away. It is much better than dragging out a bad match to spare their feelings. It will only hurt more later on.

11 Less-Known Manipulation Techniques for Seduction

Going just a step further, after you've drawn the person in, your next goal is to keep them there until they are just as committed to you as you are to them. This is not always easy, but if you've kept your EQ high, it can be easier than you think.

There are a lot of ways to keep someone by your side but if you want to employ tools that will make the **want** to be by your side, then you should pay close attention to the patterns of their behavior. Observe what they do when they are just being themselves and use these as cues as to what you can do to keep them interested. Depending on your observations you can use any one or a combination of the following manipulation techniques to advance your relationship to the next level.

Flattery: Flattery is different from giving a regular or a genuine compliment to someone. It is actually giving compliments that are not necessary. Be careful when you flatter someone; it can have dangerous repercussions. By flattering someone so as to fuel their own insecurities, they may be drawn to you or they may start to view you suspiciously. A good example of this is if you flatter a man who is not very confident in his own sense of masculinity, he may enjoy hearing your words of praise but he may be equally suspicious about the sincerity of your words. Ideally, you want to find out what makes them insecure and give them just enough support to bolster their confidence but not go overboard.

Ex: "You're such a tough guy, you intimidate everyone around you." This will flatter a man with who is insecure about his masculinity.

Ex: "You're my little baby doll." This will flatter a woman who may be insecure about her weight.

The Trojan Horse: Some might describe this tactic as a bribe. If you keep showering them with gifts, no matter how small, they will feel obligated to stay with you. This can be done very subtly as in the case of buying a meal. This will make them feel obligated to have regular conversation with you but some have actually gone to extremes. For example, some have paid to support the other's entire lifestyle, putting them in homes, giving them cars, etc. In such cases, the extent of indebtedness grows. In those instances, they may feel as if they own the other person, which carries with it its own set of risks.

The Silent Treatment: The absence of communication can have earth shattering effects when they have become accustomed to regular conversation. This type of manipulation can easily unnerve a person and make them feel they have done something wrong and they will go out of their way to fix it for you.

The Mirror: People have also put on pretenses in order to keep someone with them. They may pretend to share the same values or demonstrate that they like the same things. Manipulators have even been known to fabricate a completely new story line in order to attract others. The sole purpose of the mirror is to give the other person exactly what they need to hear to boost their emotional stability.

Make the Decision for Them: Man are usually the ones to take this tactic. In an effort to assert their masculinity, they may make decisions for the other person. By deciding what they will eat, where they will go, or what they will do, the other person over time will become dependent on them and they won't want to leave.

The Big Question: This involves asking them for something that is far more than you know they can afford to give. You know they will be forced to refuse but, in an attempt, to compromise, they will settle for the very thing you want from them in the first place. For example, you can ask them to move in with you, which you know it is too early in the relationship for that. Then you can ask for something that is less risky, like going away for a weekend together.

The Logical Fallacy: Planting the idea in their mind that if they don't do what you want then they don't have feelings for you or they don't love you. Teenagers often use this manipulation tactic quite effectively. "If you loved me you would do this or do that."

The Expected: You might attempt to keep them by telling them it is only normal that you do this or that. "We've been together for six months now. It's only logical that we start living together."

The Guilt Trip: There are often attempts to make the other person feel ashamed for not continuing with the relationship. By making them feel like they have taken advantage of you, they will feel guilty for their own behavior and will stick with you. This tactic only works when you know the other person well and you know exactly which buttons to push, but when used properly, it can be very effective.

The Remote Control: Every time the other person starts to talk about leaving change the subject to something you know they are keenly interested in. They won't be able to resist switching with you and the fated conversation will be put off to another day.

The Board Game: When they ask to do something you don't want to do, you can also shame them by questioning their motives. "Is that what you really want?" Done the right way, it can make the other person feel like they were being unreasonable for even bringing the subject up.

Keep in mind that these tactics will only work for you temporarily. There are few manipulation strategies that will keep the other person connected to do indefinitely if there is not a genuine and compatible match. So, while manipulation may have its place in a new relationship, in time, you will eventually have to work on building that relationship on honest conversation and a real emotional connection between the two of you.

Love Bombing: The art of "love bombing" does not necessarily apply exclusively to romantic relationships. In fact, it's origin started in a church setting where religious leaders developed it to attract new parishioners to their pews. They literally "bombed" them with lots of attention and affection. Over time, parents started using it as an innovative way to education their children through kindness and care. Over time, others grew to see that it could be a powerful tool that can be used to control people in all sorts of settings. Whether it's through the use of kind words, the warmth of a tender embrace, or through the corny actions the success was impressive as more and more people started being drawn into people they would never have given a second look at before.

The basis of love bombing is to display your target with lots of affection and attention in an effort to show that you are the partner of their dreams. Once they are convinced that you are a hopeless romantic and your target is convinced that you are the ideal partner for them they are ready to enter into what they expect to be an ideal relationship.

For this strategy to work, it must be done in several stages. In the initial stage, everything must be flawless in every way. This would involve performing acts specifically designed to gain their trust, giving them encouraging words to build them up emotionally, and giving them the needed support and patience when needed.

Over time, these acts can pull a person closer to you until the point when you are able to emotionally dominate them. Evil manipulators will slowly begin to extend that control and keep them tied to them through a barrage of text messages and phone calls when they're not together. By the time this begins to happen, the other person is so hopelessly dedicated that even if they do detect something is not right, their own insecurities will be so powerful that they will find it hard to break it off. They have become addicted to those large doses of praise and kindness. That's the point when a manipulator can start to take advantage of the situation.

This is an extreme form of manipulation and those who usually practice it are generally those who have a very low self-esteem to begin with. They only use love bombing because they don't believe that they can seduce a person all on their own. They feel the only way they can have a relationship is by trickery, lies, and mind control. They recognize if they have complete dominance over the other person there is no way they will ever be abandoned.

The cycle of love bombing is difficult to miss. It can be easily identified if you know what you're looking for. The resulting relationship is not based on any form of true connection but is mostly founded on the idea of a romantic relationship. The concept of "soulmates" is at the heart and the person begins to believe that everything is so perfect that it must've been fate that brought you together. Once the target accepts this belief, the relationship can quickly turn toxic.

In the beginning, everything seems like a dream come true to the victim as the manipulator dazzles them with a chaotic array of attention and affection. The onslaught of romantic words and phrases are so frequent and steady that the victim may come to believe it so strongly that they are blinded to many of the faults even when they are played out right in front of their eyes. Once it reaches this point, it is nearly impossible for the victim to break free from the hold they manipulator has on them.

There are several phases of love bombing:

Devaluation: This stage happens after the initial phase of compliments, affection, and lots of attention. In the devaluation phase, the manipulator turns that attention to disapproval and anger. This easily can escalate into threats, which is a huge part of the psychological conditional that allows them to become a dictator of the other person's behavior.

These first two cycles could repeat themselves over and over again until it reaches a major climax.

Letting go: After the relationship has escalated into abuse, victims begin to ignore their own needs just so they can stay attached to the manipulator. Given enough time, they will break away from family and friends, and give up all the things they once loved just in an effort to avoid or break away from the conflicts that may arise.

Sometimes it can take an intervention to help the victim separate themselves from the relationship. If the person has some level of emotional strength, they may find a way to break it off on their own. They may grow tired of being controlled or they may just be feeling the pressure from others to help them to break free.

If you're truly looking for a lasting relationship, you want to avoid trying the love bomb strategy. While it may draw a person to you, it won't ever be for the reasons you want. If you suspect someone is love bombing you, use your senses. They may shower you with compliments and gifts, even if you don't know them very well. They may give you a classic line like "I know we're just made for each other."

They also know how to identify someone who would be susceptible to their witty charms. They may openly talk about a past relationship on the first date. They may lament about how the other person didn't appreciate them or how they felt misunderstood, detailing all the elements of their breakup. When that happens, beware. They are trying to pull you in and play the sympathy card. Their words are carefully chosen so that you will listen to them and feel their pain. Once they can convince you of their "feelings" it is just a matter of time before they start to control you.

Breaking up from a love bomber is difficult but it can be done. However, they will continue to ply you with affections in an effort to win you back. If you want to keep separate from them there is only one way to do this. You must break all ties with them and avoid any contact whatsoever. You also need to get support so pool together those who you trust to help you resist the temptation to go back. And no matter what you do, don't blame yourself for falling for this highly effective trick. Just be happy you were able to break free and move on from there.

Chapter Seven: Advanced Manipulation Tactics

Psychological manipulation can be very subtle and it can be quite obtuse. Depending on your aim, you will decide which tactics will work best to get you what you need. Up until this point, the manipulation strategies we have discussed have been pretty simple and basic. A lot of these things can easily be picked up on your own simply by observing the interactions of the world around you. However, when these other more basic methods fail to work, there are several advanced methods you can try.

The Manipulative Power of Reinforcement

One key element of manipulation is the art of reinforcement. It's a form of behavioral psychology that allows the user to help mold his target's future behavior by giving them some form of reinforcement. By applying this strategy, you can gain a measure of control over your subject and by extension mold his conduct himself in ways that you want to see.

There are two types of reinforcement that can be applied. Positive reinforcement is the kind of stimulus that will encourage them to continue conducting themselves in a way that you approve of. Negative reinforcement would give stimulus that has been chosen to change their behavior to something else.

Of course, there are many different degrees to the type of stimulus you can provide depending on the type of results you seek. If you want them to perform the behavior more frequently or to continue the behavior for a longer period of time then you would use positive reinforcement. If you're looking for them to change their behavior or to lessen the frequency of the behavior you would use negative reinforcement. Depending on the type of reinforcement you use, you can get a wide range of results.

Rewarding Stimuli: The stimuli you use as a reinforcement must be chosen very carefully. If you hope it can be at all effective, you need to understand what your subject wants and likes. The reward has to tap into their basic needs for desire and pleasure or their use will be ineffective. We all have basic needs that drive us to do the things we do so when your reward taps into that inner need, it is more likely to encourage more of the behavior you want. In essence, reinforcement happens only if the subject sees the stimuli as a reward or in the case of negative reinforcement, as a loss.

Parents are very effective at using reinforcement to get their children to do their chores. They may offer an allowance for doing work around the house or they may offer a weekend at an amusement park for exceptionally good behavior. But when you look around you, we see the art of reinforcement playing out in every field. Few of us go to work just because we enjoy the work and it makes us feel good. We go for the paycheck/reward. Few of us are in relationships where we're not getting some form of satisfaction out of it. And we rarely spend our free time doing things we hate. When we get a moment free to ourselves, we naturally go for the things that we feel are most rewarding to us. Getting a raise or a promotion at work is a powerful incentive for getting you to work harder on your job. By the same token, losing your job for undesirable behavior can be a strong negative reinforcement as well.

In most situations, the use of reinforcement is relating to behavior but it can also relate to memory as well. A good example of this is something called "post-training reinforcement" where the reward is given after the subject has learned something new. A manipulator can use reinforcement to help improve their memory of the breadth, duration, and specific details of the lesson until it is firmly planted in their mind. In such cases, the reward needs to be something that touches the subject emotionally. That way, they connect the lesson with their personal feelings.

We've all experienced this type of reward before. If you are of the older generation, you can recall without much hesitation where you were when the Challenger exploded or the 9/11 tragedy occurred. These have been described as "flashbulb memories" because they were both events that give us intense emotions. If you look back through your own personal life, those memories that are the embedded the deepest in your mind are the very ones that have touched you emotionally. This can be an extremely powerful emotional tool when used in the right way.

In order to use reinforcement successfully, you will need to fully understand where your target is vulnerable. This information will help you to decide which type of reward you will give them in order to mold their behavior. Once decided, you must be careful not to be too over when giving the reward. When it is too obvious, the subject is very likely to understand what's going on and squash your efforts almost immediately. However, by playing a subtle and more passive role, you can gently nudge them in the direction you want them to go.

Applying Positive Reinforcement: One of the easiest forms of reinforcement is when you encourage continued practice of a desirable behavior. Your reward will be given as a means of encouraging the subject to continue or to escalate a certain act. Some examples of positive reinforcement:

- You can give words of praise encouraging them to continue.

- Money
- Approval
- Gifts
- Personal attention
- Public recognition

Positive reinforcement does not have to cost you anything. Small children for example are happy with just an approving smile from their parents. Don't get into the habit of thinking that positive reinforcement has to have a monetary value. Look for what that person needs and use that to encourage them. Even adults are not always content with monetary value. People see value in all sorts of things.

Applying Negative Reinforcement: When you want your subject to cut back or cease a certain behavior then you would apply negative reinforcement. In such a case, you would remove a reward or you would prevent them from achieving the reward they seek. Negative reinforcement could also include giving them something they don't find desirable; something that will either make them uncomfortable or find to be unpleasant. Such reinforcement is less likely to keep them continuing with the same behavior for any extended period of time.

- Nagging
- Intimidation
- Yelling
- Swearing
- Guilt trip
- Silent treatment

- Sulking

You will notice that all of the behaviors listed above can make your subject extremely uncomfortable. They play on his emotions and erode their personal self-esteem causing them to cease their behavior. Consider what happens when a parent nags their child about doing house chores. If every time the child enters the room, the parent nags, yells, screams, embarrasses, or threatens the child will eventually start doing his chores. The reward happens when the chores are done and the parent stops berating them.

Another example, an employer has a policy that all work must be completed by the end of the week or they can't have the weekend off. This is a powerful negative reinforcer and gives many workers incentive to increase their productivity during the week so that everything will be done on time.

Extinction: Reinforcement can also take a neutral position too. Positive reinforcers are used to encourage the behavior you want, negative reinforcers are designed to discourage certain behaviors. Extinction reinforcers, however, happens when you don't acknowledge the behavior at all.

For example, a child refusing to acknowledge a bully at school. With neither a positive or a negative reaction, there is no fuel for the bully to work with and he will quickly lose interest in his target. It can also be seen when employers do not recognize the work that an employee is doing. In time, the employee will lose interest in his work and will give up trying.

Keep in mind that reinforcement is not the same as punishment. Punishment is designed to correct certain behaviors and reinforcement is designed to encourage behaviors. You could think of them as the opposites of the same coin.

Charming Habits to Manipulate Anyone

Charisma can be an excellent tool for manipulating anyone. When you can be charming you are also endearing to others and they will be drawn to you. However, there is a big difference between being charming and acting charming. Some people just have a natural way of pulling people in while others may have to work at it. It's not as easy as they make it appear to be.

When you can put on the charm, it is easy to blind someone to your true intentions. By nature, people tend to listen to only those things they want to hear. They often make decisions that they know are against their best interest yet they do it anyway without giving it a second thought.

There are those who already know how to use their charm to draw us in, giving us a strong sense of confidence. Others use their charm to get you to let your guard down so you will believe everything they say. And others will use their charm to make you feel like you've been friends for years even when you've only just met. All of these people are highly skilled at turning it on and off at will making it very difficult to recognize it when it's being put to use. If you're not one of these people you will have to develop these skills that are classics for master manipulators.

Mirroring: Mirroring or matching the other person's body language sends them a signal letting them know that you are very interested in them. It builds a bond of trust that you can use later on when you want to get something from them or get them to do something for you.

In a normal setting, people will automatically do this without even realizing it. However, it can be one of the most effective ways to win someone over when you are using it to connect with the other person. Think of how many times you've smiled when you caught someone mirroring you. Perhaps you both reached for the same book at the same time. Your hands touch and you can't help but smile when you realize what happens. On a subconscious level, you are letting the person know that you have more in common than they may have realized.

Gazing Into Their Eyes: We all know how important making eye contact is when trying to communicate. It is one of the best ways to get people feel like they matter to you. When using this technique when you are trying to persuade someone you can lock your eyes with theirs with an intense gaze that can seem almost hypnotic. For the best effect, timing is important.

For example, locking eyes with them immediately after saying something that might may them feel uneasy can temper the kind of response they give you. It throws them off their game and disorients them for a minute. That will give your initial thought time to sink in.

Breaking the Rules: There is a reason why the bad guy always seems to get the girl. There is a certain charm quality they all seem to have. They may be breaking the rules but they are doing it in a playful way. They are not breaking the rules just to break them though; there is a method to their madness. They may try some intimate moves with you on the first date. Touching you in a way you would not normally permit.

This kind of behavior is really a fishing expedition. They are pushing the boundaries so they can see where you stand. How committed are you to your decisions. How you respond to these tests will determine the method of manipulation to use in the future. If you permit intimate touching on the first date, you can fully expect the intimacy to escalate in the future.

As a general rule, manipulators will use these charming qualities to invade your space, draw your attention, and to show their power over their target. Think of it as playing a game of chess where they are making a play for control over the subject's mind and heart.

Confessions: One thing charming people know how to do is talk. They are very eloquent speakers and know how to pull you into a conversation and hold your attention until they have made their point. They are avid attention seekers and to do this they need to know how to tell a story that will keep you hanging on every word.

Manipulators will do the same thing on a more personal level. Rather than telling a good story they will tell you about confidential matters to keep you coming back. They make you feel as if they trust you so much, they will share their innermost secrets with you. This is usually the first part of a manipulation strategy. They start by getting you to connect with them by confessing all their past deeds. They will continue until you are so involved you look for them to tell you more. Then they stop, literally pulling the rug right from under your feet, refusing to even discuss such things anymore. This leaves you feeling like you've done something wrong and you will do just about anything to get back to that same level of communication you had before.

Using Pet Names: On the surface, calling your significant other by pet names seems endearing and affectionate, but in reality, it is devaluing your role in the relationship. Calling someone baby, or sweetie, or darling shows that they are not seeing you as an equal in the relationship. It makes you feel lesser than you really are.

If they continue this habit for a long time and then stop, you begin to feel as if you're in the wrong and wondering what to do about it. At that point, they have maneuvered you into a position where they now have control over you and you will become their puppet and do exactly what they want just to hear those endearing words again.

Excessive Complimenting: Sometimes excessive complimenting is truly sincere but this tool in the hands of a master manipulator can be covering over questionable motives. This form of manipulation is usually done by those who are lower on the totem pole than others within the infrastructure. Children will do this to their parents, employees to their bosses, and students to teachers.

Be cautious when using this technique, most people in positions of power will be on guard so you will have to exercise a little self-control and use it gradually over a longer period of time. If you can effectively do this subtly then your chances of getting a harder more difficult person to soften up will be a lot easier than if you go in guns a blazing and gushing all over them.

Validating Negative Emotions: Helping people justify negative emotions is a powerful weapon in the hands of a manipulator. If they are feeling depressed about a mistake or something they feel they did wrong, rather than encourage you to change, a manipulator will validate those feelings so that you will stay in a negative frame of mind. Then when they have you fully committed to them, they will be your redeemer and rescue you.

This type of manipulator is not interested in making you feel better but wants you to believe that they are the solution to all your problems. They want you to believe that you cannot resolve the issue on your own so they will try to keep you trapped in that negative emotional state so they can rescue you.

It may take some time to develop these skills to a degree where you can turn them on and off without much though however, once you do, you will have all the charm and grace that you see so many others engaged in.

How to Turn Someone Into their Own Enemy

Our memories are a tricky thing. We often question whether we remember events accurately anyway, so it can be relatively easy for a manipulator to play on that natural tendency to turn someone's own recollections against them. This method of persuasion is called "gaslighting" and it is used to get someone to trust you more than they do themselves.

You can see gaslighting going on all around you. It is used by lawyers, relationship partners, religious leaders, and other with the sole purpose of making the other person believe that their memories or recollection of events is fallible. When you can convince someone that there is something wrong with how the recall events it erodes their confidence in themselves so you can then implant in them your own script for them to play out.

Addiction: It is one thing to call a person crazy and it is another thing entirely to convince them of it. They are not likely to believe you just because you said it so, you will need to start doing things to convince them of your truth. Before you can do that, you have to get them to trust you.

This starts with triggering the brain to release endorphins and dopamine. When a person gets excited a chemical reaction starts in the brain and it releases those hormones. These are the same hormones that are released when people take drugs. By doing things to trigger the same chemical release, you can cause a person to become addicted to you. Your first step in gaslighting is to create an addict by providing them with enough excitement that they will attach themselves to you just so they can continue to get that high from the chemical release in their brains.

Work on Your Own Memory: Now you have to work on yourself. It is a given that we all make mistakes but that doesn't mean that we remember them all. An effective manipulator is very meticulous and will remember every time a mistake is made by their subject and any misinterpretations or misunderstandings they may have developed. You need this so that you can use this as evidence that their memories are not legitimate and not to be relied upon.

By frequently pointing these normal flaws out, your subject will eventually begin to see how frequently they are in the wrong and will start to rely on your memory and solutions when problems come up.

Act Confused: When your subject raises an objection to your representation of the facts, you can act confused and feign a lack of understanding. Or you can dismiss his recounting as exaggerated, illogical, or completely false. Then you can present your own answer as a simple but logical account of the events. After doing this several times, the subject will start to turn to you for help more and more as they lose their own confidence in their abilities.

Forget: When they tell you they did this or that, simply tell them you don't recall it. Use phrases like, "I don't remember that," or "I didn't see you there." Be persistent even when it comes to the smallest detail. The more insistent you are the less likely they are going to resist your influence.

You could also do the opposite and convince someone that they really did do something you know they didn't do. This will confuse them even more because they will struggle to recall events that never happened. Again, if you project confidence and persistence in your belief they will begin to doubt their own memory and eventually fall in line with your thinking.

Minimize Their Concerns: Over time, gaslighting will drain your subjects to the point of frustration and depression. It will bring out a lot of negative emotions, which can be thoroughly exhausting. Once that happens, they will begin to talk about their concerns and they will turn to you because 1) they're now addicted to you. 2) they lack confidence in their own memory, and 3) you have positioned yourself to be a trustworthy ally. When they come to you with their concerns, dismiss them by telling them that they are "taking things too seriously," "overreacting, or getting too emotional."

This can turn out to be one of the most effective manipulation tools you can have in your arsenal. The best and most efficient way to use it is slowly over an extended period of time. You may not be able to master it correctly the first time, but after several tries, you will be able to turn someone's mind into his own enemy. Then you have them in a position to do whatever you want from them.

Chapter Eight: Asserting Dominance

It is relatively easy to see the kind of people that are drawn to us. We tend to gravitate towards those who are similar to us in behavior and thought. There is a lot of truth in the old saying "birds of a feather flock together." We surround ourselves with people who are going to relate to us, understand us, and support us. It saves us from constantly having to live with a defensive stance over all of our decisions.

However, as a manipulator, you will want someone around you that will behave in a certain way so you will need to exercise some level of control. You will have to assert your dominance from the very beginning so that they will follow your every instruction without question. You not only want to be able to direct their behavior but you want them to accept it too. For this you need to develop some very strong skills.

Body Language that Asserts Dominance

Your body is your largest form of communication. How you move or position it will cause others to react without question. One of the reasons to exercise dominance with your body is because it is subtle, almost invisible, so it is unlikely the other person will even realize what you're doing. We react to body language instinctively, without thought, so once they respond to you, their thoughts will naturally fall in line.

Use of Space: When people are being described as being "larger than life" it's not referring to their physical size, but the amount of space they are using. If you want to exercise dominance make sure that you are using as much space as possible. When you are standing, place your hands on your hips with the elbows pointing out so you occupy more space. When you sit, stretch your legs out as far as possible. When you lean, walk, or find yourself in any other position, make sure that your body is occupying as much space as possible.

Women however, should exercise caution with body posing. More often than not, they will be labeled as taking on a less feminine role and/or of a less reputable position with open body language. She then would want to take a more closed pose but still exercise her dominance by using her body in other ways.

It also depends on the goal of the manipulator. If it is in a business environment, she would need to consider her audience. If she is in a group with many men and few women, a closed stance can be read as being defensive and she would want to avoid that at all costs. On the other hand, if she's in a more social setting with a balanced group around her, her closed body language could make her appear to be more open to a new relationship.

Touching: There have been a number of studies that have shown how touching others while in conversation shows as more dominant. The act itself indicates that you are comfortable around them and are not intimidated or worried about invading another person's space. Of course, all of this is cultural and each environment needs to be taken into consideration. So, make sure that you understand the cultural dynamic of the people you're interacting with before you just decide to reach out a touch someone.

For women, touching men in any way could be perceived in the wrong way. If you're in a business setting avoiding even the slightest touch below the waistline. It is a powerful way to stimulate arousal. Again, women cannot use the power of touch as much as men without sending out the wrong vibes. And she should avoid touching strangers at all unless touching is viewed as acceptable in their culture.

Holding Your Ground: When you're in a small or crowded space, it is normal to give a little to allow others to navigate. To assert your dominance, try to move a little as possible. In social settings, who moves for whom lets you know exactly who is the alpha.

- If you meet an old friend and they approach you, you are on the power side: try not to move.
- If you're in a group that needs something and others retrieve it, they are on the power side: move to accommodate them.
- If you're in a meeting in your office, you are the alpha: don't move.

This same rule can be applied in all types of settings. Whether in business or social settings these guidelines are based on how people naturally move when interacting with each other. We all instinctively know that we must move for the boss but be observant when you're in groups where there is no assigned rank to each person. This is where you can assert your dominance. People will automatically move for the person who acts more dominant or for the larger person.

Eye Contact: Your eyes can also let people know that you're the top dog in the room. The longer you are able to hold eye-contact is usually an indication of your position in the setting. This is because the higher authority figures are quite comfortable maintaining eye contact with those under them. If you want to assert your dominance in a particular setting or group, don't look down.

If you do feel the need to break eye contact, make sure that you break it in the right way. If your eyes move up, it is read as a sign of dismissal. If they move to the side it is considered neutral and the two of you are on equal footing. However, if you break downwards it is always viewed as submissive, so never look down.

However, if you're a woman and looking to seduce, then looking down and then back up again is a clear signal that you want him. So, if that's your aim, then by all means, go for it.

Comfort: The more comfortable you appear the more confidence you project. Nervousness sends a message of fear and anxiety. Try taking on a calmer and slower style to exude more confidence.

It is true that people who move fast and seem to exude energy can send out a message of fear, the person who moves slowly does not reflect any type of anxiety and appears to be much more grounded and in control. The message they send is that others can feel safe and relaxed around them.

There is also the concept of "locking in" where you use the most comfortable position you can in the setting. That could mean leaning against a bar or a railing, sitting on a stool, or leaning against a desk or a wall.

Open Body Language: Asserting your dominance through open body language tells others that you are powerful. When your body is closed (hunched shoulders, crossed arms, and legs close together) it reflects an image of fear, anxiety, or unapproachable. However, when you display a more open body (arms out, legs apart, shoulders back) we appear dominant yet approachable. We let people know that we are confident and are in control.

Relaxed Body Language: Also, a body that is relaxed sends a message of authority. When you show signs of comfort you appear more relaxed. Avoid sending displacement signals like scratching, touching your face or the back of your neck, wringing your hands, or unbuttoning the collar of your shirt. All of these signals show signs of nervousness and anxiety.

Maintain Good Posture: Not only is good posture good for your health but it is also good for your image too. Your level of confidence is easily reflected in how you hold your body. When you stand erect and tall you exert a dominant and confident position but if you stand with your shoulders rounded, your head leaning forward (almost as in a permanent bow) you are taking a submissive position.

If you have been in this habit in the past, you need to start adjusting this stance as soon as possible. However, you need to be cautious and avoid over correcting. Extending your spine too far back can give you a swayback posture. Sticking your chest out too far will make you look cartoonish. Try making the adjustment in the mirror until you find the right balance.

Do the Power Walk: There is some disagreement as to whether a power walk is fast or slow. A slow walk exudes more confidence as long as it represents your natural walking style. However, if you are moving slowly in a busy work environment it may send the message that you're lazy or unmotivated. By the same token, a fast walk can also exude confidence if done correctly. Still, it can be misconstrued as nervous or anxious depending on your environment.

So, while the speed of your walk can send a strong message, it is best to focus on how you walk. Make sure that as you move your shoulders move with you. A sway of the shoulders makes them look broader taking up more space. Use your arms with a smooth back and forth movement keeping them just slightly away from your body. When your arms are too close it is a sign of fear.

Keep the legs slightly apart allowing enough room for air to circulate and keeping the thighs from rubbing together.

Always stand up erect with your feet pointing slightly outward. You don't want to do it too much because it will give off an aire of disdain for those around you.

Keep you gaze staring straight ahead and focused to give you the appearance that your walk has a purpose.

The Upward Nod: Make a habit of nodding with the chin thrusting upward rather than down. It gives you more of a rough appearance but only use it when necessary because in some crowds it can appear confrontational, which could cause more problems.

How to Talk Like a Top Dog

Your physical positioning tells others you are confident and ready to tackle anything that comes your way. People will often defer to you when you display these physical body languages even if they don't understand why. But once they do come to you, it is important for your conversation to match the message that your body is sending out. How you express yourself will further solidify your dominance in any social dynamic.

Lead the Conversation: When you speak, you must think about more than the words you choose to express your point of view. There are several variables that are important to regulating your conversation. As you assert your dominance, you need to be careful of your tone, tempo, subject matter, and who speaks the longest.

This is even more important when you are talking one on one with someone. In a group dynamic, there will always be a variety of characters to interact with however, when in a more private conversation where there are only two players, how you respond to questions and what you do will weigh heavily on who will have more dominance.

- **Tempo:** To exert dominance you need to control the speed of the conversation. You want to speak fast enough that you don't waste time but slow enough that you message is clearly understood. This means not only managing and regulating what you say, but your voice will set the tempo for the other person as well. In a group setting, it is your responsibility to make sure everyone is engaged in the same topic and on the same page. You also want to make sure to include everyone in the group. If you notice someone taking over the conversation, step in and cut them off with confidence.

In other words, you appoint yourself as the director of the conversation. Take control and gracefully interrupt when things start to go the wrong way. You could intervene in several ways.

When one person is cut off by another: "Wait a second." Then address the person who was cut off, "please, go ahead and finish your thought." Or "Let's hear what Janet has to say."

When a person is talking too fast: "Slow down, you're speaking to fast."

By taking the initiate to direct the conversation, you place yourself in a powerful dominant position and soon everyone in the group will be looking to you for direction even after the conversation has concluded and you've gone your separate ways.

- **Setting the Frame:** By the same token, directing the conversation also means deciding what's right to discuss. You decide what's fair, what's acceptable, and what's considered to be normal and appropriate conversation. The more power you exude at this stage the more people will respect and want to follow you.

- **Asking the Right Questions:** How you ask questions also plays a major role in asserting dominance. When engaging in conversation, always ask plenty of questions. In any conversational dynamic, the person who asks usually dominates the conversation and they person who answers is the subordinate.

- **Don't be Afraid to Offer Correction:** When you correct someone, you're making your power move. In essence, you are asserting your right to dictate the rules of the game. The more corrections you offer the higher your position of authority will be in their eyes. Only subordinates avoid correcting others or afraid of being viewed as taking a stand against authority.

  It is also a demonstration of your higher intellect, which is key in any dating dynamic. How you offer correction can make a difference too. For example, if you offer it in a way that shames the other person, they may see you as an authority but will lose respect for you. On the other hand, if you offer it with sincerity and with a feeling that you genuinely want to help, you will gain the respect you want.

- **Contradictions:** The same rules apply when you are contradicting another person. Whenever you are going to say something that is the exact opposite of what the other person believes, you are throwing down your dominance gauntlet. It is an extremely powerful move that if not done correctly could sever the entire relationship.

  While this may be acceptable in some settings, those who have a higher social EQ understand just how risky this move is. Instead, they may just acknowledge the other person's point of view and then redirect the conversation subtly bringing in the correct answer without pointing out his or her error. This allows the other person to save face and garner you much more honor and respect than making an outright contradiction.

- **The Conclusion:** At the close of a conversation a leader will do a quick summary of what has been discussed. If you are not the leader but are trying to assert dominance the this would be the perfect time to step up and volunteer for this role. People will begin to see you as someone who can step up and be a good leader.

Assertiveness: It is important that you speak assertively. This means that you won't want to give up or relinquish your right to speak but instead make sure that everyone not only hears you but understands it too. There are several steps to accepting this role.

- **Make sure everyone understands:** As a leader your responsibility is not just to disseminate information but to make sure that all of your subordinates are clear on what is expected. You can verify this by asking questions like, "Are we clear?" "Do you understand?" or "Did you get it?" In some situations, you might ask them to repeat your instructions back to them so you know they fully grasp your expectations.

- **Always Expect an Answer:** In some situations, people will be reluctant to answer a question or concern you have raised.

They may switch the subject or they may just pretend they didn't even hear the question. In some cases, they may even dismiss it as unimportant to the conversation. Never accept this. If you find someone who is reluctant or refuses to answer your question either repeat the question with a stronger tone that lets them know that you expect an answer or bring the conversation back around to the point of your discussion. Either way, never accept a non-answer to a direct question.

- **Repeat When Necessary:** If you find you are speaking in a group that may get too loud at times, the temptation is to raise your voice to make sure that you're heard. While this may work you run the risk of being seen as too aggressive rather than assertive. However, if you simply pause when the noise level gets too high and then repeat your message when the noise level drops again, you'll gain more respect.

  You can also remind them of your official authority position and let them know that there is no other source for which to get the information you want to share with them. Make sure you have an assertive tone and the inflection reflects the kind of position you claim to have.

- **Avoid Being Verbally Aggressive:** Verbal aggression runs rampant on the political and business front. However, this doesn't mean you have to take that road. There is a difference between asserting your dominance and the use of verbal aggression. A person who is verbally aggressive will speak over people and at times literally rob them of their right to speak for themselves. They will cut people off or force them to be defensive in their remarks. These are strong-arm tactics where you are literally railroading the other person and forcing them into submission. While this will help you to be seen as an authority, you are instilling fear and intimidation to get what you want often even shaming them into accepting your position.

If you find yourself being attacked in this manner, don't go into the defensive mode. Instead, launch your own counterattack by reframing the subject in question or refuting their statements with your own evidence. As soon as you go on the defensive you automatically relinquish your power to them. Instead, stop his attack early on in the conversation. Match their own nastiness by pushing back with equal aggression or denying any accusations they may have made.

The launch your own counterattack, pointing out their hypocrisy or any errors in their argument. Remember, the power they gain from this encounter is only as strong as their accusations against you. Your goal is not to defend your argument but to rob them of their power. Don't take a stance on any position that it would be difficult to defend or prove. Work at showing a side that your opponent doesn't want seen and force him to get back to the truth as soon as possible. Winning a heated debate like that will earn you loads of points you would have to work even harder to achieve.

- **Ignore people:** By ignoring people, you show a lot of dominance. This is an important skill that is of high quality and can prove very valuable. You can prove your dominance by ignoring people's errors or when they take an action you don't approve of. Rather than blatantly pointing out their error, ignoring them is a silent way to show disapproval.

- **Say a lot with fewer words:** The most powerful people in the world are not always full of a lot of rhetoric. They don't mind people noticing them so they are calm in the face of social scrutiny. When they speak, they usually express themselves slowly and don't hesitate to pause to let the silence drive home their point.

  When replying to another person, the general rule of thumb is to wait two seconds before speaking. Don't be afraid of the silence, it adds pressure to the other person and they are compelled to fill in the void.

- **Use Power Words:** Your speech should make good use of power words.
  - **Listen**
  - **I don't understand**
  - **Can you repeat that**
  - **Yes, that's right**
  - **No. That not right at all**
  - **Wrong!**
  - **You're mistaken.**
  - **And you're okay with that?**
  - **Before we continue, I need you to answer my question.**
  - **I don't want to talk about that now.**
  - **Tell me something more interesting.**
  - **Quiet! Silence!**
  - **The numbers speak for themselves.**

Whether you're speaking one on one or in a crowd, asserting dominance is all about projecting the right attitude. It is a very faint line that exists between being aggressive and being assertive, but if you can master these elements in asserting your dominance, you'll not only have a lot of people following you, you'll have earned their respect too.

Dominant Behavior to Show Who's Boss

Showing dominance through behavior can be very similar to using body language. In fact, some of the methods here will overlap with those in how you present yourself physically. Spend some time observing people in power and you'll begin to see what social dominance really looks like.

Take the Lead: Clearly, taking the lead in any given situation can help you to assert your social dominance. Consider the impression you leave in others when you are:

- Walking. If you are going with a group, you'll notice how the more submissive people will begin to look around for someone to take the lead. As a leader, you don't wait, you just start walking. Try it and see just how many people will start to follow you.

  If you are new to a group, don't just jump ahead. Wait and see if they already have an established leader and if no one steps forward, then you can assert your position.

- Look for ways to protect those around you. This is a classic dominant role that exudes power and is deserving of respect. Protecting and caring for others could be simple gestures like offering someone a hand when they are trying to get out of their seat to defending their decision on a business project. This strategy has no downside. A strong leader who exercises care for those in his charge is a healthy way to get any kind of relationship off to a good start.

- Expect people to follow you. If people are not sure you're the leader it will be difficult for them to follow you, but simple gestures can help them along. For example, shaking someone's hand and placing the other on their back helps direct them to move in the direction you want them to go.

- Become a good guide: Take the initiative and invite others to join you whenever possible. Not only is this a powerful way to assert dominance people will automatically see you as a leader.

- Take the lead in small things. If the entire group sits, delay sitting for at least ten seconds before joining them. If you are invited inside, delay entering. You can tell them to take one second to enjoy the view or to answer a phone call. If you are in a position that dictates you must follow, do so in a nonchalant sort of way and avoid making any eye contact with them.

- Assign tasks: Whenever possible, give tasks to others. Delegating is a sign of authority. You will notice some people assign tasks even if they don't have any formal authority. If you are assigned a task, question the command. This will make the assigner have to defend his position. The more your challenge those in authority the more power you take for yourself. However, there will be times when someone does have the authority to give you a task. If this is the case, accept the assignment gracefully but continue to challenge tasks given from those who are not in an authority position to do so.

Exert Social Pressure: Creating tension within a social environment pressures other to comply. At times you can create tension even without a reason for it, just to assert your dominance.

Use intimidation with full frontal body language or loud aggressive tones in your voice to get less important individuals to cower in submission.

Use Fewer Words: Talking too much can be a sign that you are nervous or lack confidence. Rather than expressing every thought on your mind, let your facial expressions and body language communicate for you.

Touching: You can also show dominance through touching. In fact, just the act of touching alone can put you in a more dominant position. Studies have often shown that those who touch others are automatically viewed as more dominant. However, there is the right kind of touching and the wrong kind.

- **The Parental Touch:** Parental touches doesn't necessarily mean they are exclusive to parents and their children. A boss can use a parental touch and automatically push his charges into a more submissive role.
    - Patting them on the head
    - Pinching their cheek
    - Touching their face

153

All of these touches indicate who is the parent and who is the child. They are also signaling that they are ready to take care of their subject and are ready to take charge.

Follow the Pattern: There is a distinct pattern of events that can carry you from the submissive one to the more dominant role in any type of relationship. You may start at the bottom rung of the ladder, then you move on to assertion, which will gradually slip you into a dominant role. The most effective role you can take is to follow the natural course of these patterns. The best ones to take an assertive role are those who are very good at handling those who are aggressive.

Part of that journey, however, is learning when to show aggression, punish, or intimidate. People who fall back on these dark habits when not needed usually earn the title of leader but not the respect due them. But there is a place for them in a number of interactions. Here are a few guidelines you need to follow.

- Slapping: This does not have to be a harsh type of slap that will leave your victim's cheeks burning. In fact, a light but threatening slap may be even more intimidating than outright brute force.
- Confiscating property: Picking up or taking another person's property is a very intimidating way to assert dominance. In essence, you are telling them that not only does their property belong to you but they do too. To fight back this approach, you can refuse to let them take your property or you can take theirs putting you both on equal footing.
- Territorial: Everyone feels territorial about something, but submissive people don't stand up for what they know is

theirs. To assert your dominance, you will defend property that is your own with a strong sense of confidence.

Command Attention: Exerting a quiet sense of confidence always commands attention. There is no need to be flashy or bold in order to get people to follow you. While you can certainly take that route, just following the natural course of nature will have people gravitating to you with ease. Consider being helpful to those around you. By offering to fix problems, address needs, and protect those you want in your following, you will become a natural leader without too much effort.

Asserting your dominance may not be easy at first, especially if you're used to being in a more submissive position. But, if you continue to practice these simple techniques, you'll be surprised at just how fast you can move up in your role of becoming a master manipulator.

Conclusion

Becoming a master manipulator is not as difficult as it may seem. It will take practice and commitment, and you won't master it overnight. Nothing you do well in life is ever easy, but if you stick with it through to the end you will inevitably yield positive results.

No doubt, you've heard a lot of things about manipulation. It's evil, it's dangerous, and it is demeaning, but there are both good and bad ways to view the practice. We live in a world of manipulators no matter where you look. The reality dictates that if you're not manipulating then there is a really good chance that you are being manipulated so you're going to be on one side of the coin whether you agree with it or not.

The question you really should be asking yourself is what kind of manipulator are you going to be. Parents manipulate their children as they mold them to become mature adults. Teachers manipulate their students to groom them for the future, and employers manipulate their charges to increase productivity. All of us have been manipulated in one way or another and we have all worked our magic on others. If your moral compass is triggered by this thought, then realize it is a matter of choice.

Becoming a master manipulator involves understanding how our thoughts and emotions work together. As your emotional intelligence grows so will our understanding in these areas. We've discussed how to build up our EQ and learn how to use it to identify our own emotions and those in others. This can become a powerful tool in our arsenal. Every master manipulator needs a good EQ. Without it, we will always struggle to get people to recognize us and give us what we want.

You also learned how to choose your target and the qualities that draw people to you. Everyone is not a prime target for manipulation and some can be much harder than others to convince. Especially in the beginning, you want to use the hooks listed in Chapter three to choose those who will be easier to convince. As you gain more experience, you can then try your skills on those harder and more challenging targets.

In Chapter Four we talked a great deal about body language. Learning how to read subtle cues can tell you a lot about a person and what they are thinking. Developing this skill can almost give you the power of mind reading. Learning about microexpressions and the way people walk will tell you much about what to expect and what you can ask from everyone around you.

Then we learned how to use several manipulation tools to help you get what you want. We started simply with some basic tactics that all people use and can easily be recognized. Applying the Six Laws of Persuasion can be very effective if you are well-informed about what they really are. Manipulation is a psychological game and the key to winning knowing where to position yourself to assert dominance over others. These tools are how you navigate this game.

So, whether you're looking to secretly manipulate your boss to do what you want or you're trying seduce someone into a romantic relationship the rules of the game are the same, you're just using different tools to accomplish your goals. Success can only come from asserting your dominance and staying the course.

Through the pages of this book, you have learned a lot about manipulation. No doubt, you will have to read some sections several times in order to get the full sense of them. But as you do, make sure to put them all into practice as soon as possible. This will help you to make faster progress. There will be times when you will fail miserably at your attempts to persuade others to do your bidding, but don't be discouraged; that is just part of the process. If you persist, it is just a matter of time before you can honestly say that you are truly a master manipulator.

THE POWER OF DAILY SELF-DISCIPLINE

Practical Exercises to Strengthen Your Willpower and Overcome Procrastination by Creating Atomic Habits

Table of Contents

INTRODUCTION

Have you delayed your "big" project only to delude yourself you'll do it when you're ready — and that moment never comes? Have you fallen into a loop of laziness, and can't get anything done? Maybe you started working on your dream project, only to give up 2 to 3 days later? What if you tried to learn a new language like Spanish — but gave up after the first 2 lessons because the grammar was exhausting? Have you ever dreamed of learning to play the guitar, but once you actually sat through the lessons, the chords were too hard to learn and you dropped it halfway? We've all been there!

The secret to sticking to tasks you don't want to do is self-discipline. Everyone will tell you to develop self-discipline; but how do you actually develop atomic-level self-discipline that allows you to overcome each temptation in your daily life? The kind of self-discipline that allows you to create million-dollar projects, stick through daily tasks, and get s%*t done? The secret of atomic self-discipline is revealed in this book. You're in for a journey.

This book teaches you how to handle the hardest part of human nature: Biological impulses. Biological impulses work against you. All humans delude themselves that their thoughts are their own. However,, have you considered that your thoughts are not really your own? Look at what you do instead of what you think in your head: Have you ever thought that you should get fit and should be eating broccoli instead of pizza, but found yourself ordering pizza at midnight? This is not your fault, but the fault of your biological programming. Your biology is wired to respond to immediate pleasure: food, sex, sleep, entertainment. Biological impulses are powerful, and they cannot be overcome easily. Biological impulses run nature; if you observe nature at its purest form, all animals are essentially trying to consume energy or reproduce. The same biological impulses driving us and making life great can also destroy us. This is why self-discipline is key to overcoming our biological programming.

The 5 Grand Revelations of Self-Discipline

Revelation #1: You are your own worst enemy. There are no external forces controlling you, and no one stood in your way. You created all the obstacles yourself. Accept that all your procrastination, inadequacy, failed projects and unmet deadlines are a result of your own lack of self-discipline.

The first step to obtaining self-discipline is to accept you are in a struggle with yourself. Self-discipline is the art of overcoming your own biological impulses. Once a person gets through their main obstacle — biological impulses — they can beat all procrastination, lack of focus, and laziness.

Revelation #2: Human Evolution works against you. Millions of years of evolution have wired our bodies and brains to act in animalistic ways — your nature does not work in your best interest. Essentially, we're wired to take in the most value in exchange for the least amount of effort. To reverse our biological programming, we have to train our brain on reversing the process: We have to maximize output and minimize the value we seek in return.

Once a person's brain is re-wired to exert output rather than seeking the next thing to consume, their productivity goes up and this helps them achieve all their goals. The human body is not just a reflection of two parents having a child, it's also a continuation of millions of years of evolution which you have to struggle to undo. The brain is like a horse: If you let it steer on its own, it will lead you to the edge of a cliff. If you steer it right, it will lead you to your destination. This is why self-discipline is the key to overcoming our evolution and learning to use it to our advantage.

Revelation #3: It never gets easy. Self-discipline is a daily struggle, even after years of training yourself and rewiring your brain, you're going to struggle with discipline daily. This is because you can't detach from millions of years of evolution. Your body was wired to operate a certain way; you can only accept that you're in this for the long term. Reversing evolution is easier said than done, and it's a daily struggle. Even after years of self-discipline and exercise, people will still have a daily fight with themselves. But the main difference is that the fight becomes a lot easier.

Pro Tip: Results are produced in daily increments. Movies have conditioned us to expect a big motivational moment to hit us and, all of a sudden, we're supermen. But in reality, tasks get done with focus and momentum. Once a person rewires their brain to push through daily tasks, their work becomes a breeze.

Revelation #4: Self-discipline builds momentum. People go through loops of high motivation and high downtime/resistance to work. Both of those create momentum. If a person is trying to lose weight by jogging, the first few days might be hard, but once they've gone through the first 2 to 3 days, they build up momentum and it's a lot easier for them to run.

The same applies to work — once a person "warms up" at work by having a very productive day, they can repeat that behavior tomorrow. To be successful, you have to ride the waves of momentum. And once you start you have to create the moment. Each action creates momentum: If you're lazy, you will get momentum of laziness and never do anything. On the other hand, if you are productive, you create more productive momentum. This reflects on a much larger scale. For example, countries that get rich tend to get richer while developing countries tend stay in a loop of poverty.

Revelation #5: Your brain can be rewired for self-discipline. Each action "wires" your brain to accept that as a new habit — and this applies to bad habits and good habits. If a person starts smoking, their immune system will reject the nicotine temporarily. But after a while, the brain will wire-up to accept it and start craving the substance. This creates addiction in the person's brain because their brain is rewired to that of a smoker, even if they've never smoked a cigarette before in their lives.

The brain can also be rewired for good habits. Once the brain is forced to accept a new habit, it finds a million ways to accept it. Has your boss ever threatened that you'd be fired if you fail to complete a task on time? Under pressure, your brain can find a million ways to complete a task. Once you're forced to do something, your brain starts rewiring and allowing you to do the tasks you want. The brain can be rewired to get projects done on time, to focus on hard tasks, avert temptation, and perform at peak levels. This book will teach you to rewire your brain.

How to get Motivation to Start now?

Are you still holding off your life project? Do you feel you're not ready and do you want to start next year or five years from now? Starting now is the key to making it, like the Nike commercial "Just do it."

Life Hack: The key to overcoming all procrastination is a simple mind-shift: *"You're there when you do it."* Remember that phrase. There is no magical time in the future when you'll be "ready" to start a business, to have children, to stop procrastinating, to buy a house, to own Bitcoin, to do the hard tasks. However, once you actually do these simple things, you're immediately at the finish line! When you sell your first product, you're in business. When you go out and jog, you're successful in fitness.

The premise is that you don't have to lie to yourself by setting up an arbitrary future starting point when you can shift the date to right now. The only thing holding you back is your own permission. Give yourself permission to start now and you're already at the finish line. Achieving your goals is as simple as realizing you make it once you take the action, not when the time comes! Will you take action or wait?

CHAPTER 1 – Ditch Bad Habits Now

Are you struggling with smoking, pulling your hair, eating badly, or oversleeping? If your problems are simple and come down to one bad habit, you can solve it by rooting out that bad habit.

Habits are actions we do repetitively. Once a person repeats a certain action multiple times, it becomes a habit. Once a person repeats a habit for longer periods such as months or years, it becomes their identity. Many times, people can't remember what their life was like before they assumed their bad habits as part of their identity.

Habits can be good or bad. A good habit is to wake up early in the morning, or work hard at your job, to eat moderately, to meditate. A bad habit is to wake up late, consume substances you don't need, harm yourself, or engage in activities that deplete your quality of life.

To be effective in eliminating bad habits, we have to pull bad habits like weeds by grabbing the root and removing them from the ground up. We don't want to pull at the top of the weed, giving it an opportunity to regrow. All habits can be completely rooted out by changing your identity and rewarding yourself with each milestone. This chapter focuses on the shift in identity a person should make in order to quit bad habits.

6 Surefire Ways to Quit Bad Habits

1) Create a New Identity

To root out a bad habit, you have to do one important thing — create a new identity for yourself. If you don't create a new identity and you stick to your old identity, you'll be prone to relapsing and repeating the same mistakes. Smokers who want to quit almost never create a non-smoker identity; they imagine themselves as smokers who "gave up" smoking. They've smoked for years and associate every moment in life with smoking: coffee breaks, work breaks, friend gatherings, parties, travel, etc.

However, they have to tap into the part of their brain that remembers what it used to be like as a non-smoker; they need to go back to when they were younger as most people start smoking in their teens. Could you remember the time you didn't need a cigarette in the morning when you were only happy with a cup of coffee and you weren't tempted when you saw others smoking? That was way back when you didn't assume a smoker's identity. Now that you took the identity of a smoker, you find it hard to quit.

Bad habits are essentially rooted out by reversing the clock and going back to the time when you didn't do them. If you don't remember, then you need to create a new identity that separates you from your old identity that repeated these mistakes.

Bad habits destroy lives: Alcohol, gambling, smoking, drugs, bad food. People know what they're doing is not good for them, but that information is useless — the habit is too strong and they fall back in the same behavioral patterns. In order to not fall in repetitive behavior, they have to step back and create an ANTI-IDENTITY to their current identity. Anti-identity is a method to take your current identity and live by the opposite principles. If you're a smoker, take on the identity of a NON-SMOKER. If you're a gambler, take on the identity of an ANTI-GAMBLER. If you're an alcoholic, take on the identity of a SOBER person.

Pro Tip: You don't have to "hate" your previous habit. Many people create negative energy and hate against their previous habits to cope with their new identity. However, if you really assume your new anti-identity, you can "detach" from your previous habit completely and without emotional baggage. Even years after you quit your bad habit, you might still be tempted. But the difference is that you'll be tempted at the same level as a person who was never addicted to a bad habit. This means that you will be underwhelmed in your temptation.

2) Plan Future Actions

To create a new identity, you have to have a positive outlook on your future that will allow you to take the action necessary to quit bad habits. If you have a positive mindset, you are more likely to be successful. How do you get a positive mindset? Think of the positive benefits that will come from you ditching your bad habit. Think about what your daily life will look like.

Pro Tip: Think about what your daily life will look like and write your ideal day down on a piece of paper. Write down where you'd wake up, what you would do in the morning, how you would live. Create a visual image in your head for what your new life is supposed to look like.

There are benefits to visualizing your new identity: If you're a smoker, you will get many benefits from your future non-smoker identity. You'll breathe easier, you'll become healthier, your breath won't smell, you won't spend money on cigarettes, you won't be at the mercy of nicotine addiction, etc. The bad habits probably create more negatives in your life than positives; if you want you can make a chart and compare the positives of your bad habit (the emotional value it gives you) with the negatives. If the negatives outweigh the positives, ditch the habit.

3) Push Through Resistance

This is the hardest part of quitting a habit — the initial resistance. When you stop a bad habit such as substance addiction, your body will go into "withdrawal" and have you craving for the substance.

170

This is when you're most vulnerable to relapse. People who quit for a while can maybe last a full week; but after four weeks or more, they might relapse because they're constantly tempted by external forces. For example, a smoker might see their friends smoking or a commercial of people enjoying cigarettes. They have to fight the resistance, which is the strongest the first month.

Once a person has dropped a habit for over a month, they can start to assume a new identity. The first month is the real test to your resistance and the temptation will be at its strongest. Expect it. If a person can go through a full month without a bad habit, they will likely create a new identity and sustain it for the rest of their lives. You must push through resistance, and remember that the negatives of your habit far outweigh the positives; this should be enough to keep you from repeating bad habits.

4) Replace Bad Habits

If you push through resistance, you're not done! You still have to replace a habit.

Pro Tip: People think its "willpower" that creates good habits, but good habits are created by replacing bad habits with new habits. Instead of giving your body your addiction, give it something else it doesn't crave. This will stimulate it the same, but the effect on your body won't be negative.

The best way to replace a bad habit is to create a replacement habit that will be good for the body. Many addictions are hard to shake off because they provide a high level of stimulus for the nerves and brain that make it impossible to quit. To replace those habits, you have to hit your body with equal stimulus but positive.

For example, many people who quit smoking say they did it with cold showers. Don't believe it? Cold showers that last three to five minutes in freezing cold can severely affect the nervous system to such a degree that the person feels literally no need for nicotine at all — the body has had its dose of stimulation.

Many drug addicts quit only by exercising or cold showering. This is easier said than done because a cold shower takes getting used to. You first have to smear water on your body by hand so you don't dive straight in the cold. Once you're used to it, you can go for small increments of cold. The cold will make you shiver, and it will shake up your entire nervous system. This helps with all substance addictions like nicotine, alcohol, even heroin.

Smaller bad habits like nail-biting and hair-twisting can be replaced by getting a squeezable ball that you scratch or play with instead. This will keep your hands away from your mouth and hair, and allow you to get your stimulation without harming your body.

5) Reward Yourself

Rewarding yourself is not a feel-good tactic; this is not something you do to celebrate but to re-wire your brain that the actions you're taking are good. If you're suffering all the time, if your addiction is eating you alive from the withdrawal, you must reward yourself incrementally in order to not burn out. Rewarding yourself is for the finish line: Once you've lasted a few days or a few weeks without a bad habit, it's time to give yourself a treat. You should endure suffering, and end it by treating yourself to something good.

Pro Tip: Treat yourself to a vacation if you gave up a bad habit. Book a flight to a new city or the beach, and spend a few days reminiscing at how good of a job you did. This will re-assert your new identity and keep you from slipping back into old habits.

If you suffer endlessly and you never reward yourself, you will burn out. You have to treat your brain like an animal; the horse only carries people and allows itself to be whipped because it expects a meal at the end of the day. If you promise yourself a treat after you go x amount of days without a bad habit, the reward mechanism will keep you going. This ties into a positive mindset.

6) Create a Milestone Action Plan

A long-term milestone plan is about sustaining your new identity. If you create new habits to replace your bad habits, you must keep them until the new-found identity is irreversible and part of your core being.

Planning for the long-term will allow you to create a new identity and sustain it. Think about your replacement habit: If you started with cold showers to quit an addiction, allocate a certain time of the night to repeat the cold showers. For example, your long-term strategy could be to shower at 10 PM every night: This is all you need in order to sustain your habit. The minute you make excuses or step off the habit, you will be prone to resistance and relapsing. Long-term resistance planning is all about finding a replacement habit and working on it constantly. If you achieve a 7-day milestone, give yourself a reward for that milestone. To be effective, you must assume you have a new anti-identity that is the opposite of your identity which created bad habits.

3 Essential Steps for Defeating Laziness

Do you have trouble getting out of bed in the morning for work? Do you struggle meeting deadlines of a project? Are you jobless and find it hard finding a job, or do you not feel like going to interviews at all? Laziness is a mental handicap; it can destroy your life because success is built on the opposite — work and productivity.

To stop being lazy, you have to change your mindset. Laziness cannot be treated at the surface level. If you take Adderall to focus or watch motivational videos, you're only going to last the few days or weeks until your supply runs out or you start feeling side-effects. Then your motivation will dip again, and you'll slip back to your old habits again. This is why you need a long-term identity change.

To solve laziness, you have to look at what causes it. This is an uglier side of laziness — you might be lazy because bad things have happened to you in the past. These past events/traumas or existential crisis may have created in you low self-esteem and a nihilistic mindset. Once you discover what your root cause is, you can work on eliminating it. Temporary fixes such as prescription pills will only last for a short time, and let's not even go into the negative aspects of prescription pills and other "focus" pharmaceuticals.

1) Identify the Cause of Laziness

To identify the root of your laziness; think about the history of when you started your bad habits — Did you get in a rut after you got fired from a job or you suffered from a break-up in a relationship? Did you move into a new city/country and had a hard time adjusting to the environment? How long have you been "sinking" in your bad habits? Think about the time before that, and what you used to be like. This will create a clear image for where you need to revert to. Simply take a week off to consider this, take a small trip out in nature and meditate on your behavior. You will realize where it went downhill and correct your bad habits. If you were always lazy, you will have to do the opposite — create a new identity to break the laziness.

Pro Tip: For most people, laziness is caused by a lack of mental clarity. Focus can be influenced by nutrition; food has a direct impact on the functioning of the brain. Bad food makes the brain unclear and this is why successful people overspend on good expensive foods.

2) Maximize Time in a Day

This is the most important step — not wasting time. Without realizing it, you're wasting five or maybe 10 hours of each day doing things that benefit you in no significant way. Worst of all, you might spend 10 hours a day doing nothing. How many times have you refreshed your Instagram feed today? How many times have you swiped on Tinder or talked to your colleagues when you should've been working? You might not realize this, but you've probably wasted a dozen hours you could've used productively.

To maximize time in a day, you have to shift your mindset from that of a consumer to that of a producer. A "consumer" mindset is about consuming external influences: social media, entertainment, movies, food, news, etc. A "producer" mindset is about output flowing out of you: making products, selling products, inventing, designing, creating, writing, editing. The producer mindset enables you to be at the root of life: You create the entertainment people are consuming, you create the social media content, you create the products they use, and you create the trends they follow. When you create value, people want to give you value in return. This is a key mind shift you have to make to be successful. Once you switch into a producer mindset, you'll appreciate your time a lot more.

3) Plan Productive Days

The way to do this is to act proactively. Your nutrition and bad habits could have a very negative effect on your focus and brain. High carbohydrate foods such as pasta, bread, pastries, and sugary drinks make your brain "clouded" and fuzzy. With these foods, it's almost impossible to focus. Your struggles might have come from the consumption of those foods. The worst part is that they're so widespread that the average person isn't even aware of how food can affect mental clarity. Meanwhile, foods such as broccoli, spinach, and steak reinforce your focus and simultaneously boost your mental clarity.

175

Once you've cleared your mind with good nutrition, you can plan out your daily routine. Start by waking up early and fixing your evening schedule. If you go to bed at midnight, you'll find it very hard to wake up at 6 AM. However, if you go to bed at 10 to 11 PM you'll find it a lot easier to wake up at 6 AM. You can plan your productive days by planning the nutrition you'll consume on those days, the time you'll wake up, the time you'll do your tasks and your work breaks. Once you've planned your days, it all comes down to execution.

How to Stop Procrastinating Now

Have you wasted years procrastinating on your "big" project? How about your job — do you delay work to the last second until the deadline is up, and then you rush it in an all-nighter? Do you have an idea for an invention but can't get yourself to start even after years of thinking about it? Procrastination is a disease that takes root in your brain and spreads like a cancer. Once it spreads to one cell, it spreads to your entire body and kills you. To eliminate the disease, you have to kill it at the start by not letting it take root.

1) Start Immediately

To stop procrastinating, you have to get in the flow immediately. Once your brain accepts that you've started working, it's going to find ways to keep you working. If you delay your project until the afternoon or evening, you'll probably delay it for the next day. This creates a never-ending loop of procrastination and you could waste entire months or years in this loop. Do you know of people who talk about one "business idea" or another but never do anything? They've been infected with the disease of procrastination.

All you have to do to stop procrastinating is to rewind the clock from a future "start point" to a current "start point." Do it right now! Drop everything you're doing — shut off your TV, tell your friends you're not going out, lock yourself in a room and START NOW. Don't delay this until the next day or the next week. Remember the phrase: "There is no better time to start than the present moment." You're prepared already and you must take action. Once you've started, you've done 90% of the work. The rest is all about building your momentum.

2) Optimize Your Time

The way you spend your time is unpredictable. You might think that you'll wake up in the morning and be productive, but turns out you only end up drinking coffee and watching YouTube videos until the afternoon. This is why you have to allocate key actions to exact time frames to optimize your time. If you take out a piece of paper and break down your day by the hour, you would be a lot more productive.

For example, you wake up at 6 AM, drink coffee, start work at 7 AM, work for 2 hours, take a 30-minute break at 9 AM, and continue working until 12 NN. Write this down on paper. Optimizing your time makes it impossible to fail because you'll devise a plan for every hour of the day. If you only tell yourself you'll get it done in the morning; you'll probably make up an excuse or do something else. Once your day is written in paper, you can actually execute based on that. Tell yourself that even if you don't finish your task in the time frame you allocated but you spent all that time working, that you still did a good job. Reward yourself every time you execute on your schedule.

3) Split Your Projects into Small Pieces

If you try to do everything at once, the projects will overwhelm you unless you split them in small pieces, which may mean spending a whole day working on a tiny part of a project. For example, if you have to write a 15-page business plan, start by writing 5 pages the first day, then write 5 pages the next day, and 5 pages the day after.

In 3 days, you'll be done! This is much more realistic than forcing the whole project in 1 day.

If you load yourself on too much work, you'll find it harder to focus, and you'll lose motivation because you'll think you're not making progress. However, when you split your project into multiple pieces, you can check them off like a checklist. Reward yourself every time you complete a piece of a project by taking a break, or going for a walk. Eventually, you'll tackle entire projects by learning how to allocate them in smaller bits.

The 5 Rules of Self-Discipline

Self-discipline is about beating resistance, taking control of your emotions and doing what's right for the greater good. Self-discipline is not only practiced by Buddhists, martial artists, or athletes — it's also for the average person who wants to be successful. Self-discipline is an art form, and once a person understands what it consists of, they can start implementing it in their daily lives.

1) Self-Discipline Is a Sacrifice

To discipline yourself you have to sacrifice all your comforts and pleasures. You'll no longer be able to oversleep, overeat or indulge in negative habits. You have to sacrifice everything you knew as your "comfortable life." Self-discipline is not a getaway that you do for 1 week and then revert back to your life of comfort; it's a life-long task and the art of reshaping your identity.

To develop self-discipline, you'll have to go through literal hell and you'll encounter resistance on each step. Voices in your head will tempt you to go back to your bad habits — to procrastinate and not do what's right — but if you sacrifice long enough, you will learn to ignore them. This is why self-discipline essentially boils down to sacrifice.

2) Self-Discipline Is an Identity Change

Self-discipline is not about making your current life work. People think that there are "tricks" and "shortcuts" to keep their existing way of living without making radical changes on their identity and way of operating. If you're not prepared to fully change your life by changing your sleep schedule, nutrition habits, work habits and thought patterns, the chance you'll succeed with self-discipline is very little. Self-discipline is about changing your entire modus operandi, not making your current one work.

3) If You Know Why, You'll Know How

If you want self-discipline, ask yourself: Why do you want self-discipline? Is it to become a better person? Is it to do better at your job? Is it to quit a bad habit that impacts your health? Ask yourself: Why are you trying to achieve this? If you don't know the answer, you'll only be spinning your wheels like a hamster trapped in a cage and not getting anywhere. Once you know what you're trying to achieve, your brain will know that the sacrifice is worth it. Keep your end goal in mind every time you're tempted to sip back into your old habits.

4) Self-Discipline Has to Be Realistic

Be careful not to overwhelm yourself with unrealistic goals. If you work hard daily and expect to become a millionaire in one year, you might find that it's not going to happen. If you try to quit smoking and you quit cold turkey, you might want to start by smoking less the first few weeks and then letting go completely. In order to get the motivation to stick at a new habit, your brain requires proof that you can survive the change. Your brain doesn't care that you "think" you'll do it; it wants to experience the change firsthand. Do this, and your brain will give you the motivation to stick at a new habit. Start by taking small increments and then go radical, instead of ramping up on your changes from the beginning.

5) Doing What You Don't Want Produces Results

If you look back in life at all your hard tasks — the all-nighters you had to stay up to finish a project; the gym sessions that got you 6-pack abs; the hard jobs you did to make money — they probably all came from doing tasks that you didn't want to do. They were probably difficult to do. In essence, the hardest jobs and the things we want to do the least are the ones that produce the most results for us. If you can discipline yourself to focus exclusively on productive tasks and activities that increase your output, you can maximize your life quality and productivity.

CHAPTER 2 – Develop a Self-Discipline Mindset

Self-discipline is a skill, one that can be learned like riding a bike. Learn self-discipline as if you're trying to learn to ride a bike or swim in the ocean — it takes time to cultivate the skill. If you don't know how to swim, how do you start? You dip in the water and start practicing. Then you stay afloat for a while, and repeat until you can swim. You build the momentum to practice more until you're a swimmer. Self-discipline is based on 2 things: daily practice and momentum. To obtain self-discipline, a person has to hone their skills to build consistency and small-step their way until they've mastered the skill.

Why does a person need self-discipline? The answer: it helps you achieve difficult things like giving up your bad habits or performing better at your job. In order to achieve your goals, discipline is required. Self-discipline can be trained like any other habit; the key to success is perseverance. Once you strengthen your self-discipline, you'll be able to do things in life such as get rid of your bad habits, increase your productivity, and become fit and happy. Self-discipline is hard as it reshapes your mind to go beyond your basic emotional needs.

3 Habits That Build Self-Discipline

Pro Tip: To develop self-discipline, treat your brain as if you're an athlete and you need daily training to compete in the sport championship. What happens when an athlete misses their daily training? They fall out of shape. Give yourself time if you're just starting, and kick yourself in the butt when you're slacking.

The following are the #3 essential skills to develop a self-discipline mindset:

1) The "One Day to Success" Habit

The self-discipline mindset is managed on the macro: You have to prepare your brain for the long-term, but act in small daily increments. The #1 technique to obtain self-discipline what we call the "One day to success" habit:

- **The One Day to Success Habit: "If you did it for one day, treat yourself as if you're already successful."**

If you stick to your diet for one day, be as happy as if you've already lost weight. Don't wait until you have a shiny 6-pack to give yourself a pat on the back. Long-term success is built on small daily success and it makes sense to celebrate once you've gone through a full day of discipline. Measure your success based on what you've done in a day — if you've successfully disciplined yourself, treat yourself as if you already achieved your goal. Did you do your work today? If you completed your tasks, act as if you're already at the finish line.

This is a mind shift that will get your mind to build momentum by acting as if you made it once you've gone through a full day of self-discipline. Large successes are built on daily milestones. The wrong approach is to wait for 30 days or 6 months until you reward yourself and say you've made it. The right approach is to discipline yourself for a day and then pat yourself on the back for your accomplishments that day. Base your self-esteem and happiness on your daily tasks. If you did everything you needed to do for the day, consider yourself successful. If you failed, try again tomorrow.

2) Kill Instant Gratification

Human nature wires us to consume things that provide us immediate gratification: Bad foods, alcohol, cigarettes, the news, movies, social media — what do these all have in common? They provide instant emotional relief and gratification. Self-discipline is the art of optimizing your mind for delayed, long-term gratification. If you eat a candy bar that you know you're not supposed to eat, you'll be gratified instantly. If you say no to the candy and consume broccoli instead, you'll get a better body in 30 days. The difference is that you'll be gratified later. Discipline is different from self-control because in self-control we exercise restraint, while with self-discipline we essentially re-wire our brain for discipline for the long term.

Self-discipline is a life-long task that challenges our mind continually. Accept that as long as you're alive, your mind will always push you to take the way of instant gratification — that's your biology following a survival instinct. We always want to eat because back when we used to live in tribes, if we didn't eat, we'd die. We always want to have sex because if we didn't, we wouldn't reproduce. We are addicted to substances and social media because they ping our brain with dopamine chemicals that signal we're safe. The key is not to change our biology, but to observe it objectively and take control of it.

Pro Tip: Become God. Imagine yourself as God watching your room from above. To beat our biology, we have to observe our impulsive behaviors from a 3rd person perspective: Where are you at right now? You're in a room, you are reading a book. If you go to the kitchen, observe your behavior. Ask yourself: Is this person doing something rational, or are they acting primitive? Take control of your bad behavior by removing your identity from your actions, and looking at yourself through the prism of a neutral entity.

3) Create Momentum Waves

Once you've achieved your daily success, repeat the same process by pushing through your daily milestones. This will create "Momentum Waves" that you ride like a surfer catching a wave in the open ocean. Find a big wave and catch it. If you fall off, climb back on. If you exercise for 1 day, repeat your actions diligently for a week. This will create huge momentum for you to keep going for a full month. Once you've done it for a month, keep going for a full year.

Do you remember when you used to be at peak of your productivity at work, you kept producing on time, you were making money and your clients/boss were praising your work? You were in what's called a "momentum wave." Once you get the initial momentum, it's impossible to stop. Self-discipline creates momentum. If you push a rock down a mountain, the rock will start off slow but then the speed will accelerate. By the time the rock hits the ground it can be going at an upwards of 300 mph.

Once you start with daily self-discipline exercises, you will start slow, but persevere until the momentum builds and it will become natural for you to do the tasks that you previously deemed "hard." Essentially, we're in a battle with your biological wiring and minds on the daily. Once you realize there is no "permanent fix" (i.e. a solution that alleviates you of the daily struggle against your nature), and that this a life-long task, you learn to anticipate the daily challenge and create momentum gradually. Take it one day at a time.

4 Essential Practices to Ignite Strong Willpower

What do you do when you don't feel like doing something? How do you find the energy to go to the gym at night when you feel like sleeping and staying inside? How do you get up at 5 AM to go prepare for work when you want an extra hour of sleep? How do you get the motivation to do those things you're supposed to, and do them consistently? The answer is willpower. Willpower can be the deciding factor between a successful goal and a failed goal.

What is the difference between a millionaire CEO who runs his own company and a homeless person on the street? The difference is willpower. One has the willpower to push through and be successful, while the other one lacks willpower and can barely function in life. Some people want to be successful, and they know what it takes to be successful - but they lack the willpower to do it. This chapter focuses on the importance of willpower and top 4 techniques to develop willpower to push through your daily tasks.

Willpower is like a muscle in the brain. It becomes weak when left untrained. If you do nothing to practice your willpower, you will slack and be unproductive. Treat your brain as a vehicle and willpower as the motor: If you don't have a motor, or if you have a half-functioning motor, you won't be able to drive the vehicle. However, if the motor is well-oiled and the mechanics are functioning - you'll be able to drive your vehicle through the roughest terrain in the mountains. The same applies for your brain - when you have willpower, you have a functioning brain that will get you to do anything. Want to be able to wake up at 5 AM and feel great? Want to be able to exercise at night and look forward to your trip to the gym? Want to be able to work 10 hours without breaks or distractions? Fix your willpower – and you can achieve it.

Pro Tip: Treat willpower like a bicep. To increase muscle mass, you have to lift weights in areas that target the biceps. If you stop lifting weights, your muscles shrink. The same applies to willpower: You must put pressure on your brain to develop the willpower, but once you've developed it, the practice becomes easier. If you stop working on your willpower, you lose it and you fall off. Willpower requires constant discipline and daily sacrifice.

Willpower has to be built gradually - one doesn't develop willpower overnight. Be careful not to be too overwhelmed, even if the goals seem realistic. For example, if your goal is to exercise at 9 PM sharp every night, make sure that you don't burn yourself out too much or you might not be able to exercise tomorrow. Take breaks and reward yourself once every few days, in order to not burn out. Start by taking small increments, and build your willpower using the techniques below gradually. Once you gain momentum, continue doing it and the actions will become a part of your identity.

Remember the 6-month rule: What seemed hard for you to do today will become an average day for you in 6 months. If you thought running and lifting weights in one day is impossible, once you get yourself to do it once - you might find this is an average day for you after 6 months; and you'll add another activity on top. Your willpower will peak after your brain has evidence it's possible. To give it evidence, you must throw yourself in the line of fire every day. You will naturally have dips in the process, and you must pick yourself up. Once your momentum dips, force yourself to do it again and your willpower will peak.

1) Give Your Brain Proof, Not Promises

Remember this phrase: "**Your brain wants proof, not promises.**" Your brain works like a coin machine: Once it's given proof that something is possible, it gives willpower in return. If you tell yourself "I will eat better today", your brain won't notice and give you the willpower to do it. However, if you force yourself to do it - you cook healthy food and consume it; your brain will have definite proof that it's possible. Then, it will naturally provide you the willpower to repeat it the next day. Your brain is in constant demand for proof that you can do certain things, and you must feed it physical proof if you want to get the willpower in return. Have you tried quitting smoking? If you actually stopped smoking for 1 week, your brain would have all the proof it needs to give you the willpower to be a non-smoker forever. It's not enough to think positively and make reaffirmations that you'll do it one day. You must take physical action in order for your brain to supply you with the willpower you need.

Force yourself to do what's right for one day, and your willpower will increase dramatically. If you're back from vacation and lacking willpower to go back to work, force yourself to work immediately. You will work one day faced with resistance, but your brain will have proof that it's possible. Then your willpower will return and you'll be able to go back to work the same as you used to. If you haven't exercised in 2 years, and you've fallen out of shape, you can re-set your workout routine by going out at night. Find a jogging path, get dressed and start exercising. Once you've gone through your first night, your willpower to repeat the process will rise exponentially.

2) Start With Uncomfortable Tasks

What happens when you start work in the morning? You feel discomfort. What happens when you start jogging on the track? You feel discomfort. What happens when you go for a job interview? You feel discomfort. Discomfort is what you need; it means the action is worth pursuing. Now think about what happens when you push through discomfort - you become comfortable with the habit and you start engaging with it. The discomfort you're feeling in this case is not caused by lack of ideal circumstance — it's caused by your own biological resistance. Biological resistance tries to chain you in place and conserve energy, so you must do the opposite of what you're feeling inside your body.

Remember this: **Your body does not care about your goals**. Your body rewards you for doing things that actually stall your progress: Sleeping, eating junk food, smoking, drinking, consuming media.

Your biology is wired to get you to release the least amount of energy and consume as much energy as possible. Have you ever wondered why you want to do less at work, why you sleep late, why you want to stay in bed instead of hitting the gym? It's because the resistance is there to prevent you from releasing surplus energy that would actually get you to be successful in life.

Pro Tip: To be successful, do the reverse of what your biology wires you to do. Want to sleep? Get out of bed. Want to eat pizza? Cook broccoli instead. Want to stay inside and not exercise? Go out to the gym. Want to watch Netflix and slack off? Go work 10 hours straight without taking any breaks.

Tune in with your body, listen to what it craves biologically. In most cases you're doing things based on biological impulse, and if you engineer your actions to do the reverse of your impulses, you will create the willpower you need to be successful. Start with uncomfortable tasks, whether it's waking up earlier, doing a hard project at work that you've delayed, or going to the gym. This way the uncomfortable becomes the norm and you never fall prey to your biological impulses.

3) Give 100% Effort in Every Task

Willpower is not only about starting - it's about finishing your tasks at 100% diligence. How do you develop the willpower to do a task, if not by giving your best? The wrong approach is to start an uncomfortable task and slack through, thinking that by delaying the task you can still get it done another day. The right approach is to work as if your life depends on it.

Imagine someone put a gun to your head and told you, "Go out to the gym and do 150 pushups, lift 5 reps and run 10 miles." Would you find the willpower to do it? You definitely would, as your life is under threat. Treat your regular work tasks as if your life depends on your performance, and give your best performance even if the task is unimportant. Once you get used to doing everything at 100% capacity, it leaks into other areas of your life and your willpower to do many things at once skyrockets. You'll develop the willpower to work, exercise, date and engage in fun projects without running out of energy.

4) Cut Off Distractions

Remove all distractions that restrain you from completing your work. Once you've gone through an hour or two of work, you'll feel tempted to take a break and indulge in "relaxation" periods. The downside to this is that it's usually more distractions that arise once you discover one distraction. If you're scrolling on Instagram, you'll find your ex posting something that makes you emotional or an ad that encourages you to travel to Bali. You're suddenly on a booking page searching for flights to Bali - one distraction leads to another until you've completely lost track of your original work. To avoid this, treat everything as if it has a "snowball" effect that can potentially erode your attention and harm your focus just by looking at one thing. Remember how you develop momentum in willpower? The bad side is that you can also develop momentum in distractions, so watch that you're on the right end of that spectrum.

3 Techniques to Strengthen Your Self-Control

Self-control is about controlling your emotional impulses. Look back at your impulsive decisions. Do you eat pizza at 11 PM and wonder why you did it? Do you start smoking at a party and you've been trying to quit? Do you order something on eBay when you know you should be conserving money? This is what's known as impulsive behavior. To obtain self-control over impulsive behavior, you must take control of your emotions. Most emotions that cause impulsive decisions are hard to control as they're driven by anxiety, fear, stress or even happiness. Once you're feeling high on an emotion, it's hard to make rational decisions.

Pro Tip: Self-control is a *preventive* measure. One must observe their behavior to take control of their impulsiveness. Self-control is essential and impervious to making big changes in life, as the daily struggle of self-discipline is tied to making small self-control decisions of restraint. How do you last a full day on a diet, when so many food choices are available? How do focus on work for 10 hours, when you're distracted by social media? How do stop a habit that harms you, when it provides you with good emotions? The answer is simple - overcome your impulsive behavior. There are techniques to overcome your impulsiveness, by observing your behavior and correcting it before it takes over your logical senses.

Self-control is about to averting impulsive behavior. There are 3 steps to avert impulsive behavior:

1) Identify Your Triggers

Impulsive behavior is caused by a lack of logical judgment. When you think rationally, you know what's bad and good for you. Human nature is often more powerful than the rational mind and this is why it's so hard to overcome. The struggle of overcoming nature is tied to our biology, as we've evolved to seek instant gratification. Essentially, most things that feel good are bad for us in the long run. Impulsive behavior can only be corrected on the logical level, by making your rational mind more powerful than your physical urges. How do you achieve this? Start by applying logic. Identify your triggers in advance and act preemptively — avoid putting yourself in a situation where you're tempted.

For example, if you're trying to quit smoking, you might find that partying and getting drunk makes you want to smoke more. Avoid parties — that's your trigger. If you want to eat clean, don't pass by bakeries or other food stores that tempt you to buy food. If you eat at night, get a healthy meal in advance or go to bed early. Identify your little "triggers," the small events that cause your impulsive behavior, and prevent them by completely cutting down on them. Many times, you're exposing yourself to the wrong influences, by consuming media online that serves as launch-ground for bad behavior. Humans are influenced on a subconscious level too; if one sees their friends doing something on social media their brain tempts them to repeat their behavior. Cut of all influences that trigger impulsive behavior.

If the fault of the trigger is on yourself and you can't avoid external stimulus (it's not parties or stores tempting you but your own behavior) the solution is simple: suppress your emotions. Most urges disappear within 10 minutes. If you want to have a smoke, wait it out and occupy yourself with another activity. You only have to observe your desire to smoke, and surpass your emotions. Ideally you should avoid all external triggers and suppress your inner emotions to completely avoid sipping back into impulsive behavior.

2) Restrain Impulsive Behavior

Impulsive behavior is temporary. Taking control of impulsive behavior is essential to self-control as it signifies you dominating over your primal urges. There are two ways to control impulsive behavior: 1) Let it pass 2) Engage in another activity.

Observing your impulsiveness in the 3rd person can give you insight about how you operate and the way to suppress your urges. If you can remove your identity from the equation and look at yourself as if you're neutral person - would you still feel the same urges? Feel the urge as if you're 100% there and present with it, without resisting it. In meditation this practice is known as "becoming present to the moment." This will set your mind at rest because you'll know that your addictions and impulsiveness are nothing more than the result of biological impulses flaring up. The mind attaches personal stories to your impulsiveness, but in essence, it is a behavior driven by the brain's need for fast gratification.

Utilizing replacement activities is an effective way to control impulsive behavior: Go for a shower, take a walk, have a nap, go jogging, buy a boxing bag to punch, talk to someone, etc. There are many ways to regain emotions that you seek from your addiction or impulsiveness in a manner that doesn't harm you.

3) Prevent Future Relapse

Why quit smoking if you're going to relapse after 1 month? Why eat organic food if you're reverting back to junk food a month from now? Relapse is your biggest long-term threat, so knowing how to anticipate relapse is as essential as identifying your triggers. The way you control your behavior will shape your destiny, and anticipating future relapse can help you from sipping back into bad habits.

The way to prevent relapse is simple - change your identity. Many people mistakenly hold on to their old identity and try to "make it work" by changing their habits. However, the only way to succeed in long-term change is to change who you are as a person. You must let go of your current identity and become something else, similar to a caterpillar shaping into a butterfly. For example, if you want to quit smoking you can use techniques to avoid buying cigarettes and going to the store or visiting parties. You can even tell yourself that it's bad for you mentally and that it's a terrible habit. However, the right approach is to assume a non-smokers identity. Do you have friends who don't smoke at all? Do they ever feel tempted by smokes? The answer is no. This is because their identity is fundamentally that of non-smokers. Assume the identity of a person you want to become, and you will lose your current temptations naturally.

5 Psychological Tricks to Boost Self-Discipline

To build on your self-discipline and self-control, psychology can add a layer of willpower that will help you power through the hardest days when you're pushed to the limits of your emotional capacity. What happens when you burst through a week of successful self-discipline, and then you hit a breaking point and relapse on bad habits? The way to avoid that is to apply psychological building blocks — little techniques that when stacked on top of each other, can serve as a foundation for your psychological health. Think of psychological building blocks as bricks. If you had no self-discipline in the past, you can start building your structure by making it for one day. Once you've made it past a day, you can add one more brick. At the end you'll have a whole house.

Remember the phrase: "**The mind is a creature of habit.**" Once your mind is trained to do something, it can also be un-trained. If you've fallen into bad habits, you can reverse the damage by creating entirely new habits. This is because the brain is not definite and can be altered to your ideal form, in order to take back control over your life. Self-discipline is about taking control of the mind, and psychology specializes in studying the mind.

Psychological tricks are not about going to the crazy scientist that lives next door and have them hook you on electrodes that change your mind. Instead, you need to realize that changes can be made gradually. You once didn't drink alcohol — you taught yourself how to do it. You didn't even drink coffee — now, you can't go a day without 2 cups of coffee. The mind is very flexible and can adapt to harmful habits - the same as it can adapt to new "hard" habits which you're trying to enforce that would improve your life. If you have little power over the rational mind, the following psychological tricks can help you take control now:

1) Become Present With Meditation

How do you avoid bad thoughts that lead you to impulsive behavior? The answer is to not have any thoughts at all. Meditation is the art of becoming present and dropping the conscious mind, effectively trusting that your subconscious will be enough to help you make the right decisions. Our minds are preoccupied with thoughts about the future and the past. We spend too much time thinking and little time acting.

Meditation is an exercise that helps us minimize our thoughts, and the exercise of meditation is about focusing on the breath and not thinking for 20 minutes. To visualize presence, imagine yourself in the Caveman days - you were hunting an animal, you had a spear and the animal ran from you. Once you started running towards the animal and chasing for the kill, you don't think at all but your focus was on the kill. You were completely immersed in the present moment, which is what meditation helps to achieve.

The practice of meditation can reduce anxiety, make you more confident, and give you the ability to calibrate in the moment. If you're working in a real-time environment where you have to make decisions in the moment such as the stock market or live sales, you must be present to the moment. If you're stuck in your head, your thoughts will take over and you won't be able to engage with your work.

Meditation only takes 15-20 minutes a night and all one needs is an alarm clock. Set the alarm clock to 15 minutes, sit down, close your eyes and focus on your breath. You will feel the presence sipping in within 5 minutes, and 15 minutes out, you'll feel complete presence. Once a person has meditated for months, they can naturally invoke this feeling.

2) Shift Your Prefrontal Cortex

The prefrontal cortex is a part of the brain located above the eyes responsible for controlling focus. The prefrontal cortex controls focus by identifying focus points for the brain and using the senses. Once the pre-frontal cortex is "focused" on something, it can keep the focus for a very long time. You might think it's your brain that does the focusing, but it's actually a tiny bit of the brain located at the very tip that controls your focus and you can optimize it.

The pre-frontal cortex is an evolutionary reaction to humans living in the wild, when a wild creature could attack and eat you. In response, the prefrontal cortex immediately focused on the threat and made us aware we're in immediate danger. It also helped us hunt and reproduce. The prefrontal cortex has largely remained the same, but now people are trying to alter it in order to optimize their focus at work. Even popular focus drugs such as Adderall work by alternating the prefrontal cortex.

The fastest way to shift the prefrontal cortex is to force your brain to do a hard task. If you start the activity, the prefrontal cortex finds ways to maintain it. It doesn't automatically activate when you want it, but you have to force it to activate. Want to go running but your brain won't do it? Go out and start running, and your prefrontal cortex will give you the focus to finish the exercise. Want to work on your big project? Start doing it and your prefrontal cortex will supply you with the focus and energy you need.

3) Love the Process

If you learn to love the process that gets you success, you will automatically get success. Many people are results-oriented and try to fast-forward to the end point instead of focusing on the daily process that gets them the success. This is because we live in an age of social media where people flash cars, travel destinations, and champagne. As a result, people believe that success is only about the end point and not the journey. Understand that the tiniest action you take today will have repercussions 30 days later. If you step out of your house to go to the gym, you won't see any results tomorrow but you will in 30 days later in the mirror.

Watch your steps on the way to the gym and praise yourself because you're already successful. Those tired slow steps that you take in the night, that's real success. You have to scale down your process and optimize your behavior for the small tasks that produce results. The process is essentially a set of daily milestones that you do that produce results when compounded. If you put in 30 minutes at the gym every night, you'll be fit in 1-2 months. If you work 10 hour shifts every day, you'll be successful at work. Making the tiny psychological shift that each daily action matters and contributes to the big picture will help you push through the last bit of resistance you have.

4) Optimize for Delayed Gratification

Delayed gratification is about a long-term perspective. Success may take years. This is why one must prepare for long-term thinking and the sacrifices that follow. Gary Vaynerchuk, one of the leading media marketing CEOs spent a decade locked inside a room recording wine videos for his business. He didn't go out to parties or meetups. He honed his skill and knew that if he kept at it, his success would come even if it took 10 years of non-stop work.

A scientific experiment from the 70s targeting little children called the "Marshmallow Experiment" displays this. Children were given a marshmallow candy in front of them. If they ate it immediately, they only had that one, and if they waited longer, they were given two. Many children ate the candy right away while some waited and ate two candies. Later psychologists found that children who waited to eat two candies used to display higher problem-solving capability and had much better SAT scores.

5) De-Stress Periodically

De-stressing is the final follow-up to a successful work routine. One must take the time off to remove harmful toxins and reboot by taking the appropriate time off. If you're overworked, you're under constant stress and your body is filled with a stress chemical called cortisol. Cortisol is an evolutionary chemical that is responsible for external threats - if an animal attacks you, the body pumps you full of cortisol to put you on "alert" and make you more sensitive to the world. This makes you more likely to save your life when you're running away or trying to fight off an enemy (in an evolutionary sense).

The body can't differentiate between the modern world and the Caveman days, whereas if you're under constant stress from work it fails to recognize that you're in an office tower in New Jersey, and it pumps you full of that same chemical as if you were running away from a tiger. The effective way to de-stress is to completely remove yourself from your current environment. Book a flight to a beach, camp outdoors, go on a road trip, explore your city — do anything that doesn't revolve around your current environment. Once you de-stress, you can return to work recharged.

CHAPTER 3 – The Secrets of Goal-Setting

Have you ever looked in the mirror at your extra pounds and though "I should lose weight" but never took concrete action? Maybe you took action but give up after 2-4 weeks and reverted back to your old habits? Do you dream of quitting your soul-crushing 9-5 but never do it because you're too afraid of your boss? Are you stuck in a rut and see your life going nowhere? Is there an ambitious business idea lingering on your mind, but you delayed taking action for months or years? Most people think they should do it and they know they should take action. however, their daily routine prevents them from taking right action.

Goal-setting is about one thing: **Breaking your daily routine.**

The subconscious mind knows that if you take action, your life will change and it prevents you from doing so in order to chain you to your current regimen. You're a slave to a biological impulse. Your brain wants you to remain the same — this is a protective mechanism because it finds comfort in the familiar. Quitting your job, losing weight, starting a business — that's all unfamiliar so your mind will think of every excuse and rationalization in the book to keep you from changing. This is why you must set SMART goals that are time-sensitive and break your routine to get you to do what you need to do. Re-shaping your life begins at the goal-setting stage. If you set concrete goals, you'll be able to break your routine and start living the life you always wanted, one step at a time.

Start Now: "One Day" Never Comes

Remember the phrase: **"One day never comes."** You're only there when you take action. Have you held off your "big plans" for an imaginary date when you'll be ready? Are there ideas from 5 years ago that you haven't taken action on, but you told yourself you'll do them once you feel ready? Do you have a genius business idea that you never took action on because it's too complex? SMART goals exist to give you that last "push" that you need to kick yourself in the butt and take action. SMART goals are about breaking your routine and taking huge action towards your future goals. This chapter focuses on the goal-setting mindset that will push you directly into taking action.

How to Create SMART Goals for Better Output

Pro Tip: Goal-setting is like jumping into a pool. If you don't jump in immediately, you'll be tempted to stay on the sidelines where you don't get wet. If you actually jump in, you'll find the water is not too cold and you get used to the temperature fast. The same applies for SMART goals — you can take action immediately and complete the missing pieces on the way. You will never be ready until you take action, but once you take action, your brain will find ways to keep you moving. For example, if you quit your job with an abusive boss, you will start looking for a new job immediately and eventually land a better job.

SMART goals are the action plans you plan out before you take action. There is a distinction between SMART and HARD goals: SMART goals are incremental monthly small goals a person can achieve in a short time frame, while HARD goals are more long-term oriented and require deep-level identity change. S.M.A.R.T stands for:

➔ **S-PECIFIC**

➔ **M-EASURABLE**

➔ **A-TTAINABLE**

➔ **R-ELEVANT**

➜ **T-IMELY**

SMART goals separate empty promises such as "I need to lose weight" and concrete action-plans such as "I need to lose 50 pounds in 2 months." If you set concrete goals that have action-plans and deadlines, you'll be able to achieve them categorically instead of dabbling and hoping you get motivation by instinct. If you lack motivation, SMART goals set the foundation for change by taking daily small actions. SMART goals have to contain all of the following:

1) Specific

SMART goals must be specific. The technique of is to write concrete dates and times that you can follow-through by taking action. When you write down your goal, start by writing specifics: date, time, outcome, and any other details. The more specific you are the more concrete you can be about your action taking. If you want to lose weight, write how many pounds and how many weeks/months. If you want to get a raise, write by which month and by what percent of the salary. If you want to start a business, write by what date and how many dollar sales you want to make per month. If you want to quit smoking, write when you'll have your last smoke and what you plan to do afterwards.

A Harvard Business School professor once tasked his students to write down their life goals on a piece of paper. The students quickly returned their papers to the professor. The professor read every single piece of paper and disposed them into the trash in front of the class — except one. He took the last remaining paper and read it out loud; the paper said: "I want to get a 10% raise by September of next year." He singled that out as the best paper of the class because it set a concrete action plan and deadline – instead of vaguely claiming "I want to get promoted" the student claimed that she wanted "A 10% raise by September of next year." The single difference in specific goal and time is what differentiates a failed goal from a SMART goal!

2) Measurable

Remember the phrase: "**What gets measured gets managed.**" Goals can be measured in the same way we measure our living expenses. Do you know what your rent is at the end of each month, how much your bills are and how much you owe in taxes? Think of your goals as measurable units. If you want to be successful, measure the exact increase in money you need in order to finance your future life. Let's say "success" for you entails a house. an average house in the United States in somewhere in the range of $250,000. What would it take for you to obtain $250,000? Maybe you want to start a new business to obtain that money, or get a high-paying job. Whichever it is, what gets measured gets accomplished in advance.

You can measure your fitness progress the same - if you had abs at 16% body fat, you can measure how many pounds you need to lose to fall to that level of body fat. Once you have a general measurement, you can break down your goal into small daily measurements. For instance, if your goal is to lose 20 pounds in a month, your aim should be to lose 1 pound a day. Measure your weight every day to reassure that you're losing 1 pound a day, and this will reinforce your long-term goal.

3) Attainable

SMART goals have to be realistic and attainable based on your current situation. This is why the emphasis is placed on the short term. If you want to start a restaurant, you might be 1 or 2 years away from your goal. First, you need to get the funding for the restaurant. You'll likely have to work for at least a year before you can obtain the initial funding you need for the rent location, the food supplies, the chefs and the marketing. Goals have to be split into small attainable bits that stack on top of each other.

Pro Tip: Think of goals as laying bricks for a house. You lay one layer of bricks every week, and you repeat for a year. By the end of the year, you have a full house.

Back to our restaurant example: Make it your goal to work overtime for a year until you gather the initial funding. Split that year into goals for every month, and milestones you have to reach every week. Once you have small incremental milestones, you can start taking action right away. The actions will build on each other and in 1 year you'll have achieved your ultimate goal: to own a restaurant. If you just tell yourself "One day I'll get the funding for a restaurant," you will delay your goal indefinitely. If you change your life to optimize for the daily actions that would get you the funding, the mind shift alone will ensure you're successful in the long run.

4) Relevant

Ask yourself: Is this goal true to your heart? Do you want to set goals to impress others, or is this something you've always wanted to do for yourself? Set goals that provide personal fulfillment. You will burn out if you do it to satisfy others. SMART goals are about personal satisfaction because taking action is a lot easier once it's true to your heart.

For example, if you hate your major at university and set a goal to get better grades in school only to impress your parents - you'll likely fail because it's not true to your heart. However, if you make it your goal to switch majors and pursue something that's true to your heart, you will become a lot more eager to pursue your goals. SMART goals are about concrete action, but they're also about flipping your life on its head. If you're unsatisfied with your current situation, it's time to change everything.

5) Timely

Time sets the difference between a goal that gets done and a goal that gets missed! If you have no time-frames, you have no goals. Set specific time-frames and write deadlines for all goals, the most important of which is your start date. Once you have a start date, you know that your old life is about to change. If the goal requires a big life change such as quitting smoking, delay the start date until you feel confident you'll be able to maintain your new behavior. Specify the exact day you wish to start. It's not enough to say, "I'll start next month" or "I'll start in October." The right way is to say "I'll start on the 15th of October." Timing ensures your brain won't be able to think of excuses or procrastinate the date indefinitely. Once the date is written, it's set in stone.

How to Create HARD Goals for Higher Excellence

SMART goals force you to take action; HARD goals force you to change your identity. HARD goals are the ultimate level in goal-setting: They challenge your identity and help you re-shape yourself into the person you always wanted to be. The big distinction between SMART goals and HARD goals is that SMART goals can be broken down into daily goals, weekly goals or other small incremental goals - while HARD goals can only be worked on months or years in advance. HARD goals cut deep into your soul and question whether the action you're taking is true to your identity - and if not, to completely re-shape your identity as a person. Imagine SMART goals as the goals you take action on, and HARD goals as the goals that define you:

- **SMART goal: I want to start a business in 1 year.**
- **HARD goal: I want to be a successful business owner.**

HARD goals relate to who you are as a person: Are you a fitness-oriented person, are you an action-taker, do you aspire to be a doctor/business-owner/family person? HARD goals require deep-level identity change that might take years or even decades to materialize. this is why they're as essential as the SMART goals which we use to power through action-taking processes and momentum-building. HARD goals can re-enforce your identity if you're at a crossroads in life and you have a vision of who you want to become, but lack the directions to get there.

H.A.R.D goals stand for the following:

→ **H-EARTFELT**

→ **A-TTAINBLE**

→ **R-EQUIRED**

→ **D-IFFICULT**

1) Heartfelt

Is your HARD goal one that remains true to your ambitions, values and beliefs as a person? Are you setting your goal to only make money and please other people, or is this something you've always wanted to achieve since you were a kid? If your HARD goal is to start a business, are you doing it to impress your spouse/relatives/friends or is this something you always wanted to do yourself? Ask yourself: What were you born to do? Once you have an answer to that question, you will know if your goal was heartfelt or not. From there, you can start working on your goal or you can completely change your life itinerary.

Defining HARD goals is difficult because it cuts deep in your identity and questions whether the things you're doing are what you should be doing. Often, you will see ties to your past and how you got to where you are in life. Many times, people pursue goals that are not true to who they are, and they struggle because they're going against their nature. Heartfelt goals help you become fulfilled and not just successful. This is the highest level of goal-setting because you question whether the goals relate to your core desires or if you've been misled and taken off course by influences not true to your heart.

2) Attainable

The daily reality of work is different than the imaginary action plan we create. Imagine yourself as a Roman Emperor watching the gladiators battle. It looks easy from the chair, but once you're in the ring, it becomes a completely different ball game. The same applies to goals: the actions you take on a daily basis will be different to what you wrote down. This is why you have to be as realistic as possible, in order to minimize the difference between the goals you've set and the actions you're taking in real life.

For example, if your maximum work day is 10 hours, make sure to prepare your goals for the output a 10-hour day can generate in terms of income and productivity. Many times, our projected goals fall short of our actual daily output. You'll notice that you'll want to do less work, take more breaks, and experience more distractions. This is why you may have to adjust your goals for what you can realistically do based on your historic behavior. Know yourself and your capacity.

If you feel that you're slacking off, you should optimize to improve your performance. Your HARD goals have to be adjacent to your daily SMART goals. For example, if you only exercise 1 hour a day (your SMART goal) you can't expect to become a professional bodybuilder (your HARD goal). However, if you exercise 5-10 hours a day, you can suddenly become a competitive bodybuilder after a year. The small action-steps you take on a daily basis have to be aligned to your HARD goals and big-picture perspective.

3) Required

HARD goals must be critical. They can't be a mere formality. A HARD goal has to be critical to your existence, and you must feel an immediate urge to act on a HARD goal. It has to be tied deep in your core being, or they're not worth pursuing. Ask yourself: What is itching you right now that you're not acting on? Do you have a business idea and see people opening similar businesses that you could do better than them? Is this weighing on your soul deeply? If so, you must take action.

Are you worried that you'll miss out on Bitcoin if you don't invest now? Are you worried someone will take your business idea if you don't do it now? If the HARD goal is time-sensitive and you're feeling a deep urge to act on it right now, this is something you should pursue. If you want to pursue a formality, it's definitely not a HARD goal. For example, moving out of your neighborhood to a better neighborhood is a SMART goal, but is it really a HARD goal that challenges your core identity? It's not. A HARD goal is something that changes who you are, and challenges your currently worldview on what you deem possible.

4) Difficult

If the goals aren't difficult, they're not worth pursuing. If you can get something done without changing your whole life, you must think bigger! Ask yourself: What is the hardest thing you can do right now? The task that will require the most mental energy, the longest hours at work, and the most sacrifice on your end — this is what your HARD goal should be. HARD goals are meant to be difficult and challenge your very being, in order to trigger the change that you want to extract out of life.

Avoid setting medium-difficulty goals such "lose 10 pounds of fat" or "get a promotion at work" — those are SMART goals. The right approach to setting hard goals is to aim for the top. How can you become the fittest you've ever been in your life and reach your genetic potential at the gym? How can you find the highest paying job in your industry and work for the largest corporation? How can you start a profitable corporation and become one of the most successful brands in the world?

This is a difficult task, one that might require 5 or 10 years of perseverance, but that gives your life meaning in the grand scale. A truly difficult task will challenge your existence, make you question your course in life and ultimately allow you to become what you've always dreamed to become.

Exercise: To define your HARD goals, ask yourself the following questions and write the answers down on a piece of paper:

- Where do I want to be in 5 years?
- What do I intend to do about it?
- What am I afraid to miss out on in life?
- What do I plan to do about this?
- What change will that require from me?

The answers to those questions will give you insight in terms of your real, heartfelt long-term goals. Once you have the answers written down, you can cross-reference whether your HARD goals stand for the values listed above.

The Secrets to Turning Your Goals into Achievable Steps

Have you decided on goals you're stuck at the starting point but you don't know where to start? Are you too overwhelmed with the goal-setting process, and are the multiple goals you've set confusing you? Do you have a big "bucket list" to check off and you don't know how to prioritize your goals? Goal-setting can overwhelm a person because they're making too many changes at once. If your work occupies half of your day, and you're tired at the end of the day, how are you supposed to find the energy to exercise?

Let's say you want to start a business but you need $100,000 in inventory to start. Where do you get the investment money? What about bad habits and addictions? if you're trying to quit cigarettes, alcohol and drugs, how do you know when enough is enough? The wrong approach is to try to do everything at once — you will be overwhelmed. You might last for a few weeks, but then your motivation will dip. The right approach is to prioritize your goals, and act on each one individually until your actions are working in conjunction.

Most people lose motivation after 4 weeks. The biggest reason for that is that they set their goals too high and end up overwhelmed. For example, if someone tries to lose 20 pounds in 4 weeks, they might be successful during the first week using a starvation diet, but then they'll go right back to their old eating habits once their hunger kicks back in. The smarter approach for them would be to replace their foods with healthier ones, which will take longer than a starvation diet, but it's consistent.

If you set high expectations, your goal list is going to be full. This can be a negative because if you do too many things at once you will lose track of the meaning of those things. Prioritizing your goals and allocating your action steps gradually is critical. It's better to take on fewer goals that have more meaning to you, than many goals that have lesser meaning.

Goals can be converted to action steps with a simple 4-step process:

1) Don't Aim Too High

If you aim too high, you'll be disappointed if you don't make it. For example, if you aim to make $1 million dollars in 6 months or climb

Mount Everest in 1 month, you'll likely fail. Set realistic goals based on your competency. If you're not competent, delay your goal until a point where you'll obtain the competency. If you want to climb Mt Everest, you won't be able to prepare for it in 1 month. However, if you prepare for a year in advance, there is a higher chance you'll be able to climb it given 12 months of practice.

If you want to become a millionaire, set it as a 5-year or a 10-year goal. This way you have enough time to develop and grow your business, or make it high up the corporate ladder. The right approach is to aim for moderate goals that you can achieve by preparing yourself and acting in small increments. If you aim too high, you will burn yourself out. The most effective measurement to prepare for realistic goals is to imagine an easy goal and double it.

Set goals based on evidence from the past. If you've lost 10 pounds in a month once, expect that you'll be able to repeat that. If you've made $100,000 in a year, you should be able to replicate that. In the former, it's wrong to aim for 50 pounds a month or $100,000 in a month instead of a year. Once you have evidence or a pattern you can use to judge your performance, you can plan in advance because your goals will be solidified by past evidence.

2) Limit the Number of Goals

Let's say you have 10 goals on your bucket list: 1) to move to another city 2) to lose 20 pounds 3) to quit smoking 4) to get a better job 5) to stop drinking 6) to travel to India 7) to meet a romantic partner 8) to learn the guitar 9) to wake up at 5 AM 10) to start meditating. Would those goals be realistic in 1 year? The answer is yes, but the sheer amount of goals would overwhelm you. The fact is that when you spread yourself out between dozens of goals, you won't know where to start and you will lose focus on the ones that matter.

Most people write down goals that are completely insignificant to their growth as a person — goals such as learning to play an instrument or waking up earlier. Significant goals are goals that propel you forward by helping you drop dead-weight such as addictions and help you make big moves such as finding a better job or starting a business. Limit the amount of goals you're setting by opting for a maximum of 3 goals a year - those goals should reflect your biggest desires.

3) Sort Goals by Priority

If you hate your body, make it your #1 goal to lose weight. If you're unsatisfied with your monetary situation, focus on finding a new job. If your health is suffering due to an addiction, make it your priority to quit your addiction. To prioritize goals, identify what would trigger the biggest change in your life. For instance, starting a business would make a far bigger difference than learning to play the guitar. Once you've cut down your goals to only 2-3 core goals that matter, you should sort them by your competency level.

Start with the goal that you're the most competent at, because this will build the leverage to proceed onto harder goals. If you have to choose between losing weight, finding a new job and dropping an addiction - start with whichever one you're the most confident you'll succeed at first: If you have previous fitness experience, start with weight loss. If you have experience switching jobs, find a new job first. If your bad habit is not a major part of your life, drop it first.

4) Chop Goals Down in Weekly Increments

Break down your goals in weekly increments, or small milestones that you can cross out weekly. Start by "zooming in" on your larger goal. If you have a goal that will take you 1 year to achieve, set smaller monthly milestones. Once you've set the monthly milestones, set weekly milestones that feed into your larger monthly milestones.

This way you can exclusively focus your attention on your weekly output, and that weekly output will translate to gradual monthly output until you've reached your final yearly goal.

The way to be effective with large-scale goals that take a lot of time is to start small. Remember this: **"You are the culmination of your daily actions."** If you set a milestone for each week, and you carry out your tasks on the daily, consider yourself successful. This is because the weeks will compound and you'll eventually obtain your larger goals.

How to Reward Yourself for Progress

What if you're successful for 2 weeks, you take a break and you immediately fall back in old unhealthy habits? What if you quit smoking and go right back after 4 weeks? Are you worried that if you take a break, you'll lose momentum and all your hard work will be for nothing? Many people relapse on their bad habits when they're let off the hook - this is because they've been kept on a leash for weeks or months at a time, and start craving their old lifestyle. It's extremely difficult to change your ways, but to avoid burnout a person has to take some time off and reward themselves regularly. To reward yourself without slipping back into your old habits, it's important to plan out small "rewards" accordingly.

Logistics planning your rewards is the first step. For example, if you quit smoking and you want to celebrate that fact, it's better to book a holiday abroad instead of go to a party. Once you're on a holiday you'll be able to relax on a beach and soak in the fresh air, while a party you would be tempted you to go right back to your smoking habit. If you've changed your diet and you now only consume organic food, you have to be careful not to fall to the temptation of your old unhealthy ways of living.

Why Reward Yourself Now?

Rewarding yourself is useful for two reasons: 1) It reinforces that you're successful and crossed a certain milestone 2) It helps to avoid burnout at work. People who work hard will often times spend days entire locked inside their offices in order to work harder and increase productivity. If they do this for weeks at a time they risk "burnout", and essentially start losing motivation. To avert this process, there are many ways to break the chain by rewarding yourself temporarily; until you're fully recharged and you can go back to your work schedule. If you're celebrating a small milestone, start with a small celebration. If you've achieved big success you should consider taking more time off to reward yourself and maybe even take a whole month off.

Pro Tip: Rewarding yourself is not about posting on social media. Did you lose 5 pounds in a week? Did you stop eating junk food for a week? Did you quit smoking recently? These are worthy of celebration, but a reward has to fulfill you spiritually by showing you a new side of life, one that is not prone to external validation.

The following are the best ways to unwind and reward yourself after achieving a milestone:

1) Book a Weekend Holiday

Book a weekend holiday to a place that looks nothing like your office: The mountain, beach, lake — nature of any kind. Forget about the sound of computers and phones going off, and unplug yourself from modern society. If you've been working for weeks at time, your body is full of a stress chemical called cortisol. To flush it out of your system, you have to change your environment completely. Flights can be cheap and you can book a flight for your break in advance — both cheaper and motivating as you'll expect a reward while you're working.

It's possible to travel on a budget by flying with cheap airlines and staying in cheap housing or even house shares if you're young. Make your destination as different to your current place of work as possible. If you work in a busy place, make your destination a quiet place where you can sit and do nothing. Don't overdo it. Most times, 1-2 days at the beach is enough. Sit by the ocean and listen to the waves at night. Watch the stars. Take time to think about what you did in retrospect, and what future big projects are ahead of you. Try to meditate on your thoughts. This will free you of cortisol and recharge you. You will reward yourself by changing your environment and your brain will reinforce the fact that you're successful.

2) Create a Movie Night

Humans are social creatures. Historically, we evolved to live in 150-person tribes and millions of years of evolution we spent living closely to other people. This made us crave social activity, and engaging with people socially makes us more relaxed. If you're uncomfortable at parties due to high amounts of alcohol, a movie night is the perfect reward for you. Invite your closest friends and family for a movie or a Netflix comedy. Cook some popcorn and spend the night watching movies. If you've achieved a lot of success, you can even drink and order junk for the night. You've earned it. Finish your movie night off by preparing a nice late-night bubble bath with wine. This way you can socialize and relax, and then complete your relaxation with a long relaxing therapy bath.

3) Explore the City

Go out to your city and do the first activity you come across. Watch a football game, go see a tourist attraction, go to a bar, participate in a festival. If you live in a major city where there are activities going on around the clock. Cities are full of entertainment options that can provide you with fun activities around the clock. Do you miss your childhood days when you were carefree and driving go-karts? Go find one and invite your friend. This will make you feel carefree, and you can combine multiple activities at once. How about you see a new blockbuster at the cinema, and top your evening off with a trip to your favorite bar? Your city probably has many hidden attractions and areas that you can explore. If you don't want to spend money, you can just walk and listen to music. Walking is a very meditative activity because it allows you to soak in the energy of the city.

4) Buy Yourself a Gift

Pretend it's your birthday and get yourself something you always wanted but didn't have the courage to purchase because you were conservative with your money. Did you want to get one of the new iPhones for a while, but held off from purchasing them? Reward yourself by buying a new phone. Go to your favorite book store and purchase a new book. Take a trip to the department store and try out a new pair of jeans. Go pick up a new pair of Nikes. Old-school consumerism can relax you. Appeal can make you feel new and refresh your sense of fashion. Whatever you've been missing out on, reward yourself by buying an item that you always wanted.

4 Ways to Create a Goal-Friendly Environment

Do you live in a loud household where you can't get anything done because the noises interrupt you? Are your neighbors noisy and interrupting you constantly while you're trying to get work done? Is your desk cluttered and disorganized and you struggle to organize your belongings? The environment you reside in will have repercussions on your productivity - the same as the people influencing you.

Bruce Lee used to say "If you put water into a cup, it becomes the cup. If you put water into a bottle, it becomes the bottle." In other words, you are a product of your environment. What happens when your environment is sub-par and preventing you from achieving your peak productive potential? It's time to clean house. This can mean organizing your current living space, or it could mean completely replacing your space by moving into a new neighborhood. The physical environment in which you reside in will dictate your energy output. To make the most out of your energy, you have to live in the kind of environment that is organized for productivity.

The following 4 techniques will help you create a goal-friendly environment:

1) Clean Your Room

To become productive, you have to minimize your office space to only the essential tools you need: The desk, chair, computer and/or any other tools necessary for the job. Dump everything else in the trash. If your environment is cluttered with food, boxes from eBay orders, electronics, clothes and other messy things - this will reflect in your productivity because you'll be constantly distracted by everything around you. The same applies for your computer: clear out your desktop and put every distracting icon such as games and music into a separate folder.

Only allow the most critical software on your desktop. If your room is dirty, take a full day to clean it and dispose of any items that aren't critical to your productivity. Give your old clothes away to the Red Cross. Make sure you have freedom to move your hands and that you're sitting in a forward position if you're working at an office. Your back will be exhausted from 10-hour shifts and you must give it adequate support. Once you've removed all unnecessary items and your room is clean, you'll be ready to start producing.

2) Move to a Different Area

Do you live with in an area that is too loud and distracting? If you answered yes, move out. The difference in productivity you'll experience will make up for the loss of living in a rent-free environment. Find a new apartment in a peaceful area where you can focus 100% on your work. This will enable you to minimize all distractions and maximize productivity. Moving out is a radical tactic, as many people sign contracts for rental properties that expire after 6 months or a year. However, the increase in productivity is worth it effort.

Move out even if your interior living situation is ideal but the area is too harmful to your goals. If you live in a central area of the city where bars play loud music at night, this will affect your sleep. Aim to live in an area that is suitable to your goals. For example, if you want to lose weight and you live in an area with many bakeries and fast-food joints, move to a place where there are health food stores and jogging paths. This way, you can exercise and purchase good food instead of being tempted by unhealthy food.

3) Cut Off Bad Influences

If some people such as your love partner or even your parents are holding you back by interrupting your schedule, cut them off. Our habits are formed by the people we surround ourselves with, and if the people closest to you are not aligned with your goals this can create inconvenience for both of you. It's wise to break contact with people temporarily to see if they make a difference. For example, if you're staying in your parent's place to save money but you are made to feel like a nuisance, it's better to move out. Your productivity will increase once you're free to work in your own living space. If you have friends with bad habits who influence you directly or indirectly, cut them off until you drop your bad habits and they can no longer influence you. Sometimes you can end relationships temporarily and re-start them once you've gained ground on your productivity.

4) Go to a Goal-Friendly Environment

Modern society has living spaces and environments that cater to goal-oriented people. The most notable examples include meditation clubs and co-working spaces. Co-working spaces are a relatively new invention for creative people who want to network together while they're working. A person can join a co-working space by purchasing a membership card similar to a gym. This allows them to network with like-minded individuals and focus when they need to work. There are many clubs such as meditation clubs where a person can learn a new skill and organize with individuals who are familiar with the practice. If you can't create a goal-friendly environment, you can join an existing one directly.

Chapter 4 - Techniques to Amp Up Output

Transform Your Life with the Getting Things Done (GTD) Method

Do you forget small things? Have you reminded yourself you need to get something done the whole day and then ended up forgetting about it? One day at work your boss tasks you to bring a business paper to work. You go back home and become paranoid: Your mind thinks, "Get that business paper" while you're eating, your start thinking of business papers when you're petting your dog, you go for a jog thinking about business papers at night, you almost trip on the stairs thinking about business papers, and in bed you lay awake at 3 AM thinking about the business papers.

The next morning, what happens? You get distracted by the news of the conflict in Syria, you see your dog made a mess in the kitchen, your wife starts telling you about unpaid bills — and what is the last thing you think of? The business papers. That's right, you forgot. A very popular technique that helps you remember and organize your life is the GTD method by David Allen.

The "Get Things Done" (GTD) method was invented by productivity consultant David Allen, an expert in productivity consulting with over 30 years of experience. The book became one of the most iconic and best-selling productivity books of all time. The GTD method is a 5-step method that focuses on writing down everything related to the mind, removing the unnecessary, and converting "actionable" and "unactionable" thoughts into appropriate "work tasks."

GTD is not for everyone — this is a system for people who have time to consider everything and wish to take control over their life by re-evaluating their life decisions. Example: Your boss tasks you to bring business papers at work. What is your "reminder" here? It's to bring business papers. The GTD method explains that the "reminder" has to be removed from your head by writing it down. You basically convert it to an "action item" on your big paper. We can effectively convert all planned tasks into action items and organize them down by priority. This shifts our attention from thinking about reminders to do to actually taking actionable steps. The GTD technique focuses on important tasks, so all tasks that require less than 2 minutes to complete shouldn't be written down.

The GTD Technique is a 5-step process:

Step 1: Capture

Step 2: Clarify

Step 3: Organize

Step 4: Reflect

Step 5: Engage

How it works: The GTD technique is based on taking note all your "incompletes" (things you have to do), then deciding if the "incompletes" are 1) "actionable" (ones you take action on) or 2) "unactionable" (ones you can't do anything about) and then taking action by focusing on the most important work items you've written down. The GTD technique requires a complete "brain dump" in order to jot down everything that preoccupies your mind.

Once you've completed your brain dump, you have to split the incompletes in 2 ways: actionable and unactionable. The unactionable incompletes are discarded, while the actionable ones are prioritized based on which one has the highest impact on your life and productivity. The GTD method requires a lot reflection and can't be done in a single sitting. You must be prepared to spend at least a few hours reflecting about things that occupy your mind, writing each thought down and deciding which one would have the most impact on your life.

Step 1 - Capture

The first step of the GTD method is to write down what preoccupies your brain. Effectively we're trying to complete a "brain dump" and writing everything that finds its way to our brain. It doesn't matter if the thoughts are related to work, family, business or the weather. What matters is that if something is on your mind it must to be written down. The thoughts can be of big, small, medium importance. They can be of personal, professional or other nature — write them all down. Get a piece of paper and write down 100% of everything that preoccupies your mind. This process can take a while because the average human has hundreds of thoughts, but we usually spin the same 40-50 thoughts on a daily basis and those should be written down. Write down even items that are not related to your work.

Example: Let's say you have a mole on your face that affects your self-confidence and you want visit a laser mole removal clinic. Write that down. Let's say you plan to travel to India and you've had this on your mind for years. Write that down. Let's say you're about to start a new business and you don't know how to get distributers for your product. Write that down. Dump everything — take your time and don't rush this. Imagine if an Alien species descended from another galaxy and scanned your entire brain – what would they find? Do that for yourself but only write down what's on your mind. Get your thoughts out on a piece of paper.

Step 2 - Clarify

Your brain dump should have at least solid 50 thoughts written down - proceed by sorting them into "actionable" and "unactionable" items. The difference is that for one you can take action and for another you can't do anything. Simply assign an arrow to each thought on the right and classify it as "actionable" or "unactionable." How do you know the difference? If you have a thought about how you got rejected by your high school crush, this is "unactionable" - you can't get a time machine and go back in time. If your thought was about how you need to lose 10 pounds in 3 weeks - this is "actionable." File it under "actionable" and move on.

Once you've assigned a full list of "actionable" and "unactionable" items - discard the unactionable items into the trash. This will leave only the actionable ones on the table - those are actions that you should dedicate your life on. Focus on removing the unactionable items from your head because they hinder your productivity and rob you of your mental energy.

Step 3 - Organize

You're now left with actionable items - items that you can take concrete action on. To proceed, you must sort the actionable items into items that you can achieve in the immediate future and actions that you have to delay over the long-term. This is based on your competency and time necessary to achieve the action steps.

Example: If your actionable item is to open a bookstore, you might have to delay it in favor of daily work that would allow you to save the finances necessary to open the bookstore. Both thoughts are actionable, but one takes requires more time and effort. This is why you have to prioritize your actionable plans based on which one you can do first. You can split these down to daily, weekly, monthly and yearly action-steps. The yearly actions should reflect your long-term goals while your weekly and daily actions should be updated based on the work and projects that come up daily — those are more dynamic.

Step 4 - Reflect

Micro actionable steps will require weekly changes because your weekly life is dynamic. While many large actionable steps are clear-cut and require longer commitment, the ones we handle on a daily basis will change based on circumstance. Let's say you want to save $20,000 in a year — you can't do much about this immediately. However, you can focus on making $500 a week which would ultimately lead you to saving $20,000 in a year.

If you focus on saving $500 a week, there will be daily and weekly tasks you have to accomplish in order to achieve this. For instance, you may need to increase your productivity on the daily and you must write down your actionable steps for the small weekly goals that you set, which ultimately lead to a larger goal. Take each week to review your goals and change them to ensure you remain on the right path.

Step 5 - Engage

The final step and the most crucial one — once you've completed your "brain dump," you've organized your action-steps and you have a weekly plan, all that remains is to take concrete action. Keep a weekly list of action steps that you must take action on. This will clear your brain because it's not affected by things that are unactionable, and you can focus 100% on the actionables that affect your life. Schedule weekly revisions and add new actions as your projects change, but remember to reevaluate and take a step back every 2-3 months in case you have new priorities and occupations. This will ensure that you're always on top of your life and that you're completely organized in the way you go about productivity.

Achieve More with the Pomodoro Technique

Do you burn out at work doing a 30-minute task and end up slacking off on social media? Do you maybe do 2-3 tasks in a single burst of energy and then you've had enough? Do you want to die when your boss focuses you to do multiple things at once, and you can't seem to get even one done? Many people start taking up "focus" pills and end up addicted to prescription drugs.

Even those who work from home struggle with productivity. We've all been there! The second you have to work, suddenly you also have to take a shower, have a cup of coffee, listen to that new song, clean your dirty room - anything to avoid doing the actual work. We really believe that we must do those things, but deep down we know we're procrastinating. If you're a "perfectionist" you will struggle with this even more because you set standards for yourself and it takes you hours to actually start doing something and even then, you end up with minimal output at the end of the day.

How do you get over this? The answer: Split your day into pomodoros with little breaks in between.

The brain has a limited capacity. It can't focus on a single task for an entire day and requires periodical breaks. Unfortunately, most believe that to be successful they have to do an 8-hour stint of non-stop work during the work day. This is reason modern society is addicted to prescription pills that alter our brain chemistry, and even students are taking up Adderall to focus on studies. Since altering your brain chemistry is unhealthy, the right way is to account for the brain's natural desires to relax after focusing, and to plan out a productive day in advance by anticipating the work-break balance. It's entirely possible to create your own schedule that allows you to focus on small tasks for 45 minutes and then take breaks between sessions to avoid burnout. The technique that focuses on becoming productive for a certain amount of time and then following that up with a periodic break is the "Pomodoro Technique."

Pomodoro: 25-Minute Work Sessions to Success

The Pomodoro technique is a famous productivity technique pioneered by Francesco Cirillo, an Italian chef who discovered that by observing his clock for 25 minutes and then taking a break, he was able to cook more and make better meals for his clients at the restaurant. He had a tomato-shaped kitchen timer that he used to work with.

Cirillo broke his sessions down into manageable 25-minute work bursts that he called "pomodoros," following up each burst with a short break (3-5 minutes) for relaxation. He didn't do this the whole day, but once he completed 4 pomodoros, he took a longer 30-minute break.

The Pomodoro Technique is a brain technique that optimizes your brain for work output but then relaxes it to avoid burnout. This follows a natural cycle that responds to our evolutionary nature. When we used to hunt in the wilderness millions of years ago, we would usually find an animal, struggle to kill it and then take a break. We didn't run around with spears 24/7. Our brain has to receive periodic breaks in order to preserve clarity and sanity. Ideally those breaks can be optimized after 25-minute work increments, followed up by 5-minute breaks and a 30-minute break after 4 successful pomodoros.

How Pomodoro Works: An Average Day

The easiest way to imagine an average day on the Pomodoro technique is to break your day down into 4 or 5 full pomodoros (2 hours each) that you scratch off — one full pomodoro takes 2 hours because it's split in 4 25-minute mini pomodoros and breaks. Once you've done 6 full pomodoros, consider your work day successful. 4 full pomodoros correspond to an average 8-hour work day.

For example, start with one mini Pomodoro when you wake up. Take 25 minutes to work, then 5 minutes off, and repeat this 3 more times. This should take you a total of 2 hours. Once you're done, scratch one full pomodoro off your list. Take 30 minutes off, catch some air, listen to a song and do the opposite of what you did — disengage.

When you work you must be 100% engaged with the task for maximum productivity, but once you're on break you want to do the opposite and allow your brain to recover without adding any pressure. Once you've done your first pomodoro and taken a longer 30-minute break, repeat the process 2 or 3 more times before you stop for lunch. You'll effectively have 3-4 full pomodoros completed by lunch time – this is a solid 6 hours of work in the morning. Come lunchtime, take 1 hour off to fully recover. Follow that up by completing 2 more pomodoros - this will optimize your day for at least 8 hours of work. If you wish to work a 10-hour day or even a 15-hour day, you can add 2-3 extra pomodoros to your day.

The 4 Rules of Pomodoro

1. Activities Shouldn't Require More Than 4 Pomodoros

If your activity requires more than 4 pomodoros (that is in essence over 8 hours of work) you should break it down into small actionable steps. For instance, if you have to deliver a PowerPoint presentation with 50 slides and 10 slides take you around 2 hours to complete, you should split that activity into 4 full pomodoros. This way you will complete half of the slides in 2 full pomodoros. You can't sneak in more work on your Pomodoro as this goes against the rules - once the 25 minutes are out, you must take a 5-minute break or a 30-minute break appropriately. All large tasks that require more time than is given should be broken down into small 25-minute pomodoros. Find out how much time your activities require in advance in order to optimize your pomodoros.

2. Pomodoros Must Be Protected From Interruptions

All internal and external interruptions have to be removed for a pomodoro to be considered legitimate. You can't work for 15 minutes and then browse Facebook or talk to a colleague at work. Optimally you should be focused at 100% during your pomodoro and be located in an environment that encourages productivity. Prepare your environment by minimizing clutter, removing unnecessary items and distancing yourself from influences that distract you from work, whether those are the Internet, people or any other distraction. Focus during your pomodoro to protect your productivity.

3. Recaps Count as Work Under Pomodoros

You are allowed to recap and review your work during a pomodoro because this relates directly to your productivity. Example: If you're a chef at a restaurant and you're at the end of your work day, you need to take the time to write down ingredients to shop for the next day, how much you need of x ingredient, how many pastries you need to bake and more. This helps you organize your day. This is also counted under productivity and it can be measured under a single pomodoro. If you recap and review your work, this is also considered work under pomodoro rules.

4. Optimize Pomodoros for Personal Objectives

Optimize your pomodoros to take actions that create value in return. In essence, the only time we get value is when we produce value in return. This means that to make more money and to get promoted at work, you must increase the quality of your output. How do you do that? By focusing all your attention on the little work tasks that enable you to increase your output. Most people spend 30-40% of their work day actually working - the rest is spent dwelling on work, being distracted or doing nothing at all. If you only optimize your work day to work at 80% capacity with the time given, you can double your productivity and increase your revenues by a huge margin.

4 Productive Habits of the Zen-to-Done Method

Do you struggle keeping your day-to-day habits? Do you delay your "productive" habits indefinitely and end up doing half of what you're supposed to be doing? Organizing yourself can be exhausting and confusing because we're overwhelmed by influences from the external world, and it's hard to "tune out" and focus on what's really important. We're bombarded with stimulation on social media that encourages us to go down the route of least resistance and even the opposite is true — productivity habits can clog our mind because there are too many of them and we don't know which one is the best or where to start. The "Zen To Done" Method is the most simplified and minimalistic productivity method that optimizes productivity for 4 basic habits that you do on the daily. This method was developed by Leo Babauta of "Zen Habits" in order to break a day down into step-by-step habits based on individual goals.

The Human Element of Productivity

There is a human element to productivity — we cannot function like robots that work for 30-40 minutes and then shut off consistently. In reality, we constantly experience peaks and dips of productivity, we feel a surge of energy and then we feel a diminishing of energy. Some days we're on top of the world and we can work without stopping and other days we're all out of energy and can't seem to get anything done. The question is: How do we gain consistency? If the human element prevents us from acting the same way every day and popular techniques can't work with consistency - what is the right approach?

The ZTD approach accounts for the human element by focusing on broad behavioral patterns. ZTD focuses on behaviors that can be replicated on a daily basis, irrespective of your mood or energy levels. The ZTD method begins by analyzing your broader plans, effectively mapping out your long-term and short-term goals and then focusing on scheduling action-steps that you can do on a daily basis that produce the results you're after.

The 4 Habits of "Zen To Done" Method

The original Zen To Done method featured 10 habits, but the minimalist ZTD method (which is most popular) is comprised of 4 core habits:

ZTD Habit #1: Collect

The ZTD technique focuses on letting out all ideas in one piece of paper: Making a brain dump by writing down everything that's on your mind. If you have business ideas left to accomplish, write them down. If you have things that you'd like to improve such as your health or bad habits, write down all of them. There shouldn't be any difference between quitting your smoking habit and starting a business — both are action steps you must do and they should be written down. Take out a piece of paper or open a note on your computer and write down all your goals and things you plan to get done this year.

Dedicate one page for your goals and another page for action plans that you will need to obtain those goals. Take your time as the first habit is the most crucial — it might take you hours to remember all the things you've wanted to do and things which bother you on a daily basis. If you're poor and want to take action steps to become wealthy, write that down. If you're out of shape and plan to become fit, write it down. If you're addicted to a substance and want to quit, write that down. Write down everything.

Pro Tip: To find what to write down, go for a walk late at night and let your mind unwind. Play music and let thoughts come into your head naturally. Once you have those thoughts, write them down on your phone. This is better than "forcing" your brain to come up with things to do while you're locked at home.

ZTD Habit #2: Process

Once you've successfully written down everything, it's time to convert your thoughts into daily action steps you can follow up on. Example: If your goal is to lose 20 pounds you will likely have to take multiple actions - you'll have to exercise, replace your nutrition, drink more water, de-stress, etc. To accomplish all those things at once you'll have to write down what you would have to do in an average day. Maybe you have to wake up earlier to exercise in the morning - write that down. Maybe you have to purchase gym equipment and learn how to cook healthy food - write that down. At night, if you plan to run and lift weights at the gym - write that down. In essence you have to write down the new habits that would be required of you each day in order to achieve your long-term goals.

ZTD Habit #3: Plan

Once you've written down your daily action plans and new habits, it's important to revise your action-plans based on the things you've accomplished. What we plan for and what we do in real life is a lot different. For example, we might plan to run for 30 minutes at night but our energy levels dip after 10 minutes when we actually attempt it. This is why we have to optimize to progressively ramp up the exercise by running 5 minutes more every week. This way in 4 weeks we can actually achieve a 30-minute run, once our physical condition improves. The same practice applies to productivity at work - progressively increase your work load and update your action plans based on your performance.

ZTD Habit #4: Do

Once you've planned everything - DO, DO, DO! It all comes down to action. You've removed the clutter from your head, you've written down your goals and now you have to take the actions that produce the results. Start by scheduling when you're going to do a certain action down to the hour. Example: Set your alarm clock to 5 AM and wake up early for your work. Set milestones you want to achieve by mid-day. Update your accomplishments every day and edit your action plans accordingly. Once you're actually engaged with your daily tasks, you become "self-aware" in terms of with how much work you can take on and you can increase your performance progressively in order to ramp up your output.

How to Keep Track of Productivity?

The computer. Write down your daily and weekly to-dos on a list on your computer. This is ideal if you're working from home or rely on your computer for work. You can edit your plans according to the changes in your life. Many times, we need to alter our goals once we hit milestones, and your action plan will require constant editing. The computer is the best place to do this.

Smartphone apps. Find a memo app that allows you to write down your action steps, or one that has daily reminders in case you forget something. Use the alarm clock to remind you when to take a certain action step. If you run at 10 PM each night, set an alarm clock for 9:30 PM. This way, you have 30 minutes to prepare yourself for your run, both physically and mentally.

Using the "Don't Break the Chain" Technique for Consistency

Do you manage to stay on track with a goal and can keep the habit for one month, three months or even half a year but then your output is unsatisfactory? Do you struggle increasing your yearly output and you're stuck at the same salary level for years, when you know what you need to do to increase your earnings? Do you wonder why this happens to you while your acquaintances progress?

The answer is simple: You're not doing enough. Even if you're consistent, chances are you're wasting a day or two every week and you're not maximizing your time for productivity. Consistency is a giant problem for people trying to reinvent themselves. Despite the initial "push," our biology eventually wires us to crave stability. Unless we assume our new habits as part of our identity, we eventually slip back into our old way of living. The bigger problem is when we think we're consistent, but we end up wasting days that we could spend productively. How do we not break the chain? We use every day.

Solution #1: Using Every Day in a Year

Reevaluate your off days: Even if you're killing it at work and you're satisfied with your daily performance, you should still be aware of the time lost. Let's you've kept up your work habit for a year — you've been working on your dream but you still haven't achieved your desired goal. The solution: Work every day in the year. We're given 365 days a year. If you work 5 days a week, you might think you're consistent but zoom out and take a big-picture perspective — you're losing 8 days a month or almost 100 days a year. The lost weekends add up, and once you lose 8-10 days a month due to off-days and holidays, you're robbing yourself of 100+ days you could

231

have spent working and increasing your productivity. That's almost 1/3 of the year wasted.

Solution #2: Work as If You're Being Audited

If you want to boost your productivity on the daily, implement this one trick: Work as if you're being audited. This is a huge mental habit that trains your brain to utilize every minute for productivity. Most people work 2-3 hours in an average 8-hour work day — the rest is spent browsing the internet, talking to colleagues, sitting in the lounge or doing nothing. If your work solely relies on the output — that is, your income is measured based on the product you produce and not the time spent — you must utilize this technique to produce more in the time given.

Example: Take a look at your day. If someone audits your day the same way they audit your finances, what will they discover? Have you spent every minute of your work day working, or were you slacking off on the internet? Did you take breaks that lasted longer than your work sessions? Identify your problem and fix it immediately. If you apply a rigid and thorough auditing on your daily performance, you will discover areas where you need to improve in and double your productivity.

The "Don't Break the Chain" Method

This is a reliable method for not breaking consistency and making use of every day in the year. This method is for the hardest performers who want to make a big change in their life and assume a completely new identity that re-shapes their life and prepares them for the future. The method was popularized by comedian Jerry Seinfeld, one of the biggest names in stand-up comedy and TV. Mr. Seinfeld struggled with consistency as his job commanded him to do perform in front of audiences weekly, and he invented a trick that helped him become productive every day of the year.

How it works: Take a big calendar with each day in the year, and mark the days you've worked with a giant X. You will soon realize that if you take weekends off, almost a quarter of the days each month will be left unmarked. Start marking each day you've spent working and only mark "X" on the dates if you've successfully completed all your tasks for the day. This way you'll feel inclined to increase your productivity on your off-days and prepare yourself for month-to-month consistency. This method is the final elevation in productivity because it's designed for people who want to make every day count and are ready to immerse themselves fully. If you're actively pushing yourself and productivity becomes a routine, you can use the "Don't Break The Chain" method to implement a chain of productivity that will get you what you want out of life: a higher salary, better fitness/health, more business success, and healthy relationships.

4 Science-Backed Hacks for Increased Productivity

University studies and research facilities have carried out studies that relate certain activities to productivity. Exercising, sleeping better, and walking were linked to a significant increase in productivity and the same can impact willpower in significant proportions.

Remember the saying, "What you eat is what you are"? In essence, what we consume and how we treat our bodies reflects in our mental performance. If we supply our body with the right nutrients and physical exercise it craves, it will give us mental clarity and higher performance at work. To start a life-changing process, you must start by optimizing your health and then applying the numerous productivity habits that exist. The following scientific studies prove that certain activities are linked to an increase in productivity:

1. Exercise Improves Productivity

The largest study that correlated exercise to productivity was carried out at Bristol University in the UK. The university took 200 employees and assigned exercise days and no-exercise days the same people. They observed the behavior of each individual on both days and analyzed how their performance. After the tested participants were analyzed, their results were calculated, and this is what the study revealed:

- 21% increase in concentration
- 22% increase in finishing work on time
- 25% higher ability to work without taking breaks
- 41% increase in motivation to work.

Why is exercise linked to productivity? The act of exercise is not a magic pill, but the mind reflects the condition of the body. We evolved to live out in nature and most of us were fit because we had to hunt for food and we spent our days outdoors. If we're fit, we're able to sleep less, concentrate more and we feel motivated to do more. If we're not fit, we experience constant mood swings, lack of motivation/focus and inability to stay consistent at work.

This is why improving your fitness can make a dramatic impact in your output at work. This study determined that exercise in itself increases productivity by almost 25%. Taking into account that the study was carried out on people with little/no prior exercise experience, it is safe to say that people who make fitness a part of their daily schedule will be able to perform mental tasks at 50-100% higher capacity than people who do not exercise at all.

Stanford University carried out a study that proved the benefit of walking for idea-generation. Two research professors analyzed people who were sitting and people who were walking for effects on productivity and idea-generation. The study found that people who practice walking on a daily basis experience a 60% increase in unique responses to stimuli and generate more unique ideas.

2. Sleep Improves Productivity

If you're sleep-deprived, you're likely to perform worse at work and experience low attention retention compared to people who received a full night's sleep. The minimum amount of sleep a person should have is 8 hours a night - this is optimal as it allows us to recharge. Sleep increases performance, boosts alertness and replenishes our energy. There were two notable studies that prove sleep can increase productivity.

The largest study from the American College of Occupational and Environmental Medicine determined that employees at the college who suffered from insomnia were spending thrice as much time on tasks, compared to employees who had a full night's sleep. Employees who suffered from lack of sleep were found to be less motivated to perform tasks, experienced severe lack of focus and had trouble remembering things. Sleep is tied to all mental performance: Endurance, focus and consistency. If we go without adequate sleep, we are diminishing our performance abilities by a significant margin.

Varn Bexter and Steve Kroll Smith conducted a scientific study in a corporate environment that analyzed the effect on taking power naps. Employees who took power naps at work were more alert at the job tasks and experienced increases in productivity. Employers are now encouraging their workers to take power-naps at work in order to increase their performance.

3. Music Boosts Productivity

Music is tied to increasing positive stimulus in the brain and idea-generation. A study conducted at University of Miami determined that people who listen to music at work tend to generate faster output, better ideas and had a positive mood compared to people who didn't listen to music at work. The appropriate music might vary, as certain songs can be distracting and if you use music to boost your productivity you should be careful in order to pick a record that boosts your mood without distracting you from the job at hand.

4. Green Offices Boost Productivity

Recently a study at the University of Exeter in England analyzed the impact that plants have on employees in the work space. The study was split in two groups: One group worked out of offices without green plants and another worked out of offices furnished with green plants. The study determined that people who work surrounded by plants experience a 15% increase in productivity and reduced stress levels. Humans evolved to live in forests as trees provide us with natural shade. It's no wonder most of us feel at peace when we're surrounded by plants.

Chapter 5 - Planning for Daily Success

6 Morning Routines to Start the Day on Top

Do you feel productivity highs and lows? One day you wake up productive and ready to work, and another you feel sluggish and don't feel like working at all. Ever wonder why the morning is the hardest part of the day to start working? The morning sets the tone for productivity — if you start off productive early in the morning, you'll likely keep up your productivity throughout the day. If you start off feeling lazy, chances are you won't get anything done the whole day.

Mornings are detrimental to success because the first 3 hours in the morning are when mental energy peaks. The first 2-3 hours upon waking up is when we experience peak mental clarity. This is why you must set the tone of your day in the first 3 hours! If you miss out on this short time frame, you will feel decaying mental energy throughout the day and your productivity will amount to zero. Mornings set the tone for what we do throughout the day, while evenings only prepare us for the next day. This begs the question: How do you feel consistently motivated in the morning? The solution to create morning habits that boost productivity. The following habits can double your productivity and can be implemented immediately upon waking up.

1. Wake Up at 5 AM

Waking up early is a ritual that will double or triple your productivity. The time you miss out when you're waking up late or even normal morning hours can be assigned to doing your hardest task that relieve you of the stress for the rest of the day and "rewire" your brain for productivity in the morning. Most people wake up at 8

AM or 9 AM - some even wake up at 10 AM or the afternoon. To become successful, you must wake up at least 2-3 hours before everyone else. Set your alarm clock to 5 AM or even 4 AM and start working early in the dawn. This routine will give you 2-3 hours ahead of everyone else to get the most important task of the day done.

Remember that the mind is the clearest within the first 3 morning hours upon waking up. If you use the hours before actual work hours, you can get the hardest task of your day done by the time everyone else wakes up. This gives you an edge over everyone else because you're utilizing excess hours to boost your productivity and you can assign those hours to fitness or other mind exercises such as meditation. If you're used to waking up late, this will be a daunting task for you to achieve but the body adjusts to a new habit in as little as 1-2 weeks. Waking up early won't work unless you go to bed early, so push your bed time backwards. If you go to bed at midnight and wake up at 7 AM, go to bed at 10 PM and wake up at 5 AM. This way you'll get your full night's rest and be able to start off in the early morning hours.

2. Drink a Bottle of Water

Water boosts energy to a higher degree than coffee. Most people don't realize the effects water has on energy levels in the body. We're all heard "hydration" keeps us healthy, but we never pay attention to the increase in energy high hydration produces. Our bodies were designed to consume water, and this is why we can go up to 40 days of no food if can still drink water. Without water? You'd only last a week.

Water is the most essential substance for the internal organs, and water can boost the energy levels of a person by a margin of 100%. If you wake up feeling energy less and you opt for coffee, accompany that with a bottle of water. The body is very slow in the morning because it's waking up from sleep, but when you put water into your body it's quickly assigned to the most necessary parts: the blood stream, the skin, the brain, the muscles.

Water accelerates blood flow by accelerating the bloodstream and this gives you an energizing feel. Staying hydrated also gives the skin a fresh look as opposed to a dry morning look. Water is even proven to increase sex drive in the morning by increasing the blood flow to our reproductive organs. The body adjusts to your individual consumption of water: If you drink one large bottle in the morning, you will likely have to go to the bathroom multiple times that day. However, once your body gets acclimated to consuming 3 or 4 large bottles a day, you will feel almost no inclination to flush the water out. Water consumption is a habit, one that invigorates your skin, gives you energy and supplies your internal organs with the nourishment they require.

3. Limit Time on Emails

Admit it: the first thing you did upon waking up is to check your phone for notifications and emails. If you're working in corporate America, your inbox is likely full every day. If you miss one day of emails, you may fall behind on your schedule. This makes you paranoid because you check our emails multiple times a day. Emails are productivity killers because they distract us from our main task of the morning. The emails in the morning make us think we have 20 different tasks to accomplish, but deep down we know which task of the day is the most important that would push us forward. This is why you should limit the time you spend on your emails and only check your inbox once, then go to work immediately.

If you spend more time on your emails, you'll focus on tasks you're supposed to do in the future which will further distract you from your daily goals. Give your emails one glance in the morning to make sure nothing's on fire. If things look casual, don't look at your emails until the evening and focus on work.

4. Don't Eat Breakfast

Contrary to popular belief, breakfast is not the most important meal of the day. In fact, breakfast is the biggest productivity killer for most people throughout the day. Replace your breakfast with a cup of coffee or a bottle of water to allow your body to "activate" internal organs by supplying it with essential hydration. This way the body can activate internally and flush out and debris that was accumulated from your food consumption the day before.

If you start your day by consuming food, you will load your body on items it doesn't need and lower your energy levels because you opted for food instead of water. Almost all breakfast options in the modern world contain high-carbs: bread, pancakes, cereal, bagels, and other variations of heavy breakfasts. This temporarily fills people but then their energy dips mid-day. If you want to kill your energy on purpose, start by eating a heavy breakfast in the morning. By mid-afternoon, you'll start "feeling sleepy" and you'll want to nap on your work day.

Pro Tip: When you feel like sleeping mid-day, this is your nutrition at work. The breakfast you consumed is slowly killing your internal energy and halving your sugar levels. This is why you feel a desire to sleep.

To avoid a steep decline in energy, skip breakfast and replace your breakfast with a large bottle of water and a cup of coffee. This will give you equal energy as consuming breakfast, but your energy levels won't dip mid-day. You also won't feel that fat-belly feeling but your stomach, but it will empty out and prepare you for lunch when you can consume high-nutrition foods. If you absolutely have to eat in the morning, go for a light breakfast such as a banana, apple or some eggs. Avoid all forms of pastry and sugary foods, as those are the biggest energy killers in the morning.

5. Do the Largest Task in the First 3 Hours

When you wake up, you'll know which task you must do that will require the most energy and effort - this is your "main task" of the day. This is the biggest productivity tip for people who struggle getting things done: Get that task done first, and everything else will seem like a breeze. Start working on your main task the minute you wake up. This way, your brain will get the proof it needs that the hardest task is under control, and you'll get it done in a few hours. Try to complete the task within 2-3 hours because those hours are your most prolific in the morning. The first hour upon waking up is the easiest to focus on tasks because your brain has peak mental clarity, and it progressively diminishes over the day. Start your day by doing the hardest task of the day.

Most people start by doing light tasks that don't require a lot of effort. This is a big mistake because they do a sloppy job on the first tasks and then once they "gather the courage" to do the big task they've already ran out of mental energy. The right way to stay on top of your productivity is to wake up and immediately treat work as if you're going to war: Start with the hardest project, then once you've got that off your back focus on smaller, less important projects.

6. Put a Clock in Front of You

If you're struggling starting things and you take a very long time to start a project, put a clock on your desk. Place a clock in the lower-right side of your computer, a clock on your phone or a physical clock — any clock will do. If you're reminded of the time often, you will become aware of how fast it passes and this will inject a "sense of urgency" in you that will prompt you to get things done faster. Placing a clock in front will also allow you to measure how long you take to complete tasks. This way, you can optimize your work to complete tasks faster.

Example: If you work at a call center and you call clients to pitch over the phone, you might find that you're only calling 5 people an hour. If you have a clock near you, this will tempt you to call more and you will end up making more calls and closing more. The more you're aware of time, the more you become aware of how you spend your work day. Developing a sense of urgency will give you the leverage you need to become less hesitant and take more action at work.

4 Evening Routines to End the Day Just Right

You've had a successful day — you completed all your big tasks, you closed new deals, you traveled back and forth to work. What will you do in the evening? The evening is a time to unwind and a time to prepare for the next day to make it successful. The evening is critical for the routines you set in place and forming new habits. This time of the day doesn't have to be a time for relaxation! Instead of lying in bed and watching TV in the evening, you can optimize those hours for exercise and this will improve your fitness which ultimately improves your energy levels throughout the day and making you more productive.

Night hours are ideal for re-shaping your body and mind because you're almost drained of energy, and you the little energy you have left can be assigned to activities that make an impact in your physical and mental shape. What are the best evening routines? Should you meditate, hit the gym, do yoga, prepare for work tomorrow — or do all those at once? The answer is that it depends on your situation. If you're lacking in physical activity, assign all your evening hours to fitness-related activities. If you're lacking in productivity, assign your evening hours to increasing productivity. The following are the best all-around evening routines that will help you complete your day and prepare you for another day of productivity.

1. Set up an Exercise Routine

Exercise is for the evenings, not the mornings. If you believe that you gain energy from exercise, ask yourself: Have you really exercised if you feel MORE energetic after the exercise than before? Exercising is all about draining yourself — you feel a surplus of energy and you release that energy by running, lifting weights and doing exercises that push you to your limits. Exercise stimulates endorphins, boosts blood flow and makes you look great. If you only exercise for 30 days and you've never exercised before, there's a chance you'll look very different. Your jaw will become more chiseled and defined, you'll start losing fat, and you'll feel high energy throughout the day.

If you exercise in the mornings, you'll only kill your energy because the energy that you use for productivity will diminish as it went into your morning exercise. However, if you exercise at night, you will experience the following: 1) You will be able to go "all out" because you don't have to spare any energy 2) You will tire yourself out and fall asleep more easily. If you struggle to fall asleep at night, setting up an exercise routine will tire you out and make you sleep like a baby. If you have high energy all throughout the day, it's logical to end your day by draining yourself of that energy through heavy exercise. The ideal time to exercise is 1-2 hours before you go to bed. If your bed time is at 10 PM, start exercising at 8-9 PM. This way you'll have enough time to carry out your exercise routine, shower, and prepare for bed.

The best night exercises for you are ones that cater to your current abilities and goals. If you want to lose weight fast, you should opt for HIIT — high intensity interval training. This is a method of sprinting at 90-100% capacity by running as fast as possible. The average training routine consists of 10-20 of these sprints with little breaks in-between until you run out of energy.

If you choose a less intense workout, you should aim to start jogging long-distance. Start by doing short 10-minute jogs and then progressively increase your distance every week. If you feel that you're about to faint and you're losing energy - stop. Don't over-stretch yourself on the first few exercises only because you're feeling motivated. Take your time to progressively increase your exercises.

If you want to gain weight, you should consider getting a gym membership for access to heavy equipment. The average gym is stacked with thousands of dollars' worth of technology that is inaccessible to home-gym owners. The fitter you become, the higher your energy levels will be in the office. This in turn will reflect in your productivity because you'll be able to focus for longer hours, your output quality will increase and you will tire less. Fitness also makes us less responsive to heavy weather — if you're feeling cold in the winter months, you'll feel less cold when you're fit. The opposite applies for hot weather - fit people are usually not bothered by extreme heat.

Pro Tip: Stop relying on fitness apps to track your progress. If you rely on technology you will lose touch with your body's nature: you'll think in terms of miles, hours and calories. Forget that! Start exercising and push yourself without technology and you will eventually become familiar with your physical abilities. You will instinctively know how much you can run and push yourself progressively.

2. Meditate for 20 Minutes

Do you feel unable to focus because you're distracted by everything and even when you start, you can't seem to keep your attention on one task for long? The solution is to get out of your head! We're naturally consumed by our thoughts and this gets distracting because while we're supposed to be working, we daydream about events that have no correlation to our work. How do we get out of our own head? The only way to be effective is to become present. If you have no thoughts and you immerse ourselves in the present moment, you can become more productive, more engaged with your work and produce higher-quality output. The practice that teaches the art of presence is meditation. Anyone can start meditating at home for free.

Pro Tip: You only need to assign 15-20 minutes at night to perfect your meditation. You don't have to meditate like a Buddhist Monk 12 hours a day to be successful in meditation.

The art of meditation can be summed up as "not thinking." Being present is about immersing yourself with the present moment. Imagine yourself playing basketball — you focus on shooting the hoops, you enjoy passing the ball, you anticipate fellow players passing you the ball, you're completely immersed with the game. This is what's known as "becoming present."

Do you even feel in the zone when you're out on a Friday night, you're drinking with your buddies and the conversation keeps flowing? This is also being present. People consume alcohol because it allows them to get out of their head and become present. However, the practice can be replicated naturally by teaching yourself to get out of your own way. It's easier than you think: Start by sitting on the floor of your room, preferably somewhere where you won't be distracted by noises and other people. Then, you can engage in your first mediation session.

How it works: Set an alarm clock for 15 or 20 minutes, depending on how long you think you'll last with your eyes closed. Clasp your hands together and close your eyes. Now focus on your breath and stop thinking — don't even think about not thinking, only focus your attention on the breath. Eventually, you'll start feeling a deep relaxation effect. This usually happens once you're 5 minutes in the session. You'll eventually be fully immersed in the present moment, and then the clock will ring. You'll open your eyes slowly, the world will seem like it's surreal and moving slow. This is how you know you've achieved a fully present meditation session. Once you've practiced meditation consistently for a month, you'll naturally evoke your present feeling and you'll become more confident because you'll be stuck in head way less. There are also joint meditation areas and places where you can practice meditation with other people.

3. Take a Cold Shower

Cold showers are the most extreme, but they're for people who want to push their endurance to the maximum and get in touch with their nature. Cold showers can make you stronger, more in touch with your primal nature, push your endurance and experience health benefits. Think about the old days: Humanity has evolved for millions of years and we've only had hot showers for the last hundred years. Yet, we think that hot showers are the default and cold showers are "extreme." The cold shower is how we used to shower for most of humanity's history, and this is why the practice carries numerous benefits.

The main benefits of cold showers are a rush of dopamine, stimulation of fat-burning and an increase blood flow. However, in practice cold showers have certain "invisible" benefits that manifest themselves over the long term. Cold showers shock your system and supply your nervous system with a "wake up call" similar to that of coffee in the morning. The initial shock makes the nervous system crave radical substances less, and it can help you quit chemical addictions such as cigarettes or drugs. Cold showers completely replace the need your body has for external stimulation.

One more major benefit to cold showers is that you don't feel cold in winter, as cold showers make you resilient to cold and you barely feel anything when you're out in the coldest winter months. Certain communities in Russia practice jumping in ice because cold hits their nervous system to the degree that they feel immune to cold in daily life.

Taking a cold shower should be done progressively. You can't just jump in freezing cold water without pacing yourself first. However, you also shouldn't call a shower a "cold shower" if you shower with hot water and only release 5-10 seconds of cold at the end. A cold shower has to last at least 3-5 minutes to be successful. Start by watering your legs and slowly feeling the cold water hitting your skin. You'll feel shivers all over your body because your body is experiencing the cold water. Then spread some cold water among the upper parts of your body and get used to the temperature. After you've acclimated to the cold for a minute or two, you can get under a full shower blast for a couple of seconds. This will be very shocking to you, but if you embrace it you will eventually get used to it.

Pro Tip: Imagine a cold shower like jumping in a lake. The lake has colder water than an ocean, but once you're inside for 2-3 minutes – the water doesn't feel as cold. The same applies to cold showers. Slow step them and picture yourself as if you're in a lake. You'll eventually learn to handle low temperatures.

4. Read a Book Chapter (Offline)

Go to your favorite book store and pick up a book that will help you in real life. This can be a book related to fitness, business, your profession, or anything that relates to your personal growth. Get the paperback version and get off the internet. This way you can fully engage with the book. If the book is not too large, aim to read a full chapter per day. By consuming the right information, you will improve your life and it will add a sense of "completion" once you've read a full chapter each night. This will also help you fall asleep naturally, if you struggle to get a full night's rest. It's better to read paperback editions because most tablets and laptops have light beaming into your eyes. This is harmful, especially if you're reading at night with the lights out.

Eat These 3 Foods for a Productive Brain

Does your head feel foggy and drowsy after you eat breakfast? Do you feel tired in the afternoon and want to pass out on your office chair? Do you find it hard to get out of bed, to work long hours, to exercise or do anything remotely challenging? This is not due to a lack of motivation — this is caused by your brain reacting to nutrition. The brain consumes 20% of all nutrition (calories) that enter the body, which means that the quality of your food directly reflects in the quality of your brain functioning. If you ever wondered why "organic" food is more expensive and mass-produced food cheap, the difference is due to the quality of the nutrients.

Nutrition is not about how shiny your 6-pack abs are: It's about the clarity of your mental state, the consistency of your focus, and the productivity output you leave at the end of each day. Those are all controlled by one single thing: your food intake. If you put the right foods in your body, your brain will register and function at a higher level. It will allow you to work harder, provide longer focus and enable you to do the tasks that you find challenging.

If you eat the right foods, you'll be able to perform at superhuman levels. You'll work 10-hour shifts easily, you'll run more miles without exhausting yourself, you'll think clearly and become more confident. People report that their "brain fog" disappears once they started consuming the right food. There are many foods that affect the brain positively, but the ones listed below make the biggest difference. If you want to immediately boost your performance, to feel higher energy and long-lasting focus — focus on the foods below.

1) Greens: Broccoli, Spinach, Kale

The three kings of green (broccoli, spinach and kale) are the most essential brain foods that make a night and day difference in the way your brain performs. If you had to eat only 3 foods for the rest of your life choose the top 3 greens: broccoli, spinach and kale. These 3 foods alone are better than almost every other food for removing brain fog and establishing mental clarity. Broccoli is arguably the most nutrient-rich food in the world - it contains all the right Omega-3 fatty acids that build and repair brain cells in the fraction of a millisecond, and it even has anti-aging and weight-loss properties. Broccoli's effects on the brain can be felt immediately! Once you consume a full head of broccoli, you'll feel as if a horse kicked you in the head. The effects are so powerful and they clear your brain that no other food comes close.

Pro Tip: Take 2 days to experiment the effects of food on your brain. The first day, consume the greasiest food you can find: Hamburgers, pizza, pasta. The second day, eat broccoli and spinach and mix them together. Observe the effects on your brain and your energy levels 2 hours after you consume each. You'll notice a significant upgrade in mental clarity once you consume broccoli vs. a low-energy drowsy feeling once you consume greasy food. This is why the latter cost more — they are higher quality.

The following happens when you consume greens: You start waking up, your brain starts oozing energy and you achieve maximum brain clarity. This is the effect of high nutrients penetrating your brain and supplying it with the nourishment it needs. Greens are consumed by athletes because they boost strength and endurance on the field. As a result, you can run longer and lift heavier weights if your mental state is clear. Broccoli, spinach and kale have almost identical effects and these are all premium and expensive foods. Ideally you should consume green foods at least once a day. Learn to appreciate the subtle, little flavors in greens if you currently have problems with the taste. If you can't find them due to seasoning, most supermarkets have frozen variations. You can cook them a million different ways and mix them with tasty spices.

2. Nuts and seeds

Nuts are the most nutrient-dense foods for the brain after greens. They are loaded with positive ingredients that enhance our cognitive functions. The most notable in the "nuts" category are cashews and almonds, which provide the highest stimulation for the brain and they are the perfect snack food for uplifting energy and keeping us sharp and focused. Nuts can't be consumed as a main course, but they are very effective as side-foods that which be consumed alongside main meals. Nuts such as cashews and almonds provide the highest density of fats and proteins that serve as the building block for brain muscle.

To strengthen your brain muscles, you should regularly consume nuts. Cashews and almonds are also filled with omega-3 acids and antioxidants that enhance mental clarity. Scientific studies link cashews to improved cognitive function with older age and studies discovered that they can offset old-age diseases such as Alzheimer's which are linked to the cognitive ability. They can work wonders for healthy, young individuals. Make sure not to go overboard on nuts because they are very calorie-dense and they can be fattening if consumed in copious amounts. A handful of nuts is enough for a day.

3. Fish

Fish and fish oil is essential for cognitive ability because fish contains the highest density of Omega-3 acids. Omega-3's are essential repair blocks that the brain uses to formulate brain cells and increase blood flow in the brain area. Fish have the highest density of

Omega-3's, making them essential for cognitive ability and productivity. Oily fish take the lead in terms of omega-3 rich fish, in particular canned tuna. Do you ever open a can of tuna and think the oil is bad for you? It's actually oil that your brain craves — it's linked to better cognitive abilities, increase in thinking skill and brain clarity.

Salmon is also an exceptional brain food, albeit a bit more expensive. To boost your brain function, make fish part of your weekly food consumption. You might want to take it a step further and learn how to cook fish instead of relying on canned tuna. Pick up some frozen fish from your supermarket, lay it down in some oil and let it cook for 30-40 minutes. Combine it with tasty lemons or mix it with greens, and enjoy the optimal lunch for brain power.

BONUS: 4. Coffee

Coffee deserves an honorable mention among the top brain ingredients that boosts concentration, productivity and improves our mood. Do you look forward to your morning only for the coffee? Coffee is an acquired taste because it has a bitter flavor, but once a person gets used to the taste, they learn to appreciate coffee and look forward to the bitterness. You feel "alert" when you drink coffee because caffeine has an active ingredient that blocks the brain's chemicals known as "adenosines."

Adenosine chemicals can be released in the morning and during the day as well. This is why coffee is imperative in keeping us alert and productive. One cup of coffee can supply you with an energy boost that lasts until mid-day when you have your lunch. Make sure not to go overboard on coffee — 2 cups a day is enough. Sip a cup of coffee once you've woken up, and delay the second cup until you've accomplished your work tasks and you feel ready to "reward" yourself.

15 Daily Affirmations to Teach Your Brain Self-Discipline

Affirmations are essentially self-talk that we communicate to our subconscious mind in order to demand the willpower we require to achieve our goals. The brain recognizes affirmations as crossing the border between "I want to do something" to "I will do something" — taking concrete action. Affirmations play a significant role in our transformation when set high goals because they can affect our self-belief system and incentivize us to take action. Affirmations can be applied to all areas of life. They are simple statements that you repeat to yourself when you wake up and when you go to bed.

The way to base affirmations is to consider your personal goals (not everyone can apply the same affirmations). One can create affirmations for losing weight, one can create business affirmations, one can create affirmations related to self-confidence. To determine an area where you need affirmations, think about your biggest problem in the moment. Ask yourself: What am I struggling with? Where could I improve in life? The answer to those questions is what you should base your affirmations on.

The #1 Rule of Affirmations

The base rule of affirmations is that affirmations must be positive. An affirmation cannot be negative because the subconscious mind does not recognize negative affirmations — it only recognizes positive affirmations.

✗**Negative affirmation**: I won't delay my workout anymore.

✓**Positive affirmation**: I will start working out tonight.

Affirmations must be positive, and they must be written in the first person. You must always use "I" when you write an affirmation. This registers in your brain as you referring to yourself, and it rewires your psychology for new habits. The ideal amount of affirmations per goal is between 5 or 10 affirmations. Write your affirmations down on a piece of paper and read them in the morning and before you go to sleep. You can come up with 5 affirmations for every goal. Here are some examples of affirmations based on different goals.

Example: 5 Affirmations for Weight Loss

1. I will improve my food habits and eat healthy food.

2. I will drink 3 bottles of water per day.

3. I will exercise every night.

4. I will run sprints every night at 9 PM.

5. I will get a gym membership.

Example: 5 Affirmations for Work

1. I will wake up at 5 AM every morning.

2. I will start working immediately.

3. I will do the hardest task first thing in the morning.

4. I will focus on my work completely.

5. I will work every day without taking days off.

Example: 5 Affirmations for Dating

1. I will get in shape to become more attractive.

2. I will buy better clothes to make a better impression.

3. I will start going out every weekend.

4. I will meet new people and go on dates.

5. I will find my ideal partner.

Rule #2: Must Be About the Present

The affirmations you write must relate to the present moment. You must focus your affirmations on daily actions that you can take as early as tomorrow. If an affirmation is out of your reach or too into the future, discard it. Only focus on affirmations that you relate to your present struggles.

Ask yourself: What can you do now? The answer: You can wake up early, you can eat better, you can exercise, you can meet new people. What can't you do now? You can't start a business overnight. Affirmations exist to help us after we've navigated through our goals and we know the big-picture of where we're headed; affirmations effectively re-shape our mind in order to focus on immediately achievable goals and "push" us towards taking action.

Chapter 6 - Tools for Future Success

5 Exercises to Test and Maintain Powerful Self-Discipline

Do you feel overwhelmed by big tasks that require a lot of willpower? Would you rather start small by accomplishing small tasks that give you the confidence and willpower to move on to large tasks? Willpower has to be built gradually like a muscle. If you have no weight training experience and immediately start benching 100 pounds at the gym, you will put strain on your muscles. Meanwhile benching 100 pounds bars is a piece of cake for someone who's practiced with 20 pounds bars, 50 pounds bars and 100 pounds bars progressively. Why don't you practice progressively too? To work your way up to the highest willpower goals, you must start with small goals and then once you've gained the confidence, attempt to take a swing the big ones.

Warning: **You must start now.** If you delay your big goals endlessly, time will eventually catch up with you and you'll regret not taking action now. Do you look back at things you wanted to do 5 years ago and wish you got started back then for all the years wasted? Now is the best time to start. Let's start by doing some small exercises that you can accomplish on your own. If you do the exercises here, you'll build a baseline for future willpower. You can also create your own exercises: ones that cater to your individual goals.

Pro Tip: Small exercises help set the baseline for willpower. Even a tiny exercise such as washing the dishes can increase your willpower. When we're out of willpower, we feel like doing nothing. Once we shift in gear, our willpower muscle starts growing and we gradually progress onto bigger tasks.

Treat Exercises as Monthly Challenges

Treat the following exercises the way you do challenges: Do you remember popular challenges such as the 30-day no-shave challenge? Each one of these exercises can be repeated on a daily basis and you can form your own challenges to retain the habits. Example: Create a "30-day no-TV challenge" where you challenge yourself to stop watching TV at night once you're back from work and you instead spend your time meditating or reading a book for 30 days.

Exercise #1: No-Sugar Coffee

The first challenge relates to something we all consume in the morning — coffee. You essentially have to drink bitter, sugarless coffee for 30 days. What will you accomplish? It will push you to get out of your comfort taste for 30 days. The sugar added sweetness to your coffee, but now you'll taste real coffee. Train your brain to enjoy the subtle flavors in bitter coffee and consume it slowly. This will teach you that taste is acquired. Eventually you can improve your nutrition by consuming foods that you didn't find tasty, only for their brain benefits such as broccoli and spinach.

Exercise #2: No Social Media

Deactivate your social media for 30 days. This one is tough if you have an extroverted personality. Your Facebook account? Delete it. Your Instagram? Gone. Your dating apps? Discard them all. Spend 30 days interacting with people in real life and only use your phone to make calls. Remove the pings that you get from the notifications panel during the day. What will this accomplish? It will remove your need to check your phone impulsively waiting on your next dopamine hit. This way you can effectively focus on your work and all your attention will shift to producing better output instead of watching what your buddy Brad streaming his fishing trip in Canada.

Exercise #3: Run Every Day Challenge

Let's say you exhaust yourself every night for 30 days. What will the results be? You could possibly lose between 20 pounds and 60 pounds, depending on how extreme your diet is. Contrary to popular belief, exercise does not impact weight loss as much as dieting and water consumption. The upside of exercise is the physical condition you build up.

Once your 30 days are up, this is what will happen: You will feel more powerful, you will feel increased energy in the morning, you will be able to concentrate more, and you'll refuse to stay locked inside your home at night. This 30-day exercise will build your willpower because right now you're tired and you don't feel like doing anything. In 30 days, you'll naturally crave exercise every day. Remember: It's all about the consistency. You don't have to run every night, but you must come out for the routine – take a walk instead. The part that matters is that you're consistent.

Exercise #4: Clean Your Apartment Every Week

Take one day every week to reevaluate the items in your apartment and consider everything you own. Are those items essential to your productivity or are they hindering it? Is the state of your apartment preventing you from working, exercising, meditating or cooking healthy foods that help you? Stand in the middle of your apartment and look around: Observe everything. Do you really need that Buddhist statue you brought home from your Cambodia trip? Do you really need all those clothes from 5 years ago?

Is there too much clutter in your kitchen? Do you have too many heavy snacks and food that zaps your energy? Put them in the trash.

Donate your old clothes to the Red Cross. Sell the electronics and toys. Leave only the things that are necessary for productivity — your essentials such as clothes, laptops and weights. Repeat the same for your desktop computer. Too many times we have distracting icons such as games, movies and other distractions that have no relation to our work. Remove them all. Do a clean-up every week.

Exercise #5: Meditate Every Night

Start meditating every night for 30 nights in a row. You can learn meditation in as little as 5 sit-downs, but 30 meditation nights in a row will make you a master in the practice. Meditation is about invoking the present moment and getting in touch with presence. When you meditate you feel completely at peace and you get out of your head. You think less, and you observe things as they are, not as you process them through your ego. Once you've grown accustomed to the practice, repeat it often until you can naturally invoke the feeling. If you feel that you need to delay your meditation, that's when you need it the most. Remember to take at least 20 minutes a night for the practice and cut off all distractions while you do it.

How to Create Lasting Self-Awareness

If someone told you "Go run 10 miles now" – what would you do? If you were pushed under a cold shower for 5 minutes – would you run out of the shower? Are you fully aware of your capabilities on the mental and physical level? Self-awareness is the act of discovering who you are — your own physical and mental capabilities and limits. We all have a surface-level self-awareness and know what can do approximately. However, you need to practice if you wish to develop high self-awareness and know exactly what you're capable of no matter the task.

We must test our abilities constantly to become fully aware of what we can do and can't do. Let's say you think you can run 10 miles without stopping. When is the last time you attempted to run 10 miles? What if you ran for 5 miles and you gasped for air and couldn't do it? You can't tell until you try — you need to try it out. Once you know what you can do, you can progressively increase your limits. This practice applies to all matters of life! To elevate beyond basic self-awareness, you must push yourself constantly and test your own behavior. There are practices that can help you discover lasting self-awareness.

Self-Awareness Is for Action-Takers

Self-awareness is about knowing what you can do and what you can't do by testing this on the field. This reinforces your ego in a good way because you've already tested what you can accomplish and you feel prepared to tackle your big goals. There is another underlying layer to self-awareness: How your behaviors impact people around you. Once you recognize how your behaviors and productivity are impacting people, you can adjust your output to create more of that desired feeling.

Example: If you're a musician, you can improve people's lives because your music makes them feel better. Once you recognize the kind of songs that impact people in the best way, you can create more songs that emulate that. This is because you've become self-aware. The practice applies in business: Once you learn what your clients like by testing it, you can deliver more of that product. Effectively self-awareness translates to all areas of life. It reveals how we perceive ourselves and how others perceive us.

You can't develop self-awareness by staying at home, so you must go out into the real world and discover who you are by continually taking action. The following practices will help you obtain a high level of self-awareness:

1. Travel to Foreign Countries

259

Travel to a country as opposite of your culture as possible: as long as the destination is safe, go take a few weeks off and book a hotel. Pack your bags, book the flights, get your visa stamps - go out into the world. When you get to a foreign culture, you will be tested on all levels: Your social skills when you try to communicate with people who barely speak English, your street knowledge when you end up in shady areas by accident and even the general perception of who you are. Foreign people who have no relation to you and see you for the first time will tell you their honest impressions of you. They'll try to guess where you're from, make conversation about your country/accent/fashion and this will let you know how people who are completely foreign perceive you.

In essence, you will develop a deep knowledge of your identity, your origins, the way you live life and how others perceive you. Travel will boost your self-awareness tenfold. You don't have to interact with people who are completely distant to your culture. In fact, any environment that you're not used to will suffice. The way you navigate when you get lost in a foreign country, the way you experience new cultures and the way you interact with people will reinforce your identity to the highest level. If you're still trying to "find yourself," travel is the best way to achieve that. Travel is cheap, as even inter-continental flights are now inexpensive.

2. Engage in Flow-State Activities

Why do you do some things effortlessly while you have to coax yourself into doing work? Compare how little effort it takes you to play a game vs. do a hard task at work. When you play a video game, you don't have to prepare yourself — you know it's easy and go get into the game easily. When you try to do work it's hard and overwhelming, this is why it takes patience for you to engage with that task. In both cases, you enter what's called a "flow state." The difference is that you get in a flow state with a game immediately while at work it takes longer. Imagine you're skiing down a hill. Your speed accelerates as you fly down the snow, and you can't seem to stop. This is what being in a flow state is all about.

The ideal flow-state activity is one that is hard enough to require preparation, but not hard enough that it overwhelms you: think "medium difficulty." Example: Easy difficulty flow states are flow states that you get in instantly — watching movies, playing games, cooking — those require no effort. Hard difficulty flow states are ones that require massive preparation such as launching a new product in front of a crowd or similar life-changing events. What you need are medium-difficulty flow states: Working on a project, jogging at night, sitting down for a meditation session. These "flow state" activities are perfect self-awareness boosters, because they challenge you to get out of your comfort zone continually. This builds up over time and boosts your self-awareness in terms of what you're capable of doing.

3. Do Hard Tasks Every Day

Push yourself to do things you don't want to do on a daily basis — this will maximize yourself awareness. You'll know exactly what you can do, instead of guessing what you can do. Observe your body and what it responds to. Example: You want to eat, sleep, drink coffee, socialize. What don't you want to do? You don't want to work, you don't want to exercise, you don't want to wash the dishes. These are things you should do! The more you engage with tasks you don't want to do, the highest your willpower grows. Listen to your body and do the things you don't want to do.

If you focus on doing things you don't want to do, your brain will start to develop an inclination to do these without resistance. The initial resistance you're feeling when you start doing challenging tasks is a protection mechanism from overwhelming yourself. In order to push through the initial resistance, you must assign all your energy to the tasks that generate the resistance. This way, you will proactively break through your resistance and you will become a lot more competent in your field of work. Do harder tasks progressively – eventually doing hard things will become natural for you.

3 Healthy Habits for Better Concentration

Do you have this "one" task that you know could change your life, but you end up doing the opposite of the task? Do you think about 30 unrelated things when you know you should be focused on the task at hand? Are you easily distracted and is your environment enabling you to get away without working? Lack of concentration is the biggest productivity killer and you must address this to increase your productivity and move your life in the right direction. Concentration is a flow-state activity that requires patience — it can't be achieved instantly.

To be successful in concentration, you must slowly baby-step your way into the work process. We're falsely led to believe that concentrating is about us sitting down and completing our tasks Rambo-style until the whole work day is done. The truth is that the smallest things can impact our concentration: the environment, psychology, nutrition and even our goals (or lack thereof). If we have all those aligned, we can concentrate on a single task. If one of those is missing, we'll fall in the trap and fail to concentrate. We must start by cleaning our environment of items that influence our focus, and then progressively increase our work load until we achieve maximum concentration on any given task. The following habits help you concentrate on a daily basis.

1. Hand-pick Your Influences

Turn around and look at your office: What surrounds you? Are your colleagues productive or are they slacking on social media? Are there too many distractions nearby? What about your nutrition? What are

---

---

you consuming? Cut off everything that doesn't help you: distractions, people, nutrition, non-work optimized environments – all of it. If you have a PlayStation/Xbox console and this is something you like to play, discard it in the trash. Let's say you have willpower to not play, should you still trash your console? Yes. The thought that you have it nearby will tempt you once you start working and need a break.

If you take cigarette breaks between work tasks, get rid of your cigarettes because they tempt you to think about work breaks. If your colleagues are not productive, stop talking to them. Concentration is not only about your personal output; it's also about the environment that surrounds you. If you live in an environment that is not optimized for productivity, you won't achieve anything. If you live in a productive environment that enables work, you will achieve a lot. Even minor influences such as snacks can affect your concentration. If you have snacks like chips on your desk, remove them because they increase your will to eat and make you less willing to work. Look at all the external influences that surround you and ask yourself if they're helping you or if they're distracting you from your purpose.

2. Disable the Internet

Disable the internet. This will cut off at least 50% of all your distractions. Unless the internet is absolutely imperative to your productivity (i.e. you trade stocks or sell online) completely cut it off during your work day. That's it — shut down the router and disable your phone too. The internet is the biggest concentration-killer because it gives us immediate access to everything. It's also the biggest instant-gratification tool humans have invented in history.

One distraction leads to another. Example: You start looking for medical equipment factories in Germany for your company. Suddenly you're looking up the town where they manufacture the medical equipment. You're then looking at flights to book to

Germany and hotels. After that you notice some food in the hotel pictures and you want to try that food. The internet is a slippery slope as it creates one distraction that leads to another. Disable the router and re-enable it once you're done working. You will still have access to your computer, but you'll only focus on the task at hand. If you need the internet to do research for a project, complete the research for the project beforehand and then disable the internet while you do the actual work.

3. Increase Your Hard Tasks Progressively

To maximize concentration, you have to increase your flow-tasks progressively: Start with a hard task one day, and then once you're in the flow complete the easier tasks. The "hard" task will become "moderate" the next week. This way you can do harder and harder tasks by the week. You have to habituate yourself into concentration by tackling more difficult tasks every week. On the small scale, you must do hard tasks first because this will push you into a flow state of mind. On a large scale, you want to baby-step these hard tasks and take on heavier workloads progressively every week.

This applies to other areas of life such as fitness. If you start with 5-mile run, attempt a 10-mile run the next week because you'll have built up the condition. If you attempt a 10-mile run outright, you'll likely fail because you haven't progressed to that level. Increase your "hard" tasks progressively, and start with the most essential ones. Ask yourself: What would really change my life right now? If it's fitness, focus on fitness. If it's making money, focus on your job or a business. Increase the difficulty of your tasks and tackle them accordingly.

3 Unconventional Ways to Master Self-Discipline

Do you have a more "extreme" personality than the average person and wish to test out conventional ways to achieve your goals? Are you unsatisfied with the norm and do you push yourself way above the formalities and capacities of an average person? Some people are "wired" to outperform everyone else, that's why they opt for unconventional ways to increase their productivity and achieve their goals.

Warning: Certain unconventional ways are healthier than others. In theory, an "unconventional" way to increase productivity would be to consume prescription pills. The downside is that those are unhealthy and inconsistent, so your focus only runs as long as you take the pills. If you actually reinvent yourself and you create a new persona that can focus on the tasks, you'll be able to sustain your new habits forever. This guide focuses on unconventional ways that are both healthy and sustainable — ones that everyone can implement to reflect on their life and obtain high levels of self-discipline.

1. Audit Your Time Like the Tax-Man

What does Uncle Sam ask you at the end of each fiscal year? In essence the tax authorities inquire as to how you made your money. Every April 15th us as Americans have to provide records of salaries we received, bonuses, how we spent our money, what banking institutions we used, etc. The government holds us accountable for every dollar in our bank accounts they want to know the source of our income.

What if the government audited how you spent your day? Would you know where each minute went and how you choose to spend it? What if someone analyzed your average work day? This technique alone could double or triple your productivity. If you "audit" your time the way the government audits your bank account, you will be able to identify where your time leaks and determine where you can increase your output, allowing you to patch up time leaks and optimize your time for productivity.

Put a webcam in your office and record yourself for a day. What would you find out? Were you working the whole day or did you spend half of the time browsing the internet, eating, talking to coworkers and doing nothing? If you're record every minute of your day, you'll shocked at the time you end up wasting doing unproductive things. You may spend 6 hours not working and 2 hours actually working. Most people barely spend 1/3 of their work day actually working.

To increase the quality of your output, to produce more and to waste less time, you should start by auditing your time. Keep records of every hour to see what you've accomplished and how long your breaks lasted. You only have to do this for one day. Call it an "Audit Day" and review how your day went. Once you become aware as to the way your time leaks, you can put that time to use the next day. If you spent half of the time slacking off in different ways, use that time to double your productivity.

2. Picture Your Success

What if you were assigned to become the CEO of a multimillion-dollar enterprise? What if you were the most successful doctor/lawyer/accountant in your state? What would your average day look like then? It certainly wouldn't look the same as your average day now. Think about what would happen if you were put in a high position in your field of work overnight. Now imagine what an average day would look like for you in that position. Would you be required to do more tasks, to wake up earlier, to create bigger projects? What would an average day look like for you?

Once you figure that out, write down the average day of successful you and repeat the steps as if you're successful now. Optimize your current average day to emulate the average day of your successful version. Once you replicate it, you will eventually obtain the same results they have. This is the act of "reverse-engineering" success. It's possible to tell how a person became successful by analyzing their work history and business moves. Everyone starts somewhere, but the difference is where we all end up. What did successful people in your field do to obtain their success? What did they do in the last 10 years? Did they make certain moves that you are too afraid to make? There was always something that pushed them to go beyond the average in their industry. Imagine yourself at the peak of your success and ask yourself: What did it take for you to get there? Repeat that.

3. Force Yourself to Work

When all other options fail, force yourself to do the things you don't want to do! Force is a harsh word, but in many cases it's necessary. Write down the things that you must do to be successful and gradually force yourself into the action-steps that would get you there. Example: Force yourself to wake up at 5 AM. Set the loudest alarm clock possible for 5 AM or set 2 alarm clocks that go off simultaneously. Once you hear the sounds, you will be forced to get out of bed. Every activity that you must do can be forced. Once you force yourself to do it once, your brain will receive the "proof" it needs that this is something you can do and it will become monumentally easier for you to repeat that the next day. If you can't make yourself do things the easy way, force yourself to do them the hard way.

3 Transformative Ways to Push Yourself to the Next Level

Do you feel that you're on the brink of doing something excellent? Are you feeling deep motivation and you can tell you're on the brink of changing your whole life? Maybe you need that slight little "push" that will allow you to go over the edge and make the first move towards a better life. This is how you know you're ready to elevate yourself!

So you're feeling motivated, you have your goals and to-do's written down and you're excited to get started. All you need are a few more tips that give you a better perspective as to how you should go about taking action. These transformative techniques are for the action-taker — the person who acts on their dreams daily and don't dwell too much planning. If you're ready to jump in, start by applying the following transformative techniques:

1. Be Ready, Not Prepared

If you prepare forever, you will never become prepared enough! You will always hold off until you do one imaginary obstacle, then invent another obstacle. Imagine you're ready right now and start doing the things you want right now. Let's say you want to start a restaurant but you're 10 months away from saving the money you need to open a location. Why wait the 10 months? Start by producing the dishes you will have in your restaurant today. Write down creative names for the dishes, create a menu with prices like you'd have in your restaurant and invite your friends for an "experiment" where they act as the customers and you serve them in your restaurant.

If you're trying to get in shape, why wait 3 months or 6 months from now? Even if you're loaded on work, you'll still have 1-2 hours at the end of each night that you can assign to exercise. Addictions are the worst! If you hold off the "quit date" on your addiction, you might find yourself holding it off forever. Switch your mindset from "waiting to be prepared" to "I'm ready right now." You can force yourself to be ready and remove your imaginary obstacles - start now.

2. Aim to Do More, Faster

If you have a task that requires you to do in 10 days, try to do it in 5. Let's say you have a big business pitch to make and it takes you 10 days to do the research, gather the slides, present the products and make the presentation. What if suddenly the deadline was shifted to 5 days? Would you be able to do it? Chances are, you would. Now even if the deadline is not moved and you have 10 days, act as if you have 5 days! This will create a sense of urgency and you'll be able to get your projects done in half the time.

You will be shocked at the speed in which you can tackle your "big" projects once you shorten your deadlines. Most people delay their projects or wait until they only have a few days to the deadline in order to start taking action. If you allocate every day you're given to your work, you'll be able to get things done in half the time. If it takes you 15 minutes to run the track, aim to do it in 7 minutes next time. The less time you have, the more inclined you will be to take action. Even if you have unlimited time, create artificial deadlines and make yourself achieve the tasks within those deadlines.

3. Use the Gun-to-the-Head Technique

Imagine a terrorist came and put a gun to your head and told you, "Get that task done today or I pull the trigger." What would you do? Would you delay your task and browse the internet while you casually talk to your colleagues? Or would you diligently spend every minute working on the project? The "Gun-to-the-Head" technique is to imagine that your life is in danger and that unless you do the task you're going to die. Once our body activates our survival instinct, we go above and beyond to do things that we otherwise deemed impossible.

Imagine someone put a gun to your head and told you to run 10 miles. You would run faster than an Olympic runner. However, if you had the comfort of staying inside and watching movies, running 10 miles would seem like an exhausting task for you. It's all about perspective. Once you run out of options and you're feeling unproductive, simply imagine someone put a gun to your temple and forced you to do what needs to be done. Remember the phrase: "When you have a why, you'll find a how.

Conclusion

This book is your wake-up call. It's the sign you've been waiting for!

You have the techniques. Now, it's high time to put them to use.

STOP HOLDING OUT!

This book sheds light on the biggest problems in daily motivation and self-discipline. To succeed, implement what resonated with you the most. Consume all the information. Try it out. Use this book as a reminder when you forget basic principles, to keep you on track and kick you in the butt when you start slipping.

Do you remember all those times when you told yourself, "I'll do it when I'm ready"? Now is the time — your "one day" has come! You know exactly what you need to do in order to achieve your dreams. If you've held off your purpose in life for an unknown date, if you've held back your energy and hoped for a better time — remember that there is no better time than the present moment to start.

If we leave you with anything, it's to have faith in yourself.

You will have many downturns along your journey. You will experience a lot of upsides too.

Discover who you are, discover where you're headed, and take action.

All humans are flawed, but the techniques here would help us live with our flaws. We hope you've developed a better understanding as to the mysterious ways human nature works and how our biology is wired to function against our interests. We hope you get to know who you are and grow self-awareness through trials and tribulations.

Our evolutionary nature and our goals in modern society conflict with each other. To make our evolutionary nature and modern society work, we have to apply a set of techniques that combine the best sides of both.

Use resistance as your compass.

The friction we feel on our path is resistance — the most powerful force of nature. Resistance preserves the status quo: it's a protective mechanism that protects us from stepping into the unknown. Resistance prevents from changing thinking that it's in our best interest. To do anything different, we have to shock our system and push through resistance. Resistance serves as a compass to point us towards the things we should really be doing. If you feel unwilling to work on your goals, feel the resistance in your body. The resistance tells you exactly what to do. Resistance signals that you're preparing for something great, that something is right behind the corner. If you push through it, you will come out a completely different person on the other end. Deep down, you know what that "thing" is.

Don't delay your dreams — start now.

This book covered the most important methods and techniques to help you establish daily self-discipline. Now is the time to convert all you've learned into action.

As a last note, remember this fact: We're all different.

You have to create your own motivation, your own techniques, your own disciplines. You are your own person with your own goals, your own dreams and your own circumstances. You're not forced to implement every technique we teach, and it's not important to do them all at once. It's up to you to figure out what works for you and apply your own spins on the techniques, based on your own individual experiences of operating and goals in life.

Start by doing something — anything. See where life takes you. Your journey in life is different to the journey of 7 billion other humans on the planet. Once you discover what works for you, start doing and aim for the stars.

STOICISM IN MODERN LIFE

*Discover How to Develop Your Self
Awareness, Improve Your Mental Toughness
and Self Discipline in Today's World*

Table of Contents

Congratulations on purchasing Stoicism in Modern Life: Beginner's Guide

thank you for doing so!

This guide on the philosophy of stoicism is going to support you in understanding what stoicism is, how it works, and why it is so imperative to harness stoicism for you to achieve success in your life, both professionally and personally. The ancient art of stoicism is perhaps one of the strongest philosophies that can teach you how to master the art of your mind and start taking control over your life in a powerful and meaningful way.

Thanks again for choosing this book! Every effort was made to ensure it is full of as much useful information as possible. Please enjoy!

Introduction

Throughout this book, I am going to share with you the best ways that you can harness and develop stoicism and use it in your daily life. From your relationships to your career, you are going to discover just what it takes to really change your life from the inside out and experience massive shifts as a result. I realize that changes are not something that can happen overnight; it happens gradually. But I am confident that if you begin applying the skills that I teach you right here in this very book that you will be able to start experiencing massive transformations quickly. As you continue applying these skill, you will continue to experience greater changes and transformations as you grow through life with the inner strength needed to overcome anything that you may have to face.

I encourage you to realize that your transformation is going to come from two significant places: understanding and consistency. Make sure that you take the time to fully understand and comprehend the concepts that I am sharing with you and that they make sense to you as you read through this book. That way, when it comes to discovering how you can apply these very techniques into your own life, you can do so in a complete and well-rounded manner. Once you have discovered exactly how to apply them, you are going to need to apply them consistently so that you can continue experiencing changes. As they say, "Rome wasn't built in a day, but they were laying bricks every hour." Change is not something that is achieved in one leap, but as long as you continue working towards your desires, then plenty can be accomplished.

You may be wondering what stoicism is exactly. Perhaps you have heard of the term a few times before but you weren't clear on what it was, or maybe this is your first time hearing it and you have never even considered that it might be a thing. So, before we dive in, I want to make sure that you have a clear understanding of just what it is that you are about to learn for the duration of the time that we are going to spend together! After all, your time is important, and you want to make sure that you are investing it into something that is actually going to help you have a major impact on your life.

Stoicism, according to the dictionary, is "the endurance of pain or hardship without a display of feelings and without complaint." On a surface level, this might sound somewhat harsh and outdated since we are currently living amongst a time where emotions are highly praised and are encouraged in most situations. While I am not saying that emotions should ever be discouraged or bottled up, what I am saying is that there is an appropriate manner in which emotions should be handled, especially in certain situations. By learning about stoicism, you develop a sense of emotional intelligence that enables you to both experience and express your emotions while also gaining the benefits of not letting your emotions take over you. Despite stoicism being a form of emotional intelligence, you should realize that this is only one element of what stoicism truly is. This particular philosophy not only educates you on key aspects of emotional intelligence, but also supports you in developing mental toughness, resiliency, and the ability to be more accepting of both yourself and others in your life. By embodying all of these elements of stoicism, you can develop a sense of maturity that supports you in experiencing a fuller life both personally and professionally as you equip yourself with the proper tools to navigate any situation you may face in life.

If you are ready to begin embracing the power of stoicism and learning about how you can develop it and apply it to your own life, then I would say it is time that we begin! Please take a moment to prepare yourself for what might be one of the most life-changing experiences you will ever endure. And, of course, be sure to enjoy!

Chapter 1: Understanding Stoicism

You now have a basic understanding of what stoicism is in regard to it being a form of emotional intelligence and mental resiliency, but you still do not truly understand the full concept of stoicism. Stoicism is a rather complex concept that actually has a rich history in ancient Greece. To truly understand what it is, how it works, and what purpose it is designed to achieve, you need to look at it from the earliest developments of its philosophy. From there, you can begin to understand why this particular skill is so valuable, and how it continues to relate to the modern world even though we have evolved so much from those early days.

In this chapter, we are going to explore important concepts around stoicism, such as its Greek roots and how it relates to modern-day living. You are also going to develop an understanding of what the real goal of stoicism is and why it is actually an incredibly valuable tool despite the fact that it was poorly executed for many years in our recent history. This way, you can understand exactly how stoicism relates to you and why it is such an important concept for you to grasp and comprehend.

Ancient Greek School of Philosophy

Stoicism was originally introduced to society back in the ancient Greek school of philosophy by a gentleman named Zeno of Citium. It was originally founded in c. 300 B.C.E. Inspired by Cynics, Zeno was a disciple of Socrates and spent his life as a philosopher, attempting to understand the purpose of life and the meaning of various human realities and experiences. One of Zeno's most influential followers was named Chrysippus, and it was Chrysippus who was actually responsible for molding the philosophy that is now known as stoicism.

The majority of scholars who educated themselves on Greek philosophy and stoicism typically divided the history of stoicism into three different phases: early Stoa, middle Stoa, and late Stoa. Early Stoa was the initial development of stoicism as founded by Zeno in his school of philosophy. The latter two phases were followed up by both the Greeks and the Romans who continued to try and understand the concepts of stoicism and develop upon it, molding it into modern-day stoicism. It was during the latter phase where Romans truly fostered the idea of stoicism, with some of the Empires praising it and cherishing it and others persecuting it.

Back in these early days, stoicism was a philosophy that was supposed to teach individuals how to develop self-control so that they could overcome destructive emotions. True stoicism was not designed to encourage people to extinguish or ignore their emotions, but instead to discover how they could transform those emotions through the voluntary absence of worldly pleasures, also known as "Asceticism". As an ancient leader, this would mean that you would have the self-control to feel emotions of anger or jealousy without immediately acting upon them so as to seek immediate worldly pleasure through revenge. Instead, one would willingly abstain from the pursuit of pleasure and find a resolution that worked in a less intense or cruel manner.

The usage of stoicism was intended to support a person in developing a clearer sense of judgment, a deeper sense of inner calmness, and the freedom from their suffering. It was not implemented as merely a skill or a belief system but instead was used as a way of life by those who wished to implement it into their daily living habits and rituals. Stoicism, then, was about an ethical way of living that would enable people to experience their emotions without immediately acting upon them in excessive or sometimes animalistic ways. Some argue that it was fundamental in our ability to evolve further as species to be able to live in a more civilized manner amongst other humans.

The Purpose for Stoicism in Society

Stoicism is a rather complex tool that can be used to elevate people out of many varieties of worldly suffering. To get a deeper understanding of how, we are going to look at the many ways that stoicism can help end needless suffering and promote a more positive and healthy society in general. The same concepts that allowed stoicism to be so powerful and helpful back in ancient Greece and Rome are the same reasons as to why it continues to be such a powerful concept in modern society.

Perhaps, one of the biggest benefits ancient civilizations gained from stoicism was the development of emotional intelligence which leads to individuals being able to train themselves into choosing between emotional and rational thought responses. This may have been highly fundamental in our history by preventing humans from having aggressive and violent reactions to their emotions so that they could begin having more intentional and thoughtful responses. For example, say an ancient Greek *archon*, or ruler, had been slighted by someone and experienced an intense burst of anger because he was angry that someone would defy his absolute power. Without stoicism, that ruler may simply sentence the individual to death and have him murdered publicly as a display of absolute power and to warn others off of wronging him. On an individual level, this may lead to deep inner feelings of trauma and guilt, particularly if the *archon* later regretted his decision and wished that he had spared the life of the other individual. This was not an uncommon experience back in the days of ancient Greece, where people would murder just about anyone out of anger, even their loved ones. Obviously, this leads to intense experiences of guilt and shame, and deep feelings of grief and despair which would lead to intense worldly suffering within the person who had experienced the aggressive outrage. With stoicism, the ruler would experience the intense anger but choose to experience it passively, or in a way that allows them to recognize and experience it but not act in such an intense and violent manner. As a result, they would avoid the needless endurance of guilt, shame, grief, and despair at the loss of an individual at their own hand.

While intense violent outbursts are not as common in the modern world, they still can happen from time to time, and they can still have just as negative of an impact on both parties as they ever did. While we do not exercise things like the death penalty or intense violent punishments like we once did, there are still many unkind things that people do as a way to exercise revenge against those who have upset or wronged them. Embodying stoicism can help prevent needless suffering by helping you not have such intense emotional outbursts towards those around you, thus allowing you and the other person to avoid unnecessary feelings of suffering.

Another way that stoicism can avoid feelings of suffering is by teaching a healthy detachment from feelings of loss, lack, or desperation. In both ancient and modern societies, many people have lived in conditions that are often deemed less than ideal by those living in them and by those living around them. Unfortunately, no real solutions have yet been presented to help every person in every society live a comfortable life free of any worldly sufferings such as poverty or hunger. While stoicism cannot earn you a greater income or feed a hungry tummy, it can prevent you from experiencing intense victimhood from these types of worldly experiences. In that detachment, you can see yourself as being separate from your worldly suffering and able to still experience joy and happiness despite the troubles that are happening in your life. This may not be equal to increasing your income or finding food during hungry times, but it can prevent you from experiencing these with the added stress of inner suffering and pain. For some people, the liberation from their own inner suffering is enough for them to find a solution to increase their income or find food to eat.

There are many additional types of worldly sufferings that people may have and have faced throughout the history of humankind. Stoicism may not always be the worldly answer to helping you get your hands on the resources that you need to liberate yourself from challenges, but it can certainly be a powerful tool in helping you prevent additional suffering. As such, stoicism can be a profound way to help you make the best out of any situation and use yourself as your own best tool in helping you to discover and experience a better way of living.

The Goal of Stoicism

The goal of stoicism is ultimately to end the experience of inner suffering by providing individuals with the freedom from passion (or anguish) through the pursuit of reason. By fostering the ability to be objective, unemotional, and mentally clear regarding any worldly challenges that a person may face, they can gain a greater sense of control over their worldly responses and avoid further suffering. So, in a very basic sense, the goal is to end unnecessary inner suffering in individuals through stoicism.

When you choose to embrace stoicism in your own life, your goal is not to experience no suffering at all but to detach from worldly suffering and eliminate the development of unnecessary suffering. So, instead of experiencing a great amount of anger and acting on it, thus also bringing about a great amount of guilt, you would instead experience anger and make the inner choice to experience it passively. Through this passive experience, you can overcome the feelings of guilt and shame and avoid further unnecessary suffering from within.

Of course, developing stoicism is not the easiest and most natural thing in a society that often uses shame and guilt as a way to pressure people into doing certain things throughout their lives. However, learning how to embrace stoicism will allow you to teach yourself to intentionally and willingly step back from the unnecessary suffering of these pressures and begin to take more control over yourself and your inner emotional experiences. This way, you can start experiencing the world around you more objectively and with more control over what your actual experience is, rather than feeling pushed around by the society around you.

Why Stoicism Is Not Emotional Avoidance

In recent Western history, a form of "skill" was being taught that educated people on the importance of avoiding their emotions so that they could go through life without the needless suffering of emotions. In this way, philosophies like stoicism were somewhat extorted to attempt to pressure people into accepting the often unfair realities that were being dealt with them by their superiors. Bosses, for example, would encourage an extorted form of stoicism to their employees to avoid having employees that would complain and attempt to revolt against the system in favor of staying quiet, calm, and compliant. This was taught on such a wide-scale level that to this day, many elders that continue to live in our modern world experience intense challenges when it comes to expressing or experiencing any form of emotion in a positive and healthy manner.

Anytime we discuss something like stoicism, which is the willful abstinence from intense emotional reactions, it is important that we also recognize that it is not about the *avoidance* of emotions altogether. Instead, it is about recognizing and experiencing emotions but intentionally choosing to address them more constructively and productively. This is why stoicism is often related to emotional intelligence: because it supports you in choosing reasonable and rational decisions over emotional ones.

Exercising stoicism in the modern world, free of the exploitation of those who attempted to profit and benefit off of others' complete lack of emotions, does not mean living your life void of emotions. Rather, it means living your life in harmony with your emotions and learning how to exercise them and use them in a way that empowers you but refrains from you making irrational decisions that lead to further suffering later on. In this way, your emotions, which are an important part of your human experience, continue to be honored and valued, but they do not become a hindrance for your ability to experience a positive Earthly life.

How Stoicism Relates to Modern Daily Living

The modern world is heavily driven by stress, which can be filled with unnecessary amounts of pressure and overwhelming emotions. If you live in modern-day society, chances are that you can pick apart many pieces of your daily life that are filled with stress, overwhelming emotions, and pressure from things that are considered normal or standard in modern living. For example, you might find that having to wake up early to go to a career you do not really enjoy can be stressful. Aside from work, there are many other everyday stresses that people face in their lives, too: traffic, not enough time to get everything done, messy homes, overwhelmed schedules, feeling obligated to spend time with people they may not like, and so forth. Many parts of our modern lives are plagued by stress which can lead to emotions like anger, jealousy, resentment, disappointment, guilt, shame, and other painful emotions that resemble suffering.

By learning how to apply stoicism into your everyday life, especially in the modern world, you can learn how to begin experiencing freedom from these types of suffering so that you can enjoy more freedom in your daily life. Through stoicism, you can detach from the feelings of frustration in traffic, stress in going to work, or jealousy in following people on social media who flaunt the things that you wish you had in your own life. You also allow yourself to develop mental toughness and resiliency so that you can face challenging experiences in your life, including challenging emotional experiences, without such intense feelings of suffering attached to your experiences.

As you will learn throughout this book, there are many ways that true stoicism can continue to serve us in our modern world. By embracing these methods and building your mental toughness and your ability to choose reasonable thinking over emotional thinking, you can start making decisions for yourself that will improve your quality of living. As such, your suffering associated with stress and other stress-related emotions will begin to minimize as you begin enjoying a more peaceful and positive life.

Chapter 2: Mental Toughness

The first step in becoming more stoic is learning how to build mental toughness, as mental toughness is a key tool in helping you overcome emotional responses to life. When you develop your mental toughness, you enable yourself to have the mental strength required to recognize emotional experiences and rationally think your way through the process. You also equip yourself with the tool that you need to overcome challenges without feeling defeated and allowing yourself to wallow into a victim mentality.

In this chapter, you are going to begin developing your own mental toughness so that you can begin developing the strength required to navigate challenging situations without feeling so overwhelmed and overcome by emotions. This way, you can start laying the foundation for your own personal ability to detach from challenging emotional situations and choose to passively experience your emotions in a way that reduces your personal suffering. As you go through this chapter, make sure that you understand that developing mental toughness may sound easy on paper, but in all reality, it is not always as easy as it may sound. In a society that is plagued by stress and stress-related emotional struggles, mental illness and mental chaos or overwhelming emotions are extremely common and all of these can lead to it taking longer for you to develop your mental toughness. Realize that your goal here is not to suddenly develop a "thicker skin," but instead to start understanding and enforcing the practices associated with mental toughness so that you can begin seeing results from your practice. If you remain consistent and practice these tools to the best of your ability, then in due time, you will begin experiencing all of the benefits of mental toughness. While it may not be an immediate change of pace, it will be one that is certainly worth your while, and that will pave the way for you to have many more positive experiences going forward.

Why Mental Toughness Matters

When it comes to developing stoicism, or the capacity to approach challenging emotional matters with intention and focus, mental toughness is the foundation of your practice because it equips you with the strength to control your mind. Our minds are incredibly powerful tools that have the capacity to support us or hinder us in achieving the things that we desire in life, depending on how we are using them. Many people never intentionally take control over their minds and live their entire lives being victimized by their mental processes. This often happens because people do not realize that their minds are only working instinctively and with the intention of producing survival: our minds have the capacity to be used for great things, but they do not naturally do so. The people who achieve great things have developed mental toughness by developing and harnessing the tools required to actually take control over their minds and make a difference.

See, the average human mind values pleasure over anything else. Pleasure, or feelings of positive emotions and sensations, gives the mind the belief that we are experiencing something positive and that is friendly to our survival. When we experience something that is not pleasurable, it is not believed to be supportive of our survival, and therefore the mind is either neutral or negative towards it in favor of something more pleasurable. As a result, we will often instinctively behave in ways that please us, even if the acquisition of that pleasure seems strange or uncomfortable in and of itself. A basic example of this is seen with procrastination: often people procrastinate because it is more pleasurable to do nothing or relax than it is to actually engage in the task that they are putting off. Once procrastination begins to produce stress, it stops becoming pleasurable, so the person jumps into the task and tries to accomplish it rapidly to eliminate the stress and come back to the point of pure pleasure.

The problem with the human mind favoring pure pleasure is that it can be so sneaky in how it works on a subconscious level that many people have no idea what is actually driving their pleasure-seeking behaviors. To them, their behaviors may be normal or natural, and the belief that anything should be done in any other way is unnatural and uncomfortable. They may begin to produce mental beliefs or protests to justify why *they* are incapable of changing their ways when really it is just their human mind attempting to protect its access to pleasure.

When you develop mental toughness, you learn how to put off pleasure by delaying gratification through mental skills that allow you to see the benefits in doing so. These skills are developed in a way that allows you to take control over your mind and consciously control the way that pleasure is acquired so that you are not acquiring it through ways that actually increases displeasure later on. You do so by developing tools that are capable of increasing your conscious control over your mind, such as clarity, the ability to be unbiased, the capacity to exercise rational thinking, and mental resiliency. The more you develop these skills, the stronger they become and the easier it is for you to rely on them even when times are challenging. As a result, you are able to experience greater mental toughness which will pave the way for the rest of your development of stoicism.

Developing Your Mental Clarity

The first step in developing mental toughness is developing your mental clarity, which essentially means building your self-awareness and learning how to consciously recognize behaviors that you may have. When you experience mental clarity, your capacity to have a clear understanding of your emotions, your thoughts, and the stimuli that trigger all of these experiences is increased. It becomes easier for you to understand yourself and comprehend both your instinctive responses and your rational responses because you are able to see yourself through a clearer lens.

When you experience mental clarity, you are experiencing life through mental alertness that free of stress. Because it is stress-free, you can see things as they are, rather than through your own inner perceptions that may result in you shaping the world around you in an unrealistic manner. As a result, mental clarity will also help you establish things like the ability to be unbiased or to rationally respond to situations without being hijacked by your emotions.

You develop mental clarity through a series of mental and physical practices that can help you overcome the typical triggers that lead to a lack of mental clarity in the first place. This includes mentally learning how to overcome emotions and stressors that may prevent mental clarity and physically creating a space around you that does not stimulate additional stress and mental clutter.

To begin mastering your mindset to reduce mental clutter, you need to start learning how to manage and overcome stress. The three ways that psychologists most recommend doing this is through developing a routine, learning how to tap into "flow," and preventing yourself from multitasking. Routines are particularly powerful when combined with the abstinence from multitasking because they help you get into a system where you know exactly what you need to do and when. This results in you staying focused and on-task longer because you know exactly what you need to be doing and you trust that there is enough time in your day for you to achieve everything, so you stop trying to do it all at once. At first, getting into a routine will be challenging as you are likely already used to being all over the place and living in mental chaos, but as you begin to foster a daily routine that does not require you to multitask, it will get easier. In regard to getting into your "flow" state, both having a routine and staying on track with one specific task at a time will help you get into the flow and find your groove in getting things done.

To begin mastering your physical environment for the sake of developing mental clarity, the task is quite simple: declutter. You need to maintain a clean and welcoming environment that does not have too much for your eye to focus on or look at, as this helps keep your mind clear as well. By keeping your environment clean and relaxing, you can ensure that you will not be overwhelmed by environmental distractions that may prevent you from getting focused or staying focused. This includes keeping your home clean and comforting while also favoring other environments that are more comfortable and relaxing as well, including when you go out for entertainment. Of course, enjoying upbeat and busy environments from time to time can be a great way to build excitement; spending too much time in these environments can further increase stress and decrease your mental clarity. Seek to spend more of your downtime in environments such as relaxing cafes, calm restaurants, quiet parks, and other comforting places. You should spend time in these places with friends when hanging out, but also on your own so that you can break away from the hustle and bustle of your daily life to get some calm and peace away from your normal routines. This really helps to detach your mind from everyday stress and keep you more in tune and in sync with your body and mind.

Learning to Remain Unbiased

Being biased means that you are approaching life with a very specific set of opinions and perceptions on the world around you and that you are attempting to fit everything in your life into these perceptions.

Anytime something happens in your world, you will be quick to judge it and attempt to formulate an opinion on it, which can quickly result in you generating unnecessary suffering. Think about it: how often has something happened around you that should have been irrelevant to you but generated a significant amount of stress in your life for no apparent reason? Maybe your friend did something when you were nowhere near them, and it had no impact on you whatsoever, but you were upset with them because of the very fact that they would do such a thing. Or, maybe a coworker didn't get something done the day before, so you had to do it and you were angry about it because, even though it didn't change the fact that you still had to be at your job for 8 hours, now you had one more thing to do. Perhaps your judgment and anger get even more trivial sometimes, like when you are driving and you see one person cut another person off, and you become angry because of an ignorant driver on the road. Even though they had absolutely no impact on you, your judgment on their behavior resulted in you growing angry with them and produced unnecessary suffering on your behalf.

In our society, we are not taught about how we can detach from our opinions and perceptions and see the world through unbiased eyes which often results in us developing feelings of anger, jealousy, and resentment towards other people. The problem is, these feelings are completely unnecessary because, in many cases, the experiences that lead to these emotions do not even concern us, and if they do, the impact they have on us is minuscule.

Two things work against us that impact our tendency to be biased towards negativity in our lives: negativity bias and a society of individuals who are not consciously aware of their own negativity bias. Negativity bias is a survival mechanism that allows us to recall negative experiences that we have had so that we can avoid having them again. From a survival standpoint, negativity bias makes a lot of sense and can be highly useful in helping us avoid, say, getting eaten by a cougar in the middle of the forest. Unfortunately, it doesn't do us much good living in a society where we are mostly safe from the world around us. Instead, it often leads to us feeling intensely negative about things that do not really matter, and it can grow into full-blown pessimism if we are not taught to manage our negativity bias.

What happens when you have an entire community of people not managing their negativity bias is a community of people who are negative and pessimistic. This negativity spreads like wildfire and can cause several people to feel far more intense feelings of negativity and anger within just a few minutes. You have probably experienced it yourself: when you walk into your office and your boss is in a bad mood, and then suddenly the entire office building seems to be in a bad mood as well, including yourself. Negativity bias can produce serious negative consequences when people are not consciously aware of what it is and how it is negatively impacting their lives.

The best way to remain unbiased is to become self-aware and start paying attention to how your own negativity works and how you may be contributing to your own negative feelings. By recognizing your behaviors and the way that you contribute to negativity in your own life, you can start understanding how it impacts you and how your own perceptions are impacting your mood. As a result, you can start opening your mind to seeing your daily experiences from all angles and recognizing that nothing is ever as it seems, even if you have plenty to convince you otherwise. Try and see things from everyone's perspective and, as you do, detach from your own perspective enough to be unbiased from your experiences and perception.

As you do, suddenly that person that cut you off becomes a human in your mind, and you realize that they may just be someone who is rushing to the hospital to have their baby or home to see their family that they miss so dearly. Your boss who was previously arrogant and selfish may just be someone who came from a tough youth and had to fight their way to the top and has never let go of their fighting spirit. Your friend who made a poor decision when they were out on the weekend is just a human who decided for themselves, and one that had absolutely no impact on you whatsoever. And you, you become a human who cares deeply about everyone else, to the point that you have let their actions impact your own emotions. Everyone becomes a lot more *human* when you choose to release your bias and see people, and situations, for what they truly are.

Rationally Responding to Passionate Emotions

Emotions can be *intense,* and in a person who lacks mental toughness, they can be crippling. In the psychological field, when intense emotions overcome someone and cloud their rational judgment, it is known as "emotional hijacking." Emotional hijacking is most common in people who lack the ability to remain unbiased and see things rationally, so they end up experiencing intense, passionate emotions that are difficult to navigate through. This is where stoicism comes into play: it emphasizes the importance of handling these intense, passionate emotions through the power of mental resiliency and toughness.

Learning how to respond rationally to your emotional responses takes time as it requires you to learn first how to begin changing your instinctive response to emotional experiences. For example, when you experience sadness, it is likely that you have an instinctive habitual response to that sadness that begins occurring almost immediately after the sadness is triggered. Maybe you begin crying, even if it is just a small amount of sadness, or perhaps you find yourself getting angry because you were raised to believe that sadness was something to be ashamed about. This type of immediate response can trigger an even more intense emotional response, all of which launches as a habit of the initial emotion being triggered. For that reason, the first step in developing freedom from your intense and passionate emotional responses is to start by understanding what triggers are causing them. When you can begin to identify your emotional triggers, you can start to pinpoint the exact moment that your habitual emotional responses are preparing to launch and you can interrupt them with a more conscious response.

Say you are at work one day and your boss lost a piece of paperwork that you are *sure* you gave them, but they insist that it is your fault that the piece is missing. Perhaps this is a very important piece that places a lot of pressure on both you and your boss, and the fact that it is missing and you cannot prove that it was not you who lost it means that your job could be on the line. A stressful experience like this could easily trigger you to become angry and, if you were acting passionately, it could result in a massively angry outburst. This outburst would add to the stress of the situation and may result in you losing your job because of how unprofessionally you handled yourself during a challenging experience. As a result, you would experience even greater discomfort and anger, as well as a significantly higher amount of suffering due to your own emotional response.

If, however, you were to recognize that intense anger is starting to boil up and you were to choose to respond differently, you may start regaining rational control over yourself before your emotions boiled over. You might then find yourself being able to level out your emotions and support your boss in finding or replacing the important paperwork so that you could both calm down from the stress of the experience and move on. It may seem unreasonable for you to have to correct your bosses mistake. However, if you weigh the pros and cons of both sides of the situation, you may realize that this is a significantly smaller amount of suffering than if you were to react emotionally.

Building Mental Resiliency

Part of mental toughness is being able to bounce back from challenging situations time and again. Lindsay Teague Moreno, a self-made millionaire, claims that her mental resiliency is exactly what got her to her entrepreneurial success. In her words, she claimed that she could be at work all day and get knocked down over and over all day long and still show up the next day and walk in the door ready to work. Individuals who have experienced any capacity of personal or professional success in their lives will always tell you that their ability to get back up and try again was the exact reason for their success. Our society even has a series of quotes around this very topic that are intended to help people recognize the value of mental resiliency. Quotes like "get back on the horse," "fall seven times, get up eight," "no hoof, no horse," or "it's just a bad day, not a bad life" are all meant to remind us about the power of our mental resiliency. Still, not everyone is fully aware of how to tap into this resiliency and actually use it to change their lives.

In stoicism, building mental resiliency means that you can allow yourself to bounce back from intense emotions quicker, allowing you to regain ration in even the most challenging of situations. As you begin to develop your mental resiliency, you will find that enduring emotionally trying situations becomes easier because you are capable of bouncing back emotionally. In many experiences we have in life, a lack of mental resiliency can lead to an increase in emotions because, not only do you find yourself facing emotional struggles, but you also find yourself ill-equipped to overcome them. As a result, you may fear the feeling of being trapped in your emotions or unable to overcome them. This fear or uncertainty does not rise because you truly cannot overcome your emotions, but because you are not yet equipped with what you need to do so, which leaves you feeling fearful. Rationally, you cannot think of how you can reasonably get through your emotional struggles, so as your emotions grow, your irrational mind kicks in and leaves you feeling as though these emotions may never change. For this reason, mental resiliency will help you not only overcome life challenges but also emotional challenges and develop your stoicism more strongly.

Building the type of mental resiliency that is going to allow you to bounce back from challenging times takes patience and practice, but if you keep at it, you will discover that it's actually not as hard as it may seem. In fact, in most circumstances, it is simply about shifting your perspective and realizing that not everything is as challenging as it may seem. When you can begin considering your life through a particular perspective that actually serves your growth, rather than one that keeps you trapped in the belief that you can't make it happen, mental resiliency becomes easier. This is because you begin looking at things with the desire to grow through them and succeed, rather than feeling trapped in fear of the challenges that you face.

Creating this perspective takes practice as you begin conditioning yourself to look for ways forward, rather than admitting defeat and choosing to stay where you are at. This may sound simple enough, but for many people, the practice of changing their habitual thought patterns is particularly challenging, especially if you have never consciously taken control over your thoughts before. The best way to do this is to begin by having a mantra that you can carry with you to support you in staying clear on your goals so that you can regain mental control over your experience. Your mantra can be anything from "I choose not to react until I decide how to respond" to "I can overcome this." Once you choose a mantra, repeat it to yourself every time you face challenges in your life, particularly those around your emotions. This way, you can start conditioning yourself to endure trying times so that you no longer find yourself trapped in the false beliefs of being incapable of overcoming challenges.

After repeating your mantra to yourself, you need to begin consciously changing the way that you are viewing the situation so that you can take yourself out of victim mentality and start putting yourself into a victor mentality. A common tool for reframing challenging experiences is swapping out "Why is this happening to me?" to "How is this happening for me?" or "What can I learn from this?" When you begin to look at situations with the desire to either develop a greater understanding around them or to develop a solution, it becomes easier for you to bounce back. This is because your mind becomes focused on how you can move forward, rather than fearful and afraid of moving forward at all.

Maintaining Your Mental Toughness in Challenging Times

One place where many life changes tend to fall flat is when we are faced with particularly difficult challenges that trigger us in all of the most uncomfortable ways possible. If you have ever tried to make major changes in your life, chances are you have found yourself completely abandoning all of your adjustments as soon as things got really challenging because you were ill-equipped for what you needed to stay on track. I don't want you going through all of the efforts of building stoicism in your life only to find yourself experiencing major setbacks when you face challenges, so I have highlighted some great tools for you to stay on track even when it's a challenge.

Step 1: Slow Down

The first thing you need to do any time you face a challenge in your life that has you wanting to jump into old patterns and conditioning is to slow down. When you slow down, you give yourself the capacity to ease up on your emotional reaction and restore your ability to make a rational response to the situation at hand. Sometimes, when you are really in the heat of things, drawing back on your passion can be quite challenging, and you may find yourself struggling to stay aligned with your new stoic ways. In these situations, you may do best to completely remove yourself from the situation for a few minutes before returning with a clearer, more rational frame of mind. If you are pressed on time, a simple few minutes in the bathroom intentionally calming down and gaining some perspective over the situation can help you improve your response when you head back into the friction of a passionate situation.

If you have more time, consider slowing down your approach altogether and breaking it down into smaller steps. By paying attention to the next step, and then the next step, and then the next one, you prevent yourself from looking too far out into the future and give yourself time to make better choices *now*. You also give yourself the opportunity to see that the situation is not as large or scary as it may have seemed in the first place, which can draw back on some of the feelings of fear and frustration and allow you to address it with more rational thinking.

Step 2: Get Some Perspective

Once you have slowed the situation down, you need to get some perspective around it. Start by getting some perspective on how big the situation truly is so that you can remind yourself that virtually nothing is impossible to face, even if it seems gigantic and scary early on. Instead of allowing yourself to sit and be intimidated by the challenges that you face, sit and spend some time trying to understand them and trying to reframe them for yourself. Focus on how you can frame the challenge so that it seems manageable and achievable, rather than overwhelming and scary.

Then, go on to start searching for ways that you can overcome the challenge or even parts of the challenge as soon as possible. If you do not have all of the answers yet, start in the areas that you understand and move on from there. This way, you can at least get started and begin achieving success in overcoming your challenge. As you go along, you will likely learn everything you need to overcome your challenge even further, thus allowing you to move forward completely. Before you know it, your challenge will be a thing of the past and you will have successfully overcome it.

Step 3: Ask for Help

If you are really struggling with a challenge or if you do not have the answers you need to proceed, it is never wrong to ask for help in overcoming your challenge. Reaching out for someone who knows how to help you with your specific challenge is a great way to learn what you need to move forward successfully. Whether you need a counselor to help you manage your emotions, a coach to help you manage your time or your business strategies, or a friend to help you manage your thoughts, there is always someone out there who can help you. Simply be willing to reach out and know what it is that you need, and you can feel confident that someone will be on the other side to help you. Remember, asking for help is not a sign of weakness, but recognizing that we need help is a demonstration of strength.

Chapter 3: Discipline of Self

After you have built your foundation of mental toughness, you need to build your discipline of self. This discipline is going to help you continue building your mental toughness and conditioning yourself to use that mental toughness to develop your stoicism. As you develop your self-discipline, you will discover how you can start managing yourself through challenging emotional experiences, as well as how you can create a life that avoids unnecessary suffering. This is going to enable you to have the resiliency and knowledge to help you choose to respond to situations, rather than to react to challenging situations as they arise. Through this, you will be more stoic in your responses, which will lead to less suffering and greater growth in your life both personally and professionally.

In this chapter, we are going to focus on areas of self-discipline that are going to directly support you in managing your emotions better, as well as reducing the amount of unnecessary suffering you may face directly through your actions. This way, you can start living a life that does not produce unnecessary challenges and a life that has a greater self-discipline in facing the challenges that arise.

Accepting Yourself

Self-acceptance is one of the most powerful forms of self-discipline that you can embrace because it allows you to accept yourself as you are and stop putting pressure on yourself to be someone that you are not. Self-acceptance does not mean that you are not willing to look for opportunities to grow, but instead, that you are willing to accept when you are not embodying the growth that you wish to represent in each moment. When you accept yourself, forgiving yourself for mistakes and accepting that you are human and experience human experiences, including emotions, become significantly easier because you stop resenting yourself for your human nature. This means that any time you make a mistake, fail to move forward due to a lack of understanding, or experience an unwanted emotional outburst or setback, you accept yourself in spite of what happened. With true self-disciplined self-acceptance, you accept yourself even in the times when you feel that you have acted unacceptably because you accept yourself for exactly who you are in every single moment.

Being able to accept yourself this deeply can be challenging, especially in a society where we are often taught that we are only able to be accepted when we act or behave in a certain way. However, it is imperative as it allows you to accept yourself and love yourself even when you act 'wrongly,' which prevents the unnecessary pain and suffering associated with *not* accepting yourself. It also ensures that you are willing to move on quicker because you do not hold yourself back through your own contempt and hatred towards your unacceptable actions and behaviors. So, not only does it allow you to prevent the unnecessary suffering of a lack of self-acceptance, but it also allows you to prevent the unnecessary suffering of everything that follows that lack of self-acceptance.

Accepting yourself deeply and unconditionally takes time and practice, but it is essential if you want to experience true growth in your life. For that reason, you need to devote time every day to intentionally affirming your self-acceptance to yourself and your willingness to stay in acceptance with yourself even during challenging times. Of course, this is not always easy to achieve, so you are going to need to practice this every single day, even when it feels challenging or you feel as though you truly do not accept yourself at that moment. Realize that the thing you are not accepting of when you make a mistake in your life is not *you* personally, but your behavior and the consequences of that behavior. When you realize that you yourself are not the unacceptable one but your behavior was, it becomes easier to realize that you are still worthy of acceptance, even if your behavior was out of alignment.

Another great way to start building self-acceptance is to start journaling every time you feel that you are struggling to accept yourself. Writing down the reasons why you feel like you do not accept yourself and spending some time understanding your own true feelings and experiences can help you move beyond your unwillingness to accept yourself. This is because often when you see what you are thinking on paper, you realize how unkind or unrealistic it is, and it becomes easier for you to disown that way of thinking. You grow to realize how it is not serving you or how it is actually harming you, and you discover that there may be a better way: such as choosing self-acceptance.

Accepting Things Beyond Yourself

Acceptance with self-discipline needs to go beyond self-acceptance and into the acceptance of everything and experiences that you have in your life, too. When you live a life where you frequently do not accept what is happening around you or the people who you are surrounded by, it can present many unnecessary experiences of suffering. This suffering can arise because you feel intense emotions to everything around you on a consistent basis, for a myriad of different reasons. For example, perhaps, because you are unable to accept your family as they are, you find yourself angry and annoyed every time you are in their presence. As a result, you are unable to enjoy the presence of your family even if you genuinely feel as though you love them, which can lead to suffering. You may feel as though you are obligated to see them due to your love for them and your familial connection, or because you will experience alternative forms of suffering if you do not. So, whether you choose to see your family and suffer in their presence or avoid your family and suffer in their absence, you will still experience suffering because of your own inability to accept your family.

The same can be said for your job, your financial well-being, your home, your community, and anything else that exists beyond yourself. When you cannot accept the things around you, your surroundings become a constant source of discomfort and pain which can lead to you having constant feelings of depression, disappointment, frustration, and anguish. Learn to accept situations and people as they enable you to bypass unnecessary suffering and begin cultivating a deeper sense of appreciation for the life that you have. As a result, you cannot only avoid suffering but also cultivate contentment through the very act of acceptance.

Learning how to accept the things beyond you starts with you discovering how you can tolerate the presence of various things, experiences, or people without taking everything so personally. When you realize that other people's actions or behaviors are not an attack on you personally, as well as with your circumstances and things in your environment, acceptance becomes easier. This is because you can realize that the world around you is not victimizing you, but instead, you are simply experiencing it. It is within your mind that the victimizing begins when you genuinely believe that every person, thing, and experience is intended to be a personal attack on you.

You can also develop a greater sense of acceptance by recognizing that, in many cases, your perception of other people has something to teach you about yourself. By seeking out what that lesson may be, you offer yourself the capacity to understand why you are so bothered by others and how you can stop choosing to not accept others based on who they are, or circumstances based on what they are. See why you are so deeply bothered and why it feels as though you cannot overlook these things, and choose to find ways to overlook them and move on anyway. You always have a choice in your life, and you can choose to either let go of great friendships over small things or to accept things as they are and find a way to tolerate the fact that you cannot control others around you.

Maintaining Virtue and Kindness

Stoicism is not just about tolerating those around you and ignoring your own emotions, but rather, it is about learning how to manage those emotions and find more kind-hearted ways through them. For example, if you experience anger towards a certain situation, choosing to express that anger through words and finding a resolution calmly would become your goal. This way, you can experience your anger, discover a solution, and move forward from your anger without engaging in behaviors that can cause major consequences for both yourself and those around you. In stoicism, this is the ultimate goal because, through proper and intentional management of your emotions, you can avoid engaging in major blowouts that can lead to further emotional struggles such as guilt and shame.

In life, your virtue refers to your behaviors and how they reflect your moral standards in life. If you are someone with great virtue, then you are someone who has high morals and who lives up to those morals through your behaviors and your actions. Historically, virtue also reflected ones' purity physically and mentally, so it often involved maintaining your virginity until marriage so that you would be completely pure. In modern days, a virtue often coincides with kindness because people who possess high morals believe that those around them deserve to be treated with kindness and respect, so being kind to others is a symbol of virtue in a person.

Maintaining your own virtue and kindness truly is self-discipline because we are often compelled to behave in ways that abandon virtue and kindness based on the experience of our emotions. When you experience frustration, for example, you may become snappy and harsh in your tone, making everyone around you feel as though you are not respecting them and their feelings. Chances are, this reaction is not intentional or even conscious; it is a habitual emotional response to having your feelings triggered in a particular way. Likely, it stems from not having a strong education around how to handle your emotions properly.

When you want to develop and maintain your virtue, your goal is to begin identifying what morals you desire to live by and seeking the opportunity to live by those morals in your life every single day. Common morals include or relate to humility, kindness, abstinence, chastity, patience, liberality, and diligence, which are the opposites of the seven deadly sins that are commonly taught in many religions. These virtues ultimately seek to shape people into being individuals who are willing to show up and serve not only themselves but their communities by supporting everyone around them in living in a positive life. When you consider these virtues, consider what they mean to you and how they impact your life, and then declare that you are prepared to begin living by these virtues every single day. Then, every single day, do what you can to live in alignment with these virtues and be willing to accept yourself when you do not. As you continue practicing and reminding yourself of these virtues, you will find that it becomes much easier for you to grow as a person and to maintain your virtue and kindness along the way.

Making Peace with Your Past

Many people abandon self-discipline due to guilt, shame, and residual fear that they hold onto from their past experiences. It is not uncommon to live a life where you are shaped by your past, particularly as humans who have the capacity to remember it and to remember the emotions that coincided with these memories. One of the vices of evolution is that, in being able to remember our past so that we can improve our chances of survival, we can also remember our past to the point that it retriggers trauma within us on an ongoing basis. Making peace with your past by healing unresolved traumas and challenges and accepting what you cannot change is a powerful way to release yourself from the grips of your own history and permit yourself to move forward.

When you choose to move forward without letting your past hold you back, it becomes easier for you to accept yourself more wholly and completely, including who you were in the past and who you desire to be in the future. You stop denying yourself the right to a joyful and evolutionary future because you no longer punish yourself for your experiences in the past. So, it becomes easier for you to possess even greater levels of virtue, kindness, acceptance, and mental toughness. Thus, making peace with your past directly supports your ability to develop your stoicism and become a more ethical person as a whole.

Making peace with your past takes a significant amount of emotional healing, and may not always be ideal to do on your own. Healing from your past is going to require you to personally go within and discover what needs to be healed and do some of the work yourself, while also reaching out for help whenever help is needed. By reaching out for help, you ensure that you have the support and acceptance needed to help you overcome challenging experiences in your life and grow as a person. However, the reality of inner healing is that no one else can do it for you, so you are going to need to be willing to endure the emotional aspects of healing on your own. As you do, you will find that accepting your past becomes easier because you come to peace with everything that has happened to you and how you have been impacted by various people and experiences in your life. This type of healing brings closure to painful experiences, which is often all that is needed for us to make peace with our pasts.

Overcoming Procrastination and Distractions

One of the biggest ways that people generate pain in their own lives, aside from being unwilling to accept the things beyond their control, is procrastination. Procrastination can be caused by many things, and no matter what the root cause is, it virtually always causes severe setbacks and troubles for the people who do not teach themselves to overcome this unhelpful behavior. From causing a significant amount of unnecessary stress for having to catch up last minute to causing guilt and shame for things not being completed on time, many negative setbacks can be derived from procrastination.

Overcoming procrastination in your own life requires you to start by getting to the root cause of your procrastination and finding ways to bypass that root cause so that you can get past it. In many cases, the root cause is emotional. With procrastination, you may be procrastinating something because it brings you pain, or because the alternative brings you joy. For example, you may procrastinate healing from your past because revisiting parts of your past is a painful experience for you, so you are afraid to get into it. Alternatively, you may procrastinate getting a task done for work because watching TV brings greater joy than crunching numbers or putting together presentations.

By discovering what it is that you are being motivated by more (the avoidance of pain or the desire for comfort), you can begin finding ways to work through the work that needs to be done. Some ideas include going through the process slowly so that it is not too overwhelming, breaking it down into manageable steps, or rewarding yourself for achieving success along the way. These types of small adjustments to your approach can make it easier for you to stop avoiding the process so that you can get it done and get on with your life. Once you have determined what adjustments you want to make, the last thing you have to do is get up and actually get started. For some people, this will be plenty to help them get up and get past their behavior of procrastination.

For others, these may not be enough to keep them on track, and they may find themselves backsliding into procrastination rather quickly. If you are this type of person, you need to find a way to implement some strategies to help you avoid procrastination even after you have already started. One great strategy is to find out what is distracting you or tempting you to procrastinate and avoiding that distraction as much as you possibly can. Another way is to implement a distraction time limit for yourself, as this may be more affected for people who truly cannot overcome distractions in their lives. If you are someone who gets distracted and genuinely struggle to get focused again after even a minor distraction, first off, realize that you are actually extremely normal. Recent studies have suggested that the average attention span of a human is 2.5 seconds before they become distracted once again and need to regain focus. By the way, that means that our attention span is now shorter than that of a goldfish if you were wondering!

By giving yourself a distraction break every now and again, which is simply one to three minutes to engage in a distraction and get it out of your system, you relieve your mind off the urge to get distracted and help yourself regain focus. If you find that you are getting distracted *a lot*, consider starting with frequent one-minute distraction breaks and then spacing them out further and further so that you can train yourself to increase your attention span. This way, you can condition yourself to avoid distractions without expecting yourself to be able to change your behaviors overnight completely.

Moving in Alignment with Your Goals

Another method of self-discipline that is seldom taught, but highly necessary in reducing the amount of suffering that you experience in your life, is learning how to move in alignment with your goals. Our modern society has been largely built on following a "cookie cutter" lifestyle for a long time, which means that many people are doing what they *should* be doing and are experiencing no joy or satisfaction out of it. People are pursuing jobs that they should be pursuing, getting married and having kids because they should be, engaging in hobbies because they should be, and ultimately building entire lives around the word "should." These days, there is a popular saying that goes: "Don't should all over yourself" and I think it is highly applicable here.

Doing everything in your life because you believe that is what you should be doing and because you are afraid of doing things differently only leads to you being unhappy and depressed in the long run. This is because, as humans, our emotional side needs to be nourished and taken care of and you simply cannot do that if you are constantly doing what you "should" be doing. Instead, you will find that you are building an entire life that you don't particularly care for and, because of that lack of caring, you struggle to generate motivation to actually make it happen. This all spirals into deep levels of disappointment and frustration which can ultimately lead to you living an unfulfilling life and suffering far more than you need to be.

If you want to experience true freedom and joy in your life, as well as the inner strength required to minimize your suffering, you need to start moving in alignment with your personal goals. Not only will this help you feel more fulfilled, but it will also bring a renewed sense of positivity into your life which will make acting in alignment with stoicism far easier. When you are generally a happy person, dealing with your challenging and passionate emotions becomes easier because they are not piling up and causing you to feel an intense need to release them.

You can move in alignment with your goals by determining two primary goals for yourself: who you want to be in life and what you want to have in life. By determining what these goals are, you can start setting personal rules for yourself to help you move in alignment with these goals. For example, if your goal is to be a stoic person, you will want to set rules for yourself that you will only behave in ways that cultivate your stoicism and that support you in experiencing less overall suffering in your life. If your goal is to have more money and a better house, then you would begin behaving in ways that allow you to save more money and work towards acquiring your better home.

When you set goals for yourself and you begin moving towards them, every time you see yourself making successful progress in your life, you start to feel more empowered and motivated to keep going. This can add an enriching and fulfilling feeling into your life that supports you in being happier overall. Through this, your life becomes less about suffering and more about creating one that makes you happy to wake up and enjoy your day to day experience. Many benefits can come from following personal goals, both in terms of materialistic goals and goals for yourself and your personal growth.

Chapter 4: Discipline of Action

Now that you have the inner strength and personal power required to begin moving your internal processes in alignment with stoicism, it is time for you to start bringing stoicism into your discipline of action! Your action is where you begin to allow your inner thoughts and processes develop so that you can start actually behaving stoically. This is where stoicism really comes into play because your stoic actions and behaviors will begin changing your life as you enforce them and embody them going forward. Through disciplined actions, you are going to start behaving in a way that shows emotional constraint, allowing you to use your emotions effectively, and that is ethical towards yourself and those around you.

In this chapter, we are going to discover what disciplined actions are, how they align with stoicism, and what specific actions you need to begin disciplining to embody a stoic lifestyle. Remember, stoicism heavily relies on ethical behaviors that align with virtue and morality, so your goal here is to begin acting in an ethical way that aligns with high morals. Through this behavior, you are not only going to increase your ability to embody stoicism, but you are also going to quite literally change the way that you engage with the world around you beyond your own inner thoughts and experiences.

Remember, changing behaviors like this can be quite a daunting task because you are going to be changing nearly everything about yourself likely. Since most modern humans are still highly driven by emotions, teaching yourself to become more driven by rational thought and reason without losing the value of your emotions can take time. You are truly going to be conditioning yourself into becoming a new person, which takes consistent time and practice. Furthermore, you may find that now your stoic behaviors are moving into your physical actions, the people around you start treating you differently. Those who are not benefiting from your changes may attempt to push you back into your old habits, and those who appreciate your new adjustments may start gravitating towards you in a higher degree. This means that your circle of friends and acquaintances may change as you, too, change in a rather drastic manner. That being said, deep acceptance of yourself and those around you as well as an unwillingness to revert to old behaviors will be essential in helping you completely embrace the discipline of action.

Controlling Your Emotional Passion and Expression

Where true stoicism comes into play, and not the exploitation of it that was encouraged by those who profited off of emotional repression, is when you learn how to actually control your emotional passion and expression. Through controlling your emotional passion and expression, you teach yourself to harness your emotional power and turn it into a productive tool to help you advance further in your life. For example, anger around activism that is not turned into blind rage can instead be used to passionately change people's opinions and support the true cause of the activist. Passion about the need for more love in your relationship can be harnessed to produce changes in your relationship, rather than to produce jealousy and anger around the fact that changes are not being made. When you learn how to control your emotional passion and expression, you allow yourself to use that passion alongside rational thinking to fuel the actions required to make changes in your life or the lives of those around you.

Learning how to control your emotional passion is not only a form of emotional intelligence, but it is also a form of ethical behavior. By that I mean, stoicism believes that we should always act ethically no matter what we are doing, whether it is professional or personal.

How you treat people, for example, should be ethical or of high moral standards so that you always treat people with the utmost respect and kindness in all circumstances. Behaving in this way ensures that you are always doing right by yourself and by those around you, which in turn earns you greater respect and appreciation from others.

If controlling your emotions and harnessing their power to stimulate change were easy, we would all be doing it. So it goes without saying that the balancing act of being able to experience emotional passion without expressing it intensely is challenging. Learning how to regain control over yourself amidst intense emotions requires you to slow down the experience and intentionally work with your emotions in a controlled manner. You can do this by noticing the moment an emotion begins to grow in intensity and review what the goal of that particular emotion is. For example: if you are jealous in your relationship, your goal is to develop security; if you are angry with how someone is treating you, your goal is to be treated better; and if you are grieving about a loss that you have endured, then your goal is to heal the pain.

Recognizing what your goal is with any particular emotion allows you to avoid becoming the victim of that emotion, and instead, become a person who can reasonably work his/her way through the emotion. It also prevents you from turning that emotion into a larger point of trauma or emotional suffering and enables you instead to use it to reduce your suffering overall. The next step is to begin acting in a way that works in alignment with your emotion's goal rather than your emotion itself. This is where the intense act of self-discipline comes into play: in holding yourself back from emotionally reacting and following through with your goal-based actions instead. In this situation, slowing down your approach to your resolution as much as possible will allow you to regularly check in with your goal and ensure that you are acting in alignment with it. If at any time you move out of alignment with your goal, then you will be checking in often enough to regain control over your emotions and adjust your approach.

Practicing emotional control and expression frequently enough will really be the key to developing deep control over your emotional expression. They say that you need to practice something at least 1,000 times before you completely master it, so trust that every time you have the opportunity to practice the emotional control you are working towards greater success. The more intentional you become and the more serious effort you put into regaining control over your emotions, the greater control you will have in the long run.

Acting in an Ethical Manner

In the early days of stoicism, a series of ethical actions were outlined that were intended to give stoics a set of rules to live by, so to speak. These rules were fairly simple and were intended to guide people through the proper resolutions of challenging experiences that they would face throughout their lives. The Stoics called these rules "appropriate acts" or "proper functions" and they were defined by behaving in a way that adhered to what reason persuaded them to do. So, rather than being persuaded by their emotions, the Stoics aimed to be persuaded by their rational thinking mind, or reason. Stoicism aims to achieve the process of justified, rational thinking so that every action is enacted in a way that honors both parties involved and works towards achieving a higher goal, rather than an immediate emotional goal.

For things that were not inherently good *or* bad, such as health, stoics aimed to maintain their health positively which allowed them to turn the act of maintaining good health into an ethical act. This way, they could walk in one with their human nature and harmonize their lifestyles through the act of maintaining good health. Another example was through the act of sacrificing ones' property, which could either be good or bad, depending on the circumstances at hand. If the act was done because it made a good, reasonable sense to do so, then it likely aligned with stoic's virtues and morals for ethical living. If it didn't adhere to reasonable persuasion, however, then sacrificing one's property was not an act of ethical morals and therefore was considered to be "bad". For example, someone was threatening the livelihood of your family if you did not sacrifice your property. In this case, it would make rational sense to sacrifice your property to protect the lives of your family, so sacrificing your property would be virtuous and ethical. If, however, the sacrifice was being made for personal fortune and well-being but would cost your family in some large way, then sacrificing your property would not be ethical and would be out of alignment with the stoic way of living.

If you want to act in an ethical manner true to stoic nature, you need to learn how to justify things based on rational and reasonable thinking and then act accordingly. In doing so, you bring your decision-making process into the heart of reason and out of the grips of emotions which can often lead to us doing things that are completely out of alignment with the greater good. If you want to act in true stoic nature, simply ask yourself: "Is this a reasonable decision to make? Can I reasonably justify this? Will it lead me towards my true goal, or away from it?" If the answers to these questions support your decision, chances are it is a true, ethical decision that is going to support your success. If the answer is no, then chances are you are acting out of alignment with ethics, and you need to reassess your proceedings to ensure that you are acting ethically towards yourself and everyone else involved in the situation with you.

Solving Your Problems Effectively

Learning how to act ethically and with control over your emotional passion and expression will not only help you refrain from producing unwanted consequences through your actions, but it will also help you when it comes to problem-solving. People who can bypass emotional intensity and tune into their rational thinking mind are often able to get a clearer understanding of their problems and choosing actions that will support them in discovering a genuine resolve. As you continue learning how to gain more control over your emotions and how you act on them, you should also begin diving into this major benefit of being able to tune into your rational thinking mind with greater clarity and intention.

Exercising your mind for problem-solving abilities is much easier once you have gained control over your emotions and have started tapping into your reasonable thinking mind. From there, all you need to do is begin developing the habit of looking at a problem from a bird's-eye view so that you can clearly see the entirety of the problem itself. If you are experiencing a problem that involves other people, seek to understand the problem from everyone's angle and get a clear understanding of what all your goals are so that you can work towards finding a solution that serves each of your goals. If you are experiencing a problem on your own, seek to understand the obstacles that are standing in your way and put them into perspective. See them for what they truly are, avoid making them appear larger to yourself, and get clear on what it will actually take for you to reasonably overcome these obstacles in an ethical way. That way, you can start producing action steps for you to take that will help you move towards your goal without compromising your moral standards.

After you have mentally produced a solution to overcoming your goals, the next step is to actually act that solution out. Again, you are going to need to put in a lot of work towards overcoming your personal challenges such as your emotional habits that are going to encourage you to behave in the way that you have always behaved. You will need to consistently practice and remain intentional towards changing your behavior so that, over time, it grows easier for you to behave in a more constrained and intentional manner.

Once you are able to combine your reasonable thinking and controlled emotional expression into your problem-solving abilities, you will have an incredibly powerful tool in your hands. This tends to be the most challenging time to combine emotional restraint with reasonable actions as problems can bring with them feelings of fear and desperation, in addition to the other emotions that arise. Learning how to navigate through these challenging times will put your stoicism to the ultimate test, and when you navigate these effectively, you can feel confident that your stoic development is working.

Acting with Discipline in Relationships

In relationships, it can be particularly challenging to act stoically because your emotions can be so much more intense. Love is an emotion that we all crave and need, and that can bring us great suffering and pain if we do not learn how to navigate alongside the emotion of love effectively. For many, love can be one of the most overwhelming emotions to experience because it tends to sweep through your entire body and hijack your mind with no warning signs. Then, from that state of emotional hijacking, other emotions have the capacity to squeeze into your emotional hijacking and take over how you express yourself. As a result, you can find yourself being completely backward in acting stoic in relationships, even if you are managing your stoicism well in other areas of your life.

These feelings are not exclusive to your romantic relationships, either, but instead in any relationship where love or deep admiration towards another human is present. When you experience love in your life, you need to be extra cautious and considerate towards your emotions and how you may be expressing your emotions in relation to love. For example, if you are continuing a relationship because you love the other person, but it brings you both tremendous suffering, then continuing the relationship or at least continuing it in a current way may not be ideal. You may need to adjust how you are approaching the relationship or consider terminating it altogether to eliminate the unnecessary suffering of both yourself and the other person.

Acting ethically in relationships truly requires you to deeply consider how both you and the other person are being impacted and whether or not the relationship makes reasonable sense as it is. If your relationship makes sense but the actions taking place within the relationship do not, then it may be time to reconsider how you treat each other and the respect that you have for each other. If your relationship no longer makes sense, or there is no way to restore it to a state where it can stop causing hurt, then it may be time to take a break from it or terminate the relationship altogether.

Always make sure that the way you treat your loved ones is respectful of both yourself and them, and that you never allow your emotions to persuade you to behave unreasonably. Be cautious to never let love get in the way of reason by frequently checking in with your behaviors and making sure that it makes reasonable sense to move forward in the way that you are. This way, you can always treat your loved ones, including yourself, with the respect and compassion that they deserve, whether that is experienced up close or from afar.

Moving Towards Professional Goals Ethically

Another area of your life where you need to begin developing self-discipline is in your professional life. Emotions tend to hold people back when they start behaving in an emotionally-driven manner at work, whether that is conscious or unconsciously driven. For example, being upset with your boss is one thing, but taking it out on your boss through a passionate expression of emotion can result in you being seen as unprofessional and unstable. It may even result in you losing your job due to an inability to function professionally while in the workplace. It is imperative that you learn how to manage your emotions properly so that you can behave in a controlled manner during professional experiences, ensuring to yourself and everyone around you that you are stable enough to handle professional duties.

Stoicism also needs to be reflected in your relationships with people in your professional life, no matter who they may be or what role they may play in your profession. From your boss to your coworkers or even your customers, you should always be handling yourself in a professional manner that honors your high ethics and moral standards. It may seem fun and harmless to engage in inappropriate relationships, behaviors or conversations with people relating to your career, but in the long run, it may not be the best idea. You never know how these types of seemingly harmless interactions could later impact the well-being of your career and lead to you experiencing troubles in moving forward. For example, your chummy relationship with your boss may make your present work life more enjoyable, but if it is not controlled through rational thinking, it may lead to them liking you but seeing someone else as a better fit for promotion. In this case, your overly friendly relationship may not be bad enough to get you fired, but it may cost you the professional respect and consideration of your boss.

You should always consider the reasonable reality of your professional career and how your behaviors and actions are moving you towards success. If it does not make reasonable sense to behave in the way that you are behaving, even if it seems harmless on the surface, you need to begin adjusting your behaviors. This way, you are seen as professional and competent, and it is *you* who will excel faster than anyone else due to your reasonable behaviors.

Chapter 5: Achieving the Goal of Stoicism

You are officially equipped with all of the basic understanding that you need to embody to begin achieving the goal of stoicism. Hopefully, you have already begun practicing and embodying some of the teachings from earlier in this book, but if you haven't yet, do not worry: we are going to begin applying these practices right now. In this chapter, you are going to learn about what it takes for you to actually achieve the goal of stoicism and practices you can start using right away. These tools are all powerful in incorporating into your lifestyle to help you achieve the goal of stoicism one step at a time.

Making total life changes can be trying and it takes a particular degree of devotion to officially embody the goals of total lifestyle changes, including the goal of stoicism. Be sure to proceed through this chapter while applying each step at your own pace and searching for ways to incorporate it into your personal way of living. Everyone will have a slightly different take on how they personally can develop and embody lifestyle changes, so do not be afraid to make your own personalizations to these tools. As long as the heart of the tools remains the same, your application can be done in any way needed to achieve *your* goal of stoicism.

Understanding the Goal of Modern Stoicism

Let's begin by refreshing your mind on what the goal of modern stoicism truly is. You already know that the goal of stoicism, in general, is to reduce suffering by embodying an ethical way of living, but you may wonder exactly what that means or what that looks like in a modern world. After all, the world we are living in today is significantly different from the world that existed in ancient Greek and Roman times. So, let's take a deep look into what modern stoicism looks like and the goals that it aspires to accomplish.

Despite advancing a great deal in society, many humans continue to live lives that are highly steeped in stress and suffering. It has almost become a part of the societal norm to make a joke out of living the "typical modern lifestyle", which regularly involves working at a job you dislike with a boss you don't respect and doing things out of obligation instead of personal desire. Unfortunately, just because you can make light of your suffering does not mean it does not exist any longer. If you truly want to live the stoic way, you need to start taking action towards actually reducing or eliminating unnecessary suffering in your life so that you can begin living a life of greater emotional freedom.

In modern life, this looks like finding a way to accept your life as it is right now and setting goals to improve your life so that you can start experiencing greater joy and freedom. Perhaps for you, this looks like accepting your present career and the fact that you cannot get what you want from it and setting the goal to pursue a career that you are more passionate about. Or, maybe it is learning how to accept your family as they are and learning to set new boundaries so that their behaviors no longer personally affect you, allowing you to enjoy their company more without being hurt by them so much. It may even require you to terminate some friendships and relationships and begin setting higher standards on how you are willing to let others treat you and how you are going to treat others so that you can proceed with a better life overall.

Stoicism is an opportunity to stop letting emotions drive you into suffering so that you can begin moving forward rationally. Through reasonable thinking and problem-solving, you can stop letting your emotions lead you into believing that you are trapped and start letting your sense of reason remove you from the rut that you are currently stuck in. This will likely look like a total life transformation, particularly if you are presently living a life of intense suffering and struggle. Although the endurance of this transformation may be challenging, particularly as you lose those comforts and habits that have led to your suffering so far, the outcome will be more than worth it.

Advice from Stoics

These days, stoicism is broken down into two parts: modern stoicism and ancient stoicism. Modern stoicism is still highly driven by the teachings of ancient stoicism and the advice that these early philosophers shared with those who desired to embody and embrace the stoic way of living. While there is plenty of modern advice around stoicism making waves around the Internet, I want to provide you with some powerful and profound advice from ancient stoicism which is where it all began. Of course, this advice is going to be adjusted for the purposes of modern living, but I genuinely believe that connecting with the ancient roots of stoicism will help you embody it more accurately.

Below are five pieces of advice from ancient stoics that have been modernized so that you can use them in your modern life.

1. Change Only What You Can

Humans endure a great deal of suffering by generating a false sense of control over that which they cannot truly control. The belief that we can control other peoples' actions or decisions leads to us feeling a sense of suffering when our attempts at control betray us, and we do not actually gain the control we seek. As a result, we find ourselves struggling to accept the outcomes because we believe that there is either something fundamentally wrong with ourselves or something fundamentally wrong with those around us. The reality is that nothing is fundamentally wrong here, aside from the belief that you can in any way control anything beyond yourself.

Allow yourself to stop deluding yourself into believing that you can control anything or anyone other than yourself and start focusing on how you can control yourself. Pay attention to your personal responses and reactions to the world around you and start seeking opportunities to control those responses more effectively. The more you focus on changing yourself, including your perceptions, your thoughts, and your behaviors, the less unnecessary suffering you will experience through your own behaviors and beliefs.

2. **Start Living Today**

Procrastinating when it comes to creating a life that will be more fulfilling and enjoyable is one of the biggest acts of disservice that you could possibly do for yourself. Not only does it put off your ability to acquire what you desire, but it also results in you living in unnecessary suffering even longer as you attempt to uphold a lifestyle that does not genuinely light you up. Instead of putting it off, start focusing on living a better life today by choosing to accept yourself as you are and your past for what it is.

Look for opportunities to begin showing up passionately and ethically, find ways to build a life that is filled with meaning and purpose, and pursue your meaning and purpose rationally. Practice bringing your emotion into harmony with your reason and carrying yourself in a way that is respectful and kind to both yourself and those around you, and let yourself grow from there. Each day that you invest into living a better life, you add another day into it that you get to live free from unnecessary suffering and pain.

3. **Know That You Cannot Be Broken**

We have a tendency to place a lot of power into the hands of other people by believing that they can genuinely impact us through their actions. While the actions of others may impact our physical bodies and external circumstances, our souls can never be broken. The inner part of who you are will always remain intact and whole, and you can always choose to live in a way that honors this part of you. If you find yourself being abused or taken advantage of by others in your life, choose to remember that you cannot be broken and act as though you are whole and complete in spite of their behaviors. Not only will this minimize the pain that you endure, but it will also help you remain in control over your emotions and emotional expressions.

4. **"Don't burn the candle on both ends."**

There is an old saying that goes "Don't burn the candle on both ends" which essentially means that you should never try and endure more than you can reasonably handle. Without fully relaxing your mind and body and offering them the breaks that they need, you will be attempting to overdo it, and you will likely run yourself into a state of burnout. If you want to enjoy a happier and healthier life, you need to be able to maintain your physical and mental health and truly commit to the maintenance of it.

The emotional desire may be to do the things that make you feel comfortable, but the ethical and reasonable solution is to do the things that may not be as comforting now so that you can minimize your suffering later. By fiercely protecting your mental and physical health, you can maintain it for as long as possible.

5. Focus Inward on Yourself

Stoics believe that suffering comes from within, from our own perceptions and judgments of the world around us, and that this can lead to severe pain in our lives. For this reason, stoic advice is that anytime you experience the desire to judge someone else, you look within yourself to understand what that judgment means and where it is coming from.

If you are judging someone for their ill health, for example, look within and ask yourself why someone else's health would possibly impact you to the point of having your own personal suffering. Realize that you are not that intimately connected to anyone in your life, no matter how close your relationship with them may be, and that you are not required to suffer for the sake of others. Ask yourself why you are so attached to that form of suffering, and begin doing the inner healing and growth required to detach from suffering that is in no way relating to your personal experiences.

Daily Mindfulness Practices

A great way to achieve stoicism in your life is to begin practicing daily mindfulness practices. Practicing mindfulness is an excellent way to cultivate your self-awareness and to begin to recognize areas of your life where you may be increasing your level of suffering for no apparent reason. It also allows you to begin identifying where your emotions come into play and how they are impacting your daily living. When you take the time to understand your emotions and how they are affecting you, as well as your actions and how they are affecting you, you can audit your life as a whole and seek out opportunities for growth.

In Chapter 6, we will discuss many areas where you can cultivate your daily mindfulness practice, but in essence, you are going to want to start as soon as possible by developing your self-awareness. Start asking yourself "How am I doing?" or "How am I feeling?" and begin honestly answering these questions to yourself. This way, you can easily begin to identify how you are honestly doing in life and what may be contributing to those feelings that you are having. In instances where you recognize unnecessary suffering, you can begin understanding why that suffering exists and how you are contributing to it so that you can start untangling the suffering. Then, you can begin approaching similar experiences in the future more intentionally and mindfully so as to reduce the amount of suffering you experience.

To paint a picture of mindfulness in your mind, and how this powerful tool can help you overcome suffering, let's take a look at an average daily experience that many people can probably relate to in one way or another. Imagine you were to wake up one morning and you walked into the kitchen to pour yourself a cup of coffee, only to find that there was no coffee left in the house because you forgot to purchase some when you went to the store. In this moment, you may feel a surge of frustration leap through you as you realize that your favorite morning routine has been interrupted by your own forgetfulness. When your spouse awakens and comes into the kitchen, perhaps you start taking your frustration out on him/her because you are feeling upset about the coffee situation. In this situation, you are not expressing mindfulness nor tuning into your rational thinking mind to recognize that you are simply upset that your routine has been interrupted, and not towards your spouse in any way. However, if you are not thinking mindfully and acting stoically, you might instead simply take your emotions out on your partner and increase the level of unnecessary suffering that both of you endure that morning. As you can see, bringing mindfulness into your daily practice allows you to keep everything in perspective, stay self-aware around your own experiences and emotions, and have the consciousness to choose differently. Rather than choosing to act on your emotions, you can consciously choose to act on your reason instead and be kind to your partner despite your own inner frustrations.

A Morning Meditation for Stoicism

A great way to start your day out and develop your stoicism is to begin your day with a morning meditation designed specifically to help you achieve the very goal of stoicism. Meditations are great exercises because they allow you to gain a deeper sense of emotional control over yourself, while also giving you time to visualize what you desire for yourself and making it easier for you to manifest that into your reality. For a stoic meditation, you will want to use both the releasing of unwanted emotions and the development of a vision to help you increase your stoic behaviors and cultivate a deeper sense of emotional self-control.

You can start your morning meditation by simply relaxing into a basic breathing meditation at first. To do this, relax into a comfortable seated position on the floor or on a meditation cushion and start bringing your awareness to your breath. As you become aware of your breath, start gently guiding your breath to become more rhythmic by breathing in to the count of eight and breathing out to the count of eight, too. Doing this will bring your body into a state of comfortable relaxation that will help you ease into your meditative state. When you begin to feel more relaxed, allow yourself to enjoy a few minutes of basic meditation where you can simply relax and enjoy the experience. During this first part of your meditation, you are going to develop your ability to ground your emotions and build your mindfulness, thus increasing the mental toughness that you can carry with you throughout the day. This is going to help you in tuning into your rational thinking more consistently as well, which will keep you in alignment with your goal of stoicism.

After you have spent some time relaxing in a state of meditation, you want to begin moving into the state of visualization. Here, you want to visualize what your day would look like if you were behaving stoically and how that stoicism might change the way your day would look. Envision yourself approaching your day with a greater sense of reason and ration, and with the desire to develop a stronger ability to control your emotions. Consider certain parts of your day that are typically emotionally charged and consider what they might look like if you were to take greater control over those situations in your life. When you can begin to visualize alternative habits or responses to the things that you encounter in your life, behaving in a new way becomes easier because you are essentially planning what your different responses would be. Furthermore, you envisioning yourself behaving in a completely new way actually builds your confidence in your ability to behave differently too, because you have already "seen" yourself doing it. Your ability to imagine your better responses and your better life actually creates the skills that you need to begin developing better responses and a better life.

Philosophical Diaries

Stoicism is largely based on philosophy and belief of life having a certain purpose and meaning, particularly relating to behaving in a certain way both towards yourself and towards others in your life. Stoicism itself already has a list of ethics and virtues that outlines what it is, but that does not mean that you cannot use a diary to begin developing your own belief around what stoicism is to you and what it means to you personally. When you begin to develop your own beliefs around what stoicism is and how it works, you can start really embodying and embracing this way of life in a personal manner. This allows you to make it yours and develop a personal passion, purpose, and reason for following this way of life and embodying it in your own everyday experiences.

Keeping a philosophical diary does not only support you in making stoicism more personal to yourself and your own interpretation, but it also supports you in discovering more about yourself. Through these journals, you can start digging into what life means to you, what you believe the purpose of life is, what morals and virtues you personally hold value for, and what you desire more of in life. These types of exploration topics will help you really develop an understanding around yourself and why you may behave the way you do and experience the emotions that you experience. For example, if you believe that a high moral standard is to respect your family and accept them deeply no matter who they are, then it may make sense as to why you grow so frustrated when they do something that you perceive to be unacceptable. Or, it may make sense as to why you struggle to relate with people who do not also hold their families to such great value in their own lives.

The more you understand yourself in this intimate way, the easier it is for you to develop your mindfulness even further and create reasons behind why you behave, think, and feel the way you do from experience to experience. As you explore yourself even further, identifying your own feelings and experiences from moment to moment becomes easier, and you can start carrying yourself more intentionally. Not only are you able to identify your actual habits and behaviors, but you are also able to identify how you can align them to work towards your overall goals because you now know what those goals actually are. As a result, you can experience greater growth in your life.

Studying the Art of Stoicism

When you make a total lifestyle change, such as by embodying the art of stoicism and using it in your daily life, one of the most valuable things that you can do for yourself is to continue studying that change indefinitely. For stoicism, this means that you want to continue studying the history of stoicism, what stoicism actually is, and how modern stoicism works so that you can begin applying that knowledge in your life more consistently. Ongoing education around lifestyle changes is one of the most powerful things that you can gift yourself with if you are truly serious about making permanent changes in your life.

The first reason why you want to continue educating yourself on these changes is that the more you know, the easier it is for you to actually apply the goal of stoicism into your life. As you continue to read more books, listen to podcasts, read blogs, and otherwise consume information about stoicism, you gain more insight as to how it can be applied in a variety of different experiences or situations that you may encounter in your life. As a result, you can more clearly understand how it works, what it means, and what it looks like in practical application. This means that when you encounter times that may be more trying on your emotions, you can start moving through the process of adapting to a more stoic approach easier.

Another reason why ongoing education is powerful is that it gives you a more dynamic understanding of what stoicism actually is. Every single person who has ever written on stoicism and who will ever write on it will approach the subject slightly different from everyone else who has approached the subject. This is because we all have slightly different interpretations of what stoicism is, why it is important, and how it should be applied into everyday life. As you continue educating yourself on how stoicism is being applied by other people, you can educate yourself on how you can further personalize it for your own experience as well. You may find that what has worked in the modern application of stoicism for others either fits great with you or does not resonate so much and you need to pursue a different understanding to help you achieve more.

As well, your deeper understanding of the core foundation of what stoicism is will help you begin to develop your own ideas around what it truly means and why it relates to your personal beliefs on life itself. In this way, your ongoing education around stoicism can stimulate you to begin formulating your own opinions and perspectives and even further embodying it into your own life in a way that genuinely fits you and your needs. Through this type of personalized embodiment, you grow a closer and more intimate connection to your practice which makes it easier for you to commit and devote to it in your life.

Lastly, your ongoing education around stoicism will keep it relevant to you. In a society where our average attention span is about 2.5 seconds long, it is not uncommon to read a great book, feel inspired, and then completely forget about everything you learned just a few days later. If you truly want to embody everything that stoicism has to offer, you need to be willing to stay devoted to your practice and continue keeping it at the forefront of your life. You need to put in the continued attention and effort into understanding what it is and deepening your connection with it so that you can keep growing and advancing alongside stoicism. Otherwise, there is a good chance that you will simply forget or it will become unimportant to you, and you will lack the ability to embody stoicism in your life.

Endurance Training

The last thing that you need to begin implementing into your life when it comes to achieving stoicism is developing an endurance.

This endurance can be developed by regularly strengthening the foundation of your entire lifestyle change through consistent mental toughness building. The more you work towards increasing your mental strength and toughness, the stronger your foundation will be and the easier it will be for you to maintain your stoic lifestyle. If you let your mental toughness foundation break down, the rest of your practices are going to break down alongside it, and you are going to struggle to really embody stoicism in your life. That is why we started with mental toughness training and the practices that you need to begin embodying to develop the mental strength and resiliency that you need to succeed.

I suggest that you spend several minutes per day purposefully working towards building your mental toughness. You can do this by scheduling aside time for practicing the practices given to you in <u>Chapter 2: Mental Toughness – Maintaining Your Mental Toughness in Challenging Times</u>, as well as by practicing them spontaneously when they are particularly useful in life, such as when you are going through a hard time. Practicing mental toughness on a regular basis is going to help you stay strong enough to continue choosing your rational thinking mind over your emotional thinking mind during trying times, which will keep you in alignment with stoicism.

If you are having a particularly challenging time building your mental toughness, I suggest you slow down and stay focused on your mental endurance for a while. Do not push yourself into advancing into the stoic disciplines until you have developed a deeper sense of mental toughness. Although you will likely generate some success in these disciplines, if you lack mental toughness, you may see the back-and-forth of success-then-setbacks as too much and may find yourself feeling like you would rather give up than continue. This might completely throw your entire game off, which can destroy your success and leave you feeling defeated before you ever really got the chance to begin.

Instead, take your time and really focus on building a strong foundation of mental toughness first so that your disciplines are far easier for you to uphold. When your mental toughness is developed enough that you can see the benefits of your resiliency and personal strength, then you can begin moving on to developing your disciplines as they will be much easier to develop and maintain.

In addition to building your mental toughness through mental practices, I would also suggest that you begin building a physical endurance practice as well. Physical endurance will not only support you in maintaining your health, which is an important element of stoicism, but it will also help you build mental endurance as well. Physical endurance requires a high degree of mental commitment and devotion, which is what makes it so powerful in developing your mental endurance. Furthermore, the number of challenges that you will face physically in building your endurance will teach you about just how strong you are when it comes to emotional endurance, too.

Chapter 6: Daily Application of Stoicism

Finally, you have reached the point where you can begin applying stoicism into your everyday life! At this point, you have a strong enough understanding of stoicism and all of the tools in place for you to begin developing stoicism in your life, so you are now ready to begin developing daily practices for stoicism. This is where you really get to let your practice until now shine through as you get to put the "final touches" of your lifestyle change into place. Through these daily practices, you are going to really begin to see the fruits of your labors as these practices are small yet consistent, so they pack a big punch in making real changes in your life.

In this chapter, we are going to discuss *14 ways that you can begin applying stoicism into your daily life*. This may sound like a lot, but in reality, many of these practices are simply about mindset shifts that you can focus on creating and embodying every single day. As you do, the shifts of stoicism in your life will begin to manifest rapidly as your consistent application of stoic practices begins to snowball into your successful growth. So, if you are ready to finally apply stoicism into your everyday life, let's start!

Knowing Your True Freedom

The first way that you can begin embodying stoicism in your everyday life is by generating perspective around where your freedom lies and how your freedom can be achieved. Epictetus, a Greek stoic philosopher, once quoted that "No man is free who is not a master of himself." In other words, the only true way to gain freedom is to understand yourself and begin mastering yourself regarding your emotions, your reactions, and the way that you decide to live your life. Remember, of all the things that exist in this world, the only thing that you truly have any control over is yourself. When you learn how to control yourself, you experience true freedom because you learn how to end your suffering in any circumstance that you may face.

Whenever you are faced with trying situations in your life, recognize what your instinctive reaction is and pause for a moment to hold back from that immediate reaction. Instead, slow yourself down and take the time to gather control over yourself and your emotions before proceeding. This way, you can proceed with control over your emotional passion and expression, thus allowing you to begin making conscious choices and avoiding the suffering of emotional reactions. As you do this, you begin to develop a sense of control over the way you move, the actions you take, and the way that you express your emotional self. This type of self-control and emotional constraint becomes your biggest ally when it comes to rationally moving through your life and making choices that genuinely serve your overall well-being. Through this, your life somewhat turns into a game of chess where every move is clearly thought out and, if moved correctly, can bring you that much closer to achieving your ultimate goal.

If you want to experience a better life, you need to take responsibility for your own growth and begin developing your skills around your personal growth. The more you take responsibility, the more you put yourself back in control over your own experiences and the greater you can grow in life. This pause can mean the difference between creating a new future or recreating an (ineffective) historical past.

The Circle of Influence and the Circle of Concern

One of the most powerful instruments that exist in stoicism is the circle of influence and the circle of concern. When you begin to study these two circles, you start to realize that everything in your life falls into two categories: things that you can control (your circle of influence) and things that you cannot control (your circle of concern.) The things within your circle of control or influence are things that you can actually make effective change in through your own personal choices. The things within your circle of concern are things that you cannot directly control and that you have to either accept *or* reframe using things that are within your circle of influence.

The things that fall within your circle of influence include things like: where you work, what you buy, what you read, what skills you choose to learn, what people you meet, what friends you keep in your life, and what your attitude towards life is. These are all things that you can personally control either by adjusting your mindset around them or by choosing to engage more or less with them. For that reason, these fall into your circle of influence because you can directly influence them in your life.

The things that fall into your circle of concern include things like: the news, the economy, the political views of other people, the weather, natural disasters, wars, other people's lives, and other people's opinions. These types of things are completely beyond your control, so you will never be able to influence them or change them directly. Instead, you need to decide to either accept them as they are or adjust the way that you perceive them in your life so that you can accept them. In the end, your only real option towards ending suffering around your circle of concern is to choose to change your perception around these things.

Reframing Your Attitude on Death

According to stoicism, the sooner you define how you feel about death, the less you are going to fear death, and the sooner you will begin enabling yourself to live a better life. As Socrates stated, "To fear death, my friends, is only to think ourselves wise, without being wise: for it is to think that we know what we do not know. For anything that men can tell, death may be the greatest good that can happen to them: but they fear it as if they knew quite well that it was the greatest of evils. And what is this but that shameful ignorance of thinking that we know what we do not know?" Death itself is something that many modern people fear, but the fear itself needs to be addressed if you are ever going to overcome it so that you can allow yourself to live truly. Often, the fear of death is derived from the fear of not living a great enough life before death happens, and as a result, people begin to fear what would happen if they died. The common worry is "What if I die and I did not live my best life?" which can naturally be overcome by actually choosing to live your life. However, if you are so afraid of dying that you refuse to start living, then you will always live in this fear of not living your best life because you let that very fear hold you back.

Death itself is inevitable, no matter what way you look at it, so choosing to fear it will only hold you back further. This does not mean that you have to look forward to or even welcome death, but choosing to overcome your intense fear around it will help you begin living a better life in general as you will no longer fear what could happen if you did die. Instead, you choose to come to peace with the fact that the end is coming just like you choose to come to peace with the fact that the past has already happened. As such, you move forward with a greater emphasis on *right now*.

If the fear of death is really prominent for you, rather than trying to combat your fear of death, you may find that your ability to overcome the fear is quite challenging. In this case, rather than attempting to terminate the fear itself, you may instead choose to begin reframing that fear. For example: what are you more afraid of, death or never having lived? What are you more afraid of, dying young with a great life of exciting memories or dying old with a life of regret and missed opportunities? What are you more afraid of, going out and dying in a tragic accident or never having exposed yourself to the joys of living in the first place? Do you get where I'm going with this? If you cannot completely overcome your fear of dying, make your fear of dying smaller than your fear of missing out on living.

Growing Comfortable in Discomfort

Life is filled with challenges no matter what way you choose to live your life. If you choose to sit still in your life, you are going to face the challenges of having to fight as hard as you can to avoid change and experience the pain of not growing. If you choose to grow with your life, you are going to face the challenges of obstacles that come with growth and the growing pains that are inevitable along the way. Either way, you are going to experience some degree of suffering in your life, no matter what you do. However, if you choose to endure the growing pains as they come, you can assure that they are going to be much less painful than the lifelong pain of trying to stop things from changing.

Think of your life as an old school game of Super Mario: the screen is moving and you have to keep moving with it, or else, it moves and you get left behind eventually. In the case of Super Mario, your character would simply die, and you would start again with a new life. In the case of real life, you are simply going to experience more and more pressure coming against you which will require you to grow stronger and stronger to prevent it from actually hitting you. In most cases, you will grow exhausted at some point and weeks, months, or even years of missed growth opportunities will crash upon you all at once and demand serious change from you. In this case, the pressure of waiting plus the pressure of being hit with all of your life lessons at once will produce way more suffering than growing at a natural rate would have.

Growing comfortable with discomfort now means that you will only ever have to endure manageable amounts of discomfort in your life. As long as you continue moving forward, that pressure will not build up, and you will never experience the need to hold a mountain over your head while praying that it doesn't crush you when it all falls down at once. The suffering that you experience when you choose to grow instead of standing still is far less than if you were to never change at all.

Recreating Yourself as a Person

Until now, you have likely held fairly tightly to the identity of who you are as a person. You probably have an identity that you have clung to all of your life, or at least for most of your life, that has been shaped by significant memories and experiences that you have shared with other people. Maybe the combination of your Mother telling you that you were too sensitive and you crying after being bullied off the high school basketball team has left you believing that you are too sensitive as a person. Maybe your Dad telling you that you are special and your teachers always putting unique stickers on your work has led you to believe that you are more special than those around you. Whatever your belief about yourself may be, you can guarantee that it is not accurate as to who you truly are.

Psychology says that there are three elements to our identity: how we experience the world, our inner voice, and our persona that we share with people around us. Each of these parts of our identity is slightly different from the other two parts of our identity, thus leaving us with our true identity falling somewhere in between these three moving parts. When you realize this to be true, you realize that not only has your belief around your identity been wrong all this time but also that you can completely recreate those beliefs and your identity within yourself.

As you embody the goals of stoicism in your own life, seek to learn how you can embody it in a way that truly changes who you are. Rather than being a person who is heavily driven by emotion or who engages in irrational behavior, become a person who is driven by rational thinking. Reinvent yourself as the person who is reliable, trustworthy, and stable. Begin to develop trust in yourself and learn how to rely on yourself as being the one person that you can turn to when you are in need of genuine change in your life. Start building your relationship with yourself and everything in your life will change.

Embodying Your Own Philosophies

Remember your philosophy journal? Now is a great time to begin digging into it and embodying everything that you have been writing inside of that journal, including your own philosophies on what life is and what it means. When you begin embodying your own philosophies in life, you begin to create an intimate and personal connection with life itself. Rather than simply embracing what someone else says is true and believes is right, you can start embracing what you believe to be true and right for you.

If you believe in stoicism, chances are that your personal philosophies and beliefs somehow connect to stoicism as well. So, not only will this help you live more in alignment with your personal truth, but it will also help you embody a deeper connection to the stoic way of life and embrace it in a more personalized manner. Choose what your purpose is in life, discover your mission, and choose to live in alignment with your purpose and mission every single day. Seek the opportunity to make your own life and the lives of those around you better through your actions and infuse your everyday living with your purpose and mission.

When you embody your own philosophies, you not only start living life on your own terms, but you also start distributing your own knowledge and understanding more powerfully. What if people like Epictetus, Zeno, and Socrates never shared their philosophies in life with those around them? Had this never happened, the Greek school of philosophy would have never been established and stoicism, amongst many other philosophies, would have never come into existence. It does not serve to keep your beliefs and philosophies to yourself when they can serve better when they are being shared with the world around you.

Always Work Towards Your Personal Mission

One of the goals of stoicism is to always be working towards achieving your personal mission in life. When you have identified what it is that you truly want to achieve with your life and what purpose you serve here on earth, choosing how to respond to challenging situations becomes a lot easier. With a clear vision, you can see what it is that you are working towards and you know exactly what you need to factor in when it comes to choosing the reasonable solution to move forward with. This makes navigating emotional challenges more manageable because you know what it is that you are working towards, so there is more at stake if you *don't* manage your emotions and respond stoically.

As you grow, your goals and dreams are going to change in your life, but your mission is always going to stay the same. Your mission is what it is that you want to achieve in your life overall, and it tends to remain consistent throughout your goals and your dreams. When you consistently work towards an overall mission in your life, it becomes easier for you to know yourself and handle yourself in virtually any situation that you face even unexpected or challenging ones. You automatically start considering your mission and that which matters most to you in the face of challenges and rationally thinking about how you can honor your mission and work in alignment with it while still proceeding. In the goal of stoicism, this prevents irrational emotional outbursts because you know what it is that you desire to achieve, so you are not caught in emotional turmoil with no clear understanding as to what is causing it or why. Instead, you can easily tell which of your primary missions or values has been compromised or is being threatened by the situation at hand, and you can rationally choose action steps that will help you proceed in alignment with your mission.

Be a Student of Life

Seneca, a Roman stoic philosopher, once said: "As long as you live, keep learning how to live." Being able to recognize that you are never going to know all that there is to know about life is imperative in allowing yourself to always remain open to all that life has to offer you. If you want to live your best life, you need to live a life with humility by realizing that you will always be learning, as long as you are alive. Every day will present you with new challenges, opportunities, changes, and lessons. As long as you are willing to, you can awaken to these lessons and embrace them and learn how to implement them so that each day is better than the last.

You may think that some days have nothing to teach you or find yourself feeling as though sometimes it isn't *you* who needs to embrace the lessons being presented. Trust that any time you attempt to push the responsibility onto someone else, you are not paying attention to life with an open enough mind because you are allowing your ego and emotions to cloud your judgment. You need to be willing to admit that the lessons being presented in life are also being presented to you.

If you find that you are genuinely going through your days with nothing to learn, your lesson may be that you need to challenge yourself more. Seek opportunities to learn and grow and put yourself in circumstances where you can start embracing greater challenges in your life. You may feel that being free of challenges is a blessing, but in reality, it is a sign that you are either ignorant towards everything around you or you are not doing enough to present yourself with growth opportunities. Use this as an opportunity to take responsibility for yourself and your personal growth and well-being and create your reality in a new and exciting way.

Create Happiness, Don't Dream of It

One of the biggest teachings in stoicism is that your goal is not to dream of having happiness, but to create it instead. Rather than placing your happiness into worldly things like materialism, place the development of your happiness into yourself. According to Epictetus, the less you need to be happy, the happier you are going to be because fewer conditions will need to be met for your happiness to be achieved. Learning how to master your mind is a profound way to begin generating your own happiness and taking responsibility for your own contentment.

Happiness in and of itself is an illusion; it is merely an emotion that we experience just like anger and jealousy. When you realize this, you realize that just like anger or jealousy, happiness can be triggered by small things as well. This reality means that it does not need to be so challenging for you to experience happiness and that there are no certain circumstances that need to be met for you to be happy. Stop telling yourself things like "I will be happy when I have more money" or "I will be happier when I live in a new house", and instead, start realizing that you can be happy *right now*.

Beyond creating your own happiness, learn how to create your own contentment. Happiness, like other emotions, will come and go, so developing an attachment to living in a state of happiness can be challenging in and of itself. It can make the pursuit of happiness so cumbersome that you find that you truly cannot experience happiness at all and so, you are endlessly chasing something that you simply cannot catch. Instead, realize that in some situations, you are not going to be happy, and being content is just as pleasant as being happy, as it means that you are at peace with all that surrounds you and all that you embody.

Learn How to Be Present

The power of presence has been talked about a lot in the self-help industry over the past few years, but the reality is that presence is not a new concept nor is it one that was modernized by recent trends. Instead, the power of presence is something that has been talked about and taught about for years, including all the way back in ancient Greek times where stoicism was originally developed. That being said, the modern trends in the self-help industry means that learning about the art of presence and how to practice being in the moment is widely taught about and easy to educate yourself on.

The ability to remain present is something that needs to be addressed differently for different people. The reality is that not everyone is going to have the same thought processes or approaches to their realities in the same way, which means that everyone is going to need to hear the information in a particular way for it to actually *click.* That being said, do not shy away from reading and consuming all of the materials that you need to consume around presence to help you learn about what it means and how to embody presence in your own life. In fact, fully immerse yourself in the practice because once you get it, everything will absolutely change.

When you live your life in the present moment, forgiving the past and seeing everything as a new experience is effortless because you are in *this* moment, not one that has already passed you by or one that has yet to arrive. This means that your emotions attached to previous memories and challenges in your life no longer drive you through current experiences, which prevents you from responding to things with an excess of emotional passion. For example, if your spouse forgets to change the toilet paper roll, you do not feel compelled to get angry at him/her for the past three years of things that he/she had done wrong in your eyes over one isolated incident. Instead, you recognize that it was one isolated incident you can treat it as such, without the intense emotional response that you may instinctively attempt to respond with if you are still living in the past.

Always Take 100% Responsibility for Yourself

Learning how to take responsibility for yourself is not only a way to eliminate your suffering but is also a way to promote your growth and success in life, too. When you take responsibility for yourself, you put the control of your life back into your own hands and give yourself the tools that you need to heal, grow, and change throughout life. It may feel difficult, but when you take responsibility for yourself, you take responsibility for your feelings and your behaviors, and you give yourself exactly all of the power you need to make changes in your life.

From a perspective of looking back on your past, taking responsibility means that you take ownership for any role that you may have played in any challenges that you may have faced and that you recognize that you could have done things differently. Then, it means accepting yourself for the choices you made and realizing that you did your best with the knowledge that you had. For the challenges you faced that you could not have changed, you take responsibility for the feelings that you continue to face and the way that this may continue challenging you now in your present life. By taking this type of fierce responsibility for yourself, you give yourself the power that you need to change your life by healing, accepting, and moving on from your past.

From a present and futuristic standpoint, taking responsibility for yourself means accepting the behaviors and actions that you are taking right now in your everyday life and how they are impacting you right now and the future version of yourself. This means taking responsibility for the fact that when you do things such as wake up late, you face the consequences of being late to your engagements. This means taking responsibility for the fact that when you do things such as consistently show up late, you set your future self-up for failure by making it nearly impossible for you to hold down a job or earn an income. When you take responsibility for yourself, it means that you are taking responsibility for every single thing that you do or do not do and how it impacts you now and the future version of yourself that is yet to come.

If you truly want to live in alignment with the goals of stoicism you need to be willing to take responsibility for your personal growth, your emotional intelligence, and your ability to develop your rational thinking. You need to be willing to identify areas in your life where you could improve, and then actually take action necessary in moving forward and improving your life. When you take responsibility for yourself and your behaviors, it is like giving yourself the keys to your brand new life, and you have the choice to either make it something truly amazing for yourself.

Grow Beyond Materialism

Mahatma Gandhi once quoted, "Increase of material comforts, it may be generally laid down, does not in any way whatsoever conduce to moral growth." Materialism is an attitude that can produce a significant amount of suffering in anyone's life. Materialism is a constant source of stress in many modern societies where the mindset of "more, more, more" is basically bred into people from the beginning and is continuously injected into people's minds. In Western society, people are taught that they need to purchase new things on a constant basis to keep up with everything else. Fashion, housewares, trendy toys or gadgets, and many other consumerism-style products are constantly being produced and marketed to people through the power of emotions. Marketers market to people knowing that they want to fit in, be cool, enhance social status, experience happiness, or experience the sentimental or nostalgic value that the object may be able to offer. Of course, true consistent emotional happiness and support does not come from materialistic items, so it leads to people constantly going through cycles of buying things for joy and then feeling empty when the novelty wears off. As they say, the best things in life are not things.

Rather than exposing yourself to this suffering and being captivated by your emotions that fear being left behind or ridiculed for not having the latest and greatest things, learn how to deny materialism in your life. Purchase only what you need and what you genuinely desire, and leave everything else behind. Base your emotions on things that you can control, such as your thoughts and behaviors, and not on things that you can acquire like toys and fashion accessories. This way, you always feel truly in control over your emotional well-being, and you do not feel as though you are constantly at the mercy of corporations that are profiting off of your emotional instabilities.

Be of Service to Others

True love is a powerful thing, and with it can come experiences such as true joy, true contentment, true fulfillment, and true excitement.

353

When you experience true love in your life, it opens up a world of other opportunities that you can enjoy through that love directly. It does not only open it up for you, but it opens it up for those around you as well, who are being loved through your service. Through this, a significant amount of pain and suffering ends because you are opening yourself and others up to a world of love and gentleness. Studies have shown that when you express love and kindness to one person, it often creates a ripple effect as they then express it to someone else, and the act carries on over many people.

In life, one of the greatest things that we can do for ourselves and for others is to serve. If you put anyone in the position of being able to serve genuinely, they will always say that they feel infinitely happier and more abundant as a result of their service. At the end of the day, we are always trying to serve someone in addition to ourselves: our family members, our friends, our audiences, our coworkers, or our employees. Some people make it their life mission to serve as many people as possible, whereas others are perfectly content just serving a small number of people in their lives. No matter what, though, if you ask anyone about what is important to them, some form of service will virtually always come to their mind.

We feel best when we serve because the act of giving love aligns us with the act of receiving love, and that genuinely feels good. When you can rationally think about how love improves your life and the lives of those around you in this way and act in a rational way around love, your ability to serve and generate true sustainable love increases. As a result, your suffering decreases and your genuine overall happiness grows.

Embody the Lighter Side of Life

There is nothing humble about living a life that is overwhelmed with seriousness. Just because the goal of stoicism is to be rational and reasonable does not mean that you are not able to experience humor and comedy in your life. In fact, one of the best ways that you can grow mental toughness and develop your stoicism is by learning how to make light of challenging situations. Seeing the brighter side of things and allowing yourself to embody the lightness helps you overcome the suffering that is attached with being too serious all of the time.

People who are too serious take things personally, feel the weight of the world on their shoulders, and struggle to let go and experience true joy and happiness in their lives. They find themselves feeling trapped in the energy of seriousness, and it can weigh them down and leave them feeling pessimistic in the long run. Not knowing how to laugh and see and embody the lighter side of life is just as damaging on your soul as never allowing yourself to overcome the suffering that you have endured in your life until now.

Learn how to laugh at yourself when you make mistakes, and laugh at the irony of challenging situations when you cannot overcome them with ease. Learn how to see life as something that is light and joyful, and discover how you can smile at the things that are beyond your control. Give yourself the gift of being gentle in your perspective and your opinion, and avoid trying to make everything so heavy and overwhelming all of the time. In seeing the lighter side of life, you give yourself the ability to avoid getting weighed down by seriousness, and you start enjoying yourself once again. Rather than holding you back and keeping you feeling overwhelmed, your emotions instead become an ally that helps you lead a greater life when you learn how to experience the lighter side of life itself.

Conclusion

You have officially read the entirety of *Stoicism: A Practical Guide for Beginners to Practice Stoicism: Complete Guide of Self-Discipline, Mental Toughness, Productivity, and Mastering Confidence, Jealousy, and Anger Management, and Everything You Need to Know About Stoicism*! Thanks for making it through to end of this guidebook. Let's hope it was informative and able to provide you with all of the tools you need to achieve your goals whatever they may be.

By now, you should have a strong understanding of what stoicism is, where it stems from, and how it has evolved to serve the modern world. Stoicism is a powerful art that, when appropriately applied, can help you master one of the most valuable tools that evolution has granted us: your rational mind. By applying the lessons that were taught to us by ancient Greek and Roman philosophers, you can discover powerful ways to move through your challenges and experience greater success in your personal, social, and professional lives. Through the proper application of stoic ways of life, not only can you find the opportunity to experience greater success, but you can also help your own personal evolution along. The more you refine and harness the power of your rational mind, the more you work in alignment with the very nature of being a human being. As a result, you can tap into the entire power of the human mind and experience more of just about everything you desire out of life.

Stoicism is a powerful lifestyle that teaches you about the importance of reducing your own personal suffering through embodying an ethical way of living that values high moral standards. When you embody stoicism, you teach yourself how to harness the power of your emotions and use them to inspire yourself to respond to things with a more rational approach. Through this rational approach, you can work towards effectively achieving the goals that your emotions had in the first place without the unnecessary implication of further suffering.

Despite how far we have evolved, humans continue to find themselves falling into the temptation of satisfying their emotions immediately and suffering for that satisfaction in the long run rather than managing their emotions effectively and benefiting overall. Stoicism continues to support us in overcoming this need for instant gratification by encouraging us to embody the pillars of high moral standards and ethical living by favoring our reasonable mind over our emotional one. This does not mean that you should be ignoring or avoiding your emotions, but instead that you should be working in alignment with your nature and discovering how you can move forward with a whole approach.

As you move forward from this book, continue working on building your mental toughness and resiliency so that you can experience a stronger foundation to build your practice of stoicism upon. Teach yourself how to stay dedicated by staying consistent in educating yourself about stoicism and developing a personal practice that aligns with your stoic development, too. In the early stages, you may benefit from keeping this book handy so that you can refer back to Chapter 6: Daily Applications of Stoicism and inspire yourself to embody stoicism on a daily basis. At least, early on, this chapter will be handy in reminding you about how simply you can apply it in your everyday life. From learning to manage your anger at work more effectively so that you can continue to carry yourself in a productive way to learning how to accept your family and friends as they are and choosing to love them anyway, stoicism will help in many ways. The more you practice, the more this empowered way of living will have the capacity to change your complete life.

I encourage you as well to really take advantage of using your own philosophy diary where you, too, can begin discovering what life means to you and what you feel your purpose in life is. As you continue looking into your own inner studies, developing your personal mission, and sticking to it through your rational, decision-making becomes easier. In no time, you will discover just how easy it is to stick to the power of rational thinking when you have a genuine and powerful reason that inspires you to do so.

www.ingramcontent.com/pod-product-compliance
Lightning Source LLC
Chambersburg PA
CBHW071855090426

42811CB00004B/619